OXFORD READINGS IN PHILOSOPHY

Series Editor G. J.

LOCKE ON HUMAN UNDERSTANDING
SELECTED ESSAYS

Other volumes are in preparation

LOCKE ON HUMAN UNDERSTANDING

Selected Essays

Edited by
I. C. TIPTON

OXFORD UNIVERSITY PRESS
1977

Oxford University Press, Walton Street, Oxford OX2 6DP

OXFORD LONDON GLASGOW NEW YORK
TORONTO MELBOURNE WELLINGTON CAPE TOWN
IBADAN NAIROBI DAR ES SALAAM LUSAKA ADDIS ABABA
KUALA LUMPUR SINGAPORE JAKARTA HONG KONG TOKYO
DELHI BOMBAY CALCUTTA MADRAS KARACHI

Introduction and selection © Oxford University Press 1977

British Library Cataloguing in Publication Data
Locke on human understanding: selected
essays—(Oxford readings in philosophy)
1. Locke, John—Knowledge, Theory of—
Addresses, essays, lectures
I. Tipton, Ian Charles   II. Series
121'.092'4   B1298.K/
ISBN 0–19–875039–0

*Printed in Great Britain by
Cox & Wyman Ltd
London, Fakenham and Reading*

ACKNOWLEDGEMENTS

Permission to reprint the papers in this collection has been obtained from the publishers or editors of *Philosophy*, *Ratio*, *Theoria*, *The Locke Newsletter*, *The Philosophical Quarterly*, and *The Journal of the History of Ideas*, as recorded at the start of each essay. Minor corrections have been made in all the papers and significant changes have been made in some. I wish to record my thanks to the various contributors for their co-operation in this, and in particular to Douglas Greenlee and Laurens Laudan for providing additional material at very short notice.

My colleagues Dr. O. R. Jones and Mr. Peter Smith read my introduction and made helpful comments on it.

All references to, and quotations from, Locke's *Essay* have been checked against the two-volume *An Essay Concerning Human Understanding*, edited by John W. Yolton (London, 1961: revised 1965).

CONTENTS

INTRODUCTION

I

In introducing their collection of essays *Locke and Berkeley* (London, 1968), C. B. Martin and D. M. Armstrong noted that it was not practicable to devote a volume to each of these philosophers, this 'partly because there did not seem to be enough papers of high quality to make two separate volumes and partly because in discussing either philosopher it is profitable and almost inevitable to oppose him to the other'. Martin went on to say:

The serious study of Locke is not in fashion. Until recently, unabridged versions of Locke's *Essay* had been out of print for many years. Generations of students were taught from Pringle-Pattison's abridged edition. This was good enough to give them target-practice. However, too many crucial arguments and distinctions were omitted, and as a result the student was unable to know what Locke *said*, let alone what he meant.

Another result was that there was 'a deplorable shortage of good articles on Locke's *Essay*'. Berkeley could (surely) have been given a volume to himself. But the time was not yet ripe for one on Locke.

The justification for publishing the present collection is that the situation has now changed. The serious study of Locke is again in fashion. Not that it should be suggested that anything dramatic happened in or after 1968. Fraser's unabridged edition of the *Essay*, first published in 1894, had been made available again by Dover Books in 1959, and Everyman's Library substituted an unabridged for an abridged version in 1961. Doubtless this both reflected and stimulated the renewal of interest that is by now very apparent. Recent books on Locke have included Yolton's influential *Locke and the Compass of Human Understanding* (1970), Woolhouse's *Locke's Philosophy of Science and Knowledge* (1971), Duchesneau's *L'Empirisme de Locke* (1973), and a collection of original essays edited by Yolton under the title *John Locke: Problems and Perspectives* (1969). At a more introductory level there is Mabbott's *John Locke* (1973). And a third, revised, edition of

Aaron's *John Locke* appeared in 1971. Even more significantly, the first of the thirty proposed volumes in the Clarendon Edition of the Works of John Locke was published in 1975.[1] Nor must we ignore the excellent *Locke Newsletter* which first appeared in 1970. Published annually by Roland Hall at the University of York and distributed free to Locke scholars and to institutions throughout the world, this journal (for it is too modest in describing itself as a newsletter) contains short articles, queries, replies, corrections to the editions of the *Essay* in print, book reviews, and so on. It also keeps the Locke bibliography up to date. The books by Mandelbaum, Buchdahl, and Bennett which are listed in my bibliography have been highly influential, though these are not devoted entirely to Locke. And another sign of the growing interest in Locke is the number of articles on him in the journals. Some of these are reprinted in this volume. Those chosen all originally appeared in the ten-year period 1966–75.

II

Exciting though the present time may be for students of Locke, it is none the less a time of approach towards a proper understanding of the *Essay* rather than one in which all has suddenly been made clear. On almost every topic there is disagreement over what Locke *meant*. And not surprisingly there are various ways of approaching him. For many the principal concern is to understand what Locke is saying and to separate out various strands in his thought. Others want to develop some insight which they think they discern, perhaps with difficulty, in his writing on a topic. And others continue to use him for target-practice. But one feature of the present scene deserves special comment. This is that there is a widespread conviction that the *Essay* is worthy of study in its own right and that it is not always profitable, let alone almost inevitable, to oppose Locke's philosophy to that of Berkeley.

Writing in 1933 (his paper is reprinted in Martin/Armstrong) Gilbert Ryle observed that Locke had suffered from the tendency of historians of philosophy —'abetted, it must be confessed, by those who set examination papers in philosophy to students'—to pigeon-hole philosophers. Locke of course was pigeon-holed as an *Empiricist* and as founder of a school to be continued by Berkeley and Hume: this school being set against that of the *Rationalists*, containing as its great names those of Descartes, Spinoza and Leibniz. It is perhaps unfortunate that there were three of each and that the Channel divided Britain from the Continent, for this encouraged those responsible for

---

[1] The volume already published is devoted to the *Essay*. In corresponding with Locke scholars I have found that this edition is already proving influential, and had this been a collection of new essays I might have thought it appropriate to ensure that all quotations were taken from it. The General Editor, P. H. Nidditch, has provided an outline survey of the project as a whole in the *Locke Newsletter*, 5 (1974).

course construction to arrange things in such a way that the impression was given of an ideological gulf greater than any that actually existed.[2] As one result of this, there is always the danger that Locke will be expounded in a way that will make him a suitable target for Berkeley and Hume who, the story goes, revealed the inadequacy of his principles and thus prepared the way for the Kantian synthesis of the two great *isms*.

Serious students of Locke and Berkeley have of course usually been aware that this approach was in many ways inadequate. Nobody could doubt that Locke was an important influence on Berkeley, but, as Luce and Popkin revealed, the influence of Malebranche and Bayle was crucially significant too. So far as Locke is concerned, the positive influence of Descartes on Book IV of the *Essay* in particular was obvious to any attentive reader. Yet the facts of course construction continued to encourage people to concentrate too exclusively on Locke as founder of a school and on Berkeley as his successor, thus doing an injustice to both. Berkeley has certainly suffered as a result of this, and the suggestion that he has misunderstood or misinterpreted Locke on some issue may well result on occasion from a too easy assumption that Locke is always the target. But Locke has suffered more. The conviction that Locke can be profitably examined in isolation from Berkeley is reflected in the fact that Yolton's important book contains only four brief references to Berkeley.

Berkeley is not prominent in the present volume. He is not even mentioned in some of the papers, and he is not in the forefront of *any* of them. Writing on primary and secondary qualities, Alexander for example notes that 'Locke has been seriously misrepresented in various respects ever since Berkeley set critics off on the wrong foot', but he stresses that to reach a correct understanding of Locke on this topic we need to forget about Berkeley and see him in relation to Boyle. The paper by Laudan concentrates further on the relationship between Locke and the science of the day and opens with criticism of those who 'by reading history backwards, have written as if Locke accepted the view of Berkeley and Hume that the empiricist philosophy should not be based on a "scientific" metaphysics'. Allison does mention a criticism Berkeley had to make of Locke on personal identity, but he is much more interested in tracing a line of thought from Locke to Leibniz and Kant. And on language Kretzmann claims that 'Berkeley's second thoughts about the thesis that

[2] Ryle again warns against the danger of taking the two-camp theory too seriously in a review in the *Times Literary Supplement* of 19 Sept. 1975. 'The idea that the literate world was excited by a fight between the dragon of Rationalism and the St. George of Empiricism ignores two facts, first, that neither "ism" was going to be mentioned as such until the nineteenth century; and, secondly, that Locke's account of knowledge proper, as distinct from judgment, opinion, guess-work and fancy, was hardly distinguishable from that of Descartes. Indeed Locke, going far beyond Descartes, promised that Ethics would join pure mathematics as a demonstrative science.'

words signify ideas mark the beginning of a tradition of criticism so uniformly and intensely negative that the thesis seems now to be considered beneath criticism'. Kretzmann's belief is that 'the main thesis of Locke's semantic theory is not as bad as it looks; and it looks as bad as it does because it looks simpler than it is'.

III

But at this point I should like to concentrate on one particular issue: this being whether Locke was or was not a *representative realist*. Did he believe that when I take it I am seeing or touching a rose I am aware not of the rose but of an *idea*, a quite distinct object, which is produced in me by the rose? If we want to set Locke up as a target for Berkeley—or for 'nearly every youthful student of philosophy' who, Ryle has recently reminded us, 'both can and does in about his second essay refute Locke's entire Theory of Knowledge'[3]—we will have him believing this. For Berkeley reaches his position by claiming that *given* the only things we are aware of are ideas it must follow both that we can have no evidence for the existence of outward objects and that, ultimately, we cannot even make sense of talk of such objects. But *did* Locke hold that the ideas received from sense perception are, as it were, images in our minds and that we are aware of them rather than of the objects he supposed produced them in us? And if he did think in this way, how is it that he could so often talk quite happily of our observing things in the world around us and indeed fail to be more worried about the sort of challenge Berkeley was to make? If our concern is to set Locke up for Berkeley's attack we will not dwell on these questions. However, if we are concerned with *Locke* they will interest us, as they have recently and increasingly interested Locke scholars.

In his paper 'Locke's Idea of "Idea"' Douglas Greenlee casts doubt on the view that 'Locke regarded ideas as "entities" of a very special sort, customarily called "mental", that these entities are "in the mind", that they are images, that they, rather than what they are images of, are what the mind "directly" or "immediately" knows, and hence that they serve as screens or barriers intervening between the mind and the world it is trying with a certain measured success to understand'. And it is interesting that when he wrote this (his paper was originally published in 1967) he could see himself as opposing the *standard* interpretation and one that was seldom questioned. For the pendulum has now swung in the opposite direction. It is now widely, though not universally,

---

[3] The words come from Ryle's 'John Locke', an address delivered in 1965. The address has been printed twice, but it will be most easily located in Vol. I of Ryle's *Collected Papers* (1971). The paper contains a lively working-out of the truth behind an at first sight implausible (and provocative) remark made by Russell in casual conversation. 'No one ever had Common Sense before John Locke—and no one but Englishmen have ever had it since.'

held that whatever Locke believe it was not what has been traditionally supposed. In the book referred to earlier, Yolton for example denies that 'Locke thought of ideas as entities'. In Yolton's view 'the way of ideas was his attempt to formulate perceptual realism', while ideas were 'his way of characterising the fact that perceptual awareness is mental'. And in another paper reprinted in the present collection we find Woozley reaffirming the view, which he first put forward in his introduction to the abridged edition of the *Essay* published by Fontana in 1964, that 'the accepted interpretation of Locke's epistemology . . . is itself hardly to be taken seriously at all'. The debate however continues. Thus we find Gunnar Aspelin writing in opposition to Greenlee, and Greenlee replying in a note specially written for this collection. We also find Eric Matthews suggesting (in one of two pieces I have taken from the *Locke Newsletter*) that the traditional criticisms 'were not . . . based on a total misreading of Locke, but are justifiable in terms of a tenable interpretation of his text'.[4]

Readers will have to make up their own minds on this issue, and a number of the papers in this collection may help them to do this. They may for example be impressed by Matthews's observation that early critics of Locke 'did, after all, live in the same intellectual atmosphere as Locke' and that it may be 'more likely, therefore, that they would interpret him correctly than that his perhaps over-subtle modern defenders should do so'. Berkeley was not the only one, nor was he the first, to interpret Locke in what became the 'standard' way. But the issue is a tricky one and it is perhaps only fair to point out that even were we able to call Locke back from the grave it is not clear that we should immediately get wholly satisfying replies to our questions. As Woolhouse notes in his book, Locke differs from Berkeley in being 'little interested in the philosophical problem of perception as understood today'. He often showed a reluctance to take criticism as seriously as his critics would have wished, but it is not hard to detect a particular tetchiness when he is questioned about the nature of ideas: a tetchiness which results in part from a simple lack of interest in the issue. Anyway, I shall not attempt to settle the matter here, contenting myself instead with just three additional points.

The first is that given that Locke was prepared to argue that 'since the extension, figure, number, and motion of bodies of an observable bigness may be perceived at a distance *by* the sight, it is evident some singly imperceptible bodies must come from them to the eyes, and thereby convey to the brain some *motion*, which produces these *ideas* which we have of them in us' (II, viii, 12),

---

[4] Matthews's main concern is to criticize one argument which he finds in Woozley's introduction to the Fontana abridgement of the *Essay*. The argument is that as an objection Locke made to Malebranche's theory would apply equally to his own position *if* he were a representationalist, he cannot have seen himself as committed to this position. The reader will note that Greenlee also uses this argument.

then he clearly should not have held that we perceive the ideas rather than the outward objects 'of an observable bigness'. Rather he should have held, as in Yolton's view he did hold, that what is produced in us is an awareness of the outward object. Indeed it may seem so obvious that he should have thought this that we may be tempted to argue straight off that this must be what he always did think. I should not myself accept this argument, if only because other reputable and even important philosophers have quite clearly been subject to confusion at just this point. What we should I think accept is that there are *many* passages in which Locke assumes acquaintance with outward things, and that if, as Greenlee concedes, there are passages that may *suggest* a 'dualist' reading, there is no excuse for ignoring a definite 'non-representationalist vein of thought in the *Essay*'.

The second observation is that, whatever Locke's view of the matter, the texts provide surprisingly little by way of evidence to settle·the issue one way or the other. Those like Aspelin who hold that he was a representationalist seize, for example, on the well-known passage in IV, iv, 3 in which he says that the mind 'perceives nothing but its own *ideas*', that our knowledge is real 'only so far as there is a conformity between our *ideas* and the reality of things', and that we therefore need to ask how the mind can know that its ideas 'agree with things themselves'. But we must agree with Greenlee that it is rare for Locke to go so far. As the debate between Greenlee and Aspelin again illustrates, there is disagreement over how the passage should be interpreted;[5] and even if we do read it (as I suspect we should not) as *committing* Locke to intermediary entities, it is not obvious that we should not see this as an aberration rather than supposing that he is departing from his real view when he suggests that we perceive outward things. Again, there is a significant passage in Draft A in which Locke talks about the 'simple Ideas or Images of things . . . which are noe thing but the reviveing again in our mindes those imaginations which objects when they affected our senses caused in us'. This may seem impressive enough, but of course it *is* in a draft written nearly twenty years before the *Essay* was published, the passage *was* revised, and the printed versions do seem to suggest that Locke has taken pains to avoid committing himself to anything so definite. Further, if I read Yolton aright I think that he at least might argue that even this is compatible with perceptual realism. Perhaps the most that a reading of the *Essay* taken as a whole may suggest is that Locke never wholly freed himself from the notion that ideas of sense might be thought of as 'imaginations' and entities, this even though he

---

[5] Few passages in the *Essay* can have been referred to more than IV, iv, 3, usually to suggest that Locke was a representationalist and not unaware of the difficulties inherent in the position, but sometimes (and usually more recently) by those reacting against this interpretation. As well as looking in the obvious places, the reader might consult for example the paper by Butler listed in the bibliography under 'Substance', esp. pp. 150–1.

was certainly not concerned to promote this view and never seriously doubted that sensation does provide us with every assurance we could wish of the existence of outward things. It remains the case, however, that some would not want to go even this far; and readers who want more on the topic might look for example at Ch. 5 of Yolton's book, or at a paper by Douglas Lewis (mentioned in my bibliography) which considers 'three main aspects of Locke's philosophical speculation that have been taken as supporting the contention that in Locke the only things with which we are acquainted in experience are ideas', and argues that 'none of these three aspects of Locke's view support this interpretation'.[6]

The third point is perhaps the most important. It is that it is now very widely conceded even by those who suppose that Locke did reify ideas (or that he sometimes slipped into doing this) that he was not enthusiastic about it and that we are going to miss a lot that is of importance if we continually ask ourselves whether claims he makes are claims he can properly make given his representationalism. Usually, as for example when discussing primary and secondary qualities, substance, and, I would argue, scepticism with regard to the senses, Locke is not just thinking out the implications of the view that we perceive objects in our minds rather than outward objects; and the questions that do concern him would have remained questions even had he been totally convinced that in having an idea of sense we are acquainted with the outward thing. Jonathan Bennett is one commentator who has done much to make this clear to us, and Matthews in effect concedes the point when he observes that 'any criticisms which might be made of his (alleged) representationalism do not seriously affect the value of his philosophy as a whole'.

IV

Turning now to the topic of primary and secondary qualities, there are a number of things many people have believed about Locke's position that are either false or suspect. One is that Locke held that 'secondary qualities' are only in us. Another is that he held that there were certain arguments, and in particular the argument from the relativity of perception, which *proved* that colours, say, were in us, but which left shapes etc. as genuine qualities of outward things. And another is that Locke's position is hopelessly vitiated

---

[6] On the other side, another relevant paper is the one by Nathanson (see bibliography). Nathanson says: 'Locke certainly did not advocate that percepts are images, but I think it fair to say that a consideration of his system suggests that such an assumption lies close to the heart of much that he held. At the very least, he is committed to holding that percepts represent things, and he provides no other model for understanding the representative relationship.' I should however point out that Nathanson uses 'percept' to cover more than the immediate object of sense perception, and that Locke's general ideas will for example be *percepts*. But this only makes his judgement more interesting.

(a) because the arguments which are supposed to prove that colours, tastes, etc. are in us would (if cogent) prove the same for *all* qualities and (b) because no representationalist can justify, even if he can make sense of, the claim that certain phenomenal qualities are like, and others unlike, qualities in outward and unperceived things. These mistakes have persisted in part at least because Berkeley 'set critics off on the wrong foot', and I believe that we must again resist the temptation to see Locke through Berkeleian spectacles if we are to get him right. Setting the record straight is, however, no easy task, and here too I will have to be content with a few observations.

The first concerns terminology. Berkeley presents the materialist as holding that colours and the like are *secondary qualities* and as conceding that these are only in the mind, so the issue for Berkeley is whether figure, for example, is in the mind in just the way that 'secondary qualities' are allowed to be. And the point here is that this involves an unannounced departure from Locke's terminology which is such that 'secondary qualities' can only be located in objects, this because they are either *textures*, as Alexander would have it, or, as is I think more usually the case, *powers*: 'powers to produce various sensations in us by . . . the bulk, figure, texture, and motion of their insensible parts' (II, viii, 10). Corresponding to these secondary qualities *in objects* there are the ideas produced *in us*; but the secondary qualities remain *in things*, and if we suppose otherwise it will be because Berkeley's way of talking has misled us. Berkeley either misunderstood Locke or decided, not necessarily improperly, 'to give to the term "secondary qualities" a meaning other than that which Locke, when he is speaking exactly, gives to it'.[7] So much is plain, but one tricky question remains. The question is whether Locke identified colours, sounds, smells, tastes, etc. (a) with the secondary qualities (i.e. with the textures or powers) alone, or (b) only with the ideas produced in us, or (c) with the ideas and with the secondary qualities. Of these (a) receives least support from the text. I have always felt myself that there is a lot to be said for interpreting Locke (and indeed Boyle too) in the light of (c), and for seeing him as distinguishing between colour, say, as experienced or as an idea, and colour as a secondary quality or power in things. So it is interesting that it is (b) that Alexander opts for. He claims that 'for Locke, ideas, all of them, are in the mind, and qualities, all of them, are in objects', and at the same time that 'colours and tastes are ideas'. It may be, however, that it does not matter too much which side we come down on as between (b) and (c). Locke is not consistent in his talk about primary and secondary qualities, and even in II, viii we find him distinguishing between *ideas* 'as they are *ideas* or perceptions in our minds, and as they [i.e. ideas] are modifications of matter in the bodies that cause such perceptions in us' (§7). It is in the very

[7] The quotation is from the paper by W. H. F. Barnes listed in the bibliography.

next section that he goes on to warn that when he talks of ideas as being in things 'I would be understood to mean those qualities in the objects which produce them in us'. And this is just one of the passages in the *Essay* which suggest considerable uncertainty on Locke's part over how best to express the sort of point he wants to make. For example in II, xxiii, 8 he tells us that 'secondary qualities . . . are nothing but bare powers' *and* that 'the colour and taste of *opium* are, as well as its soporific or anodyne virtues, mere powers'. But elsewhere the analogy is quite different. Thus in II, viii, 18 the sweetness and whiteness of manna are identified not with powers, but with the *effects* of powers, 'as the pain and sickness caused by *manna* are confessedly nothing but the effects of its operations on the stomach and guts'.[8]

I need not dwell here on Locke's supposed use of the argument from the relativity of perception to *prove* that colours and so on (as perceived) are only in us and that there is nothing like them in outward bodies, because Alexander argues forcefully for the conclusion that 'Locke was not attempting to *make* the primary/secondary quality distinction but was accepting it, ready-made, from Boyle as an essential part of the corpuscular hypothesis, which was already well on the way to being established'. Locke, Alexander tells us, 'was reporting scientific findings to the layman and showing how we could make sense of some superficially puzzling features of our everyday experience and our everyday descriptions of the world'. I believe that this is both true and important. It does however raise the more general question as to Locke's attitude to hypotheses and to the corpuscular hypothesis in particular, and on this I can only refer the reader to the paper on this topic by Laudan which is reprinted below; to the paper by Yost which he criticizes; to Ch. 1 of Mandelbaum's *Philosophy, Science and Sense Perception*; to Yolton's criticisms of Laudan's account in *Locke and the Compass of Human Understanding*, pp. 64–78; and to Laudan's comments on Yolton's criticisms in the 'postcript' specially written for this collection. We have in fact reached another area where there is vigorous debate, though there is also a fair measure of agreement. As Woolhouse points out (*Locke's Philosophy of Science and Knowledge*, p. 113), there is agreement that Locke should be seen 'against the background of the science of his time rather than as a person whose importance was to have been followed by Berkeley and Hume' and there is agreement 'that Locke thinks that the qualities and properties of things are dependent on

---

[8] Alexander returns to the topic of primary and secondary qualities in his 'Curley on Locke and Boyle' (see bibliography). This paper is concerned with whether Locke thought of powers as *intrinsic* to objects, and with what he thought it was for an object to have a power. Complex issues are involved here, but they must be faced by anyone wanting an adequate account of Locke's view on secondary qualities. For example, we need to face up to these issues before we can decide exactly what we should make of odd claims such as that 'yellowness is not actually in gold, but is a power in gold to produce that *idea* in us by our eyes, when placed in a due light' (II, xxiii, 10).

corpuscular mechanisms'. The debate is about 'how much Locke thinks we can infer about them and whether he would agree with a practising scientist's attempt to work in terms of them'.

The final point I want to make concerns the relationship between the primary/secondary quality distinction and Locke's (alleged) representational-ism. For it is now I think very widely recognized that there is no close relation-ship and that the point he wants to make in II, viii should be evaluated independently of any formulation that may suggest a representationalist stance. Briefly, and I am afraid very roughly, what Locke needs is not a dis-tinction between ideas as perceptual objects on the one hand and the unper-ceived qualities of real things on the other; but rather a distinction between (1) what we can call the *phenomenal* qualities of perceived macroscopic objects, which are those the object characteristically appears to have when it is perceived by creatures who are constituted as we are constituted, and (2) those that would feature in a scientific account of the object, which are those Locke thinks it has in itself. Thus we cannot explain how the orange char-acteristically appears round to us (or has the phenomenal quality of roundness) without conceiving it as occupying space in such a way that it *is* round,[9] though we cannot account for its appearing orange by attributing to it a certain surface texture (or corpuscular structure) such that when light strikes it we (though not necessarily other creatures) see it as orange. There is no need for Locke to assume that when I perceive the familiar colouring I am perceiving something in my own head which is genuinely coloured but which fails to resemble anything in the outward object, any more than there is any need for him to suppose that the apparent shape is the actual shape of a mental item. His unfortunate talk of resemblance and lack of resemblance between ideas and qualities does, surely, sidetrack us from the true import of what he has to say.

V

I cannot comment in detail on all the topics covered by papers in this collec-tion. I shall however just introduce the topic dealt with by M. R. Ayers before going on to say something about personal identity and about the innate knowledge issue.

[9] It might be objected here that: 'no atomist can consistently hold that the specific qualities which we perceive when we look at or when we touch material objects are identical with the qualities which these objects, when considered as congeries of atoms, actually do possess. For example, the continuous contour which characterizes the perceived shape of an object such as a table cannot be considered by an atomist to be a wholly adequate representation of that object's true shape.' The quotation is from Mandelbaum's book (see bibliography), p. 15. Mandelbaum's development of this point leads him to a very interesting interpretation of Locke's position, but if Yolton's criticisms of Mandelbaum in pp. 47–9 of his book are sound, my admittedly brief and rough account will stand.

No collection of this sort would be complete without something on Locke's account of substance in II, xxiii, so I am happy to be able to include Ayers's paper on the puzzling question concerning the relationship between what Locke says about our notion of substance as the substratum of qualities and what he says about real essences or the internal (corpuscular) structures of things. Students approaching Locke with some of the standard guides must often be puzzled by the fact that he seems to be vulnerable to, and sometimes sensitive to, sceptical attack on so many different levels. One we have to some extent dealt with in looking at representative realism. Two others are covered by Ayers. Basically the problem is this. Locke has things to say about substance and about real essences which have been taken as suggesting that we have *two* somethings-we-know-not-what which are ontologically distinct and which he believes in for quite different and unconnected reasons. The notion of pure substance on this view will be a hangover from his training in philosophy, it will be such that anyone who considers it will find that 'he has no other *idea* of it at all, but only a supposition of he knows not what support of such qualities which are capable of producing simple *ideas* in us' (II, xxiii, 2), and its nature will remain unknowable basically because, as commentators have suggested, it can *have* no nature. Real essences on the other hand will be more closely related to Locke's scientific background. These *we* cannot know, basically because our senses and instruments are not acute enough to acquaint us with the inner workings of things. It does not help us much to be told, as O'Connor tells us in his *John Locke*, that the two notions are 'analogous'. But obviously it would be helpful if we could discern some clear *relationship* between Locke's view on substance and his view on essences. Ayers attempts to do just this.

Ayers makes a strong case for supposing that Locke did *not* distinguish ontologically between real essence and substratum substance, that the latter is not supposed to be 'an entity distinct from *all* its properties', and, further, that Locke sees the notion (like that of power) 'as operating in everyday thought as a sort of dummy concept, *faute de mieux*'. If Ayers is right, the real essence comes in because talk of a substratum or support for the phenomenal qualities of observed objects can, for Locke, 'only be interpreted intelligibly as alluding to this unknown intrinsic nature which is causally responsible for the relational, phenomenal properties'. Ayers covers some difficult ground in this paper, but he is worth following, for if he has succeeded 'agreement will now prove possible on Locke's theory of substance'.

In introducing the topic of personal identity I must start by pointing out that it is now almost inevitable that anyone writing on Locke's thoughts on it will have what Flew says in his paper 'Locke and the Problem of Personal Identity' very near the front of his mind. A word on Flew's paper (which is reprinted in Martin/Armstrong) may then be in order. Flew sums up Locke's position by saying that for him 'X at time two is the same person as Y at time one if and only if X and Y are both persons and X can remember at time two (his doing) what Y did, or felt, or what have you, at time one'. He points out that this formula might be interpreted in various ways, but that whatever interpretation we give it formidable objections will arise. Thus, for example, on one plausible interpretation there will be the objection (derived from Reid) that, while on this criterion an old man will not be the same *person* as a certain youngster if he does not remember the youngster's doings, it would seem that on the same criterion he must be the same person, *given* (a) that he is the same person as a middle-aged man whose doings he does remember and (b) that the middle-aged man did in turn remember having performed the acts of the youngster. Flew also suggests that one of the reasons Locke had for attempting to make a fundamental distinction between 'same man' and 'same person' lay in his 'Platonic–Cartesian conviction that people essentially are incorporeal spirits'. It was another mistake to look for a 'talismanic definition' of 'same person', but Locke would have avoided at least some of his difficulties had he not held that '"person" refers to some bodiless and intangible inhabitant of the dark room of the understanding'.

Flew argues powerfully and his paper will remain required reading for anyone interested in the topic. Indeed Allison concedes in the paper I have included in this collection that objections such as those made by Flew are 'fatal' to Locke's theory. However, if our concern is to understand Locke, there is, I think, more to be said, and without necessarily accepting every detail of Allison's analysis I would suggest that he is clearly on to something important when he stresses that Locke was concerned *not* to identify the diachronic person with an incorporeal spirit or indeed, and as we shall see, with any kind of substance. Locke *does* argue (most improperly) that because we think, we must draw the conclusion 'that there is something *in us* that has a power to think' (I I, i, 10, my emphasis), but the 'infallible' conclusion is not that there is something *immaterial* in us. Allison quite rightly draws attention to the notorious passage in Book I V in which Locke argues that *for all we know* God might have added the power of thought to matter,[10] but it needs stressing that the same agnosticism about the nature of the thinking thing is apparent throughout I I, xxvii. Thus for example the self is said to be 'that conscious thinking thing (whatever substance made up of, *whether spiritual or material, simple or compounded, it matters not*) which is sensible or conscious' (§17, my italics). Admittedly Locke does continue to believe in a thinking substance within the man, and he does think it 'more probable' that the substratum of thought is immaterial (§25), but at the same time he allows that

---

[10] For some pertinent remarks on what Locke says about the possibility of 'thinking matter', see the paper by Ayers reprinted in this collection, pp. 99–100.

we are quite right in thinking that the limbs of our bodies are, for the present at least, *parts of* us as persons (§§11 and 17). And this is not all. More significantly still, Locke holds that our ignorance of the thinking thing is such that we do not even know whether it could perform its operations 'out of a body organized as ours is', or indeed whether each self may not be naturally and inextricably allied to one particular body (§27). To this extent it is true to say that for Locke we *may* be essentially corporeal. Aaron is very much on the right lines when he says in concluding his treatment of the topic in his *John Locke*: 'It is not possible to say what Locke thinks a person to be. He offers us a criterion for testing whether A is one and the same person yesterday and today, yet he does not at all enlighten us on what it is to be a person. Accordingly, the chapter is inadequate both as an analysis of identity, and as an analysis of the self.' Locke is clearly of the opinion that we have here entered an area where the candle that is set up in us does not shine anything like as brightly as we might wish, and I think we must hold that it is his uncertainty about the nature of the thinking thing quite as much as his *belief* that it is probably immaterial, his opposition to dogmatic dualism quite as much as his predilection for dualism, that explains the muddles he gets into over the person and personal identity.

Developing this in my own way, I would suggest that Locke believes that our uncertainty about the nature of the thinking thing must mean that we have to countenance a number of *possibilities*. Thus for example the possibility that thinking, deciding, and so on might be done by an immaterial thing *in* a body leaves open the possibility that the spirit could travel from body to body or subsist in a bodiless state; so in Locke's view we cannot assume that wherever we have the same man we will have the same person. Equally, however, there may be no such immaterial thing, so the concept of personal identity must be distinguished from that of the identity of such an item. Further, given that we do not know what sort of stuff it is that is the substratum of thought, it follows (again in Locke's view) that if we are to have, and use, criteria for personal identity, these must be kept distinct from those for the identity of any kind of stuff. As is well known, Locke ties the concept to *consciousness*, encouraged in this by the conviction that what matters here is not whether there must be substantial identity (which we cannot know) but whether an individual at time two is to be held responsible for the doings of an individual at time one, this not in the weak sense that the same man or the same soul was operative, but in a sense which would make praise or blame and reward or punishment appropriate. It may, I think, be worth pointing out here that just as a reading of II, xxiii has seemed to some to suggest a most unfortunate dual ontological commitment to substance and to real essences, so II, xxvii might *seem* to pose a similar problem. For here we have not just the same man (the physical organism) but also the thinking thing within the man *and* the diachronic person which might, apparently, be allied at different times to different bodies or to different material or immaterial substrates. From this point of view Allison's paper has it in common with Ayers's that it thins out Locke's ontology. Allison argues that the view that emerges in Locke is that the person 'is not in itself an entity of any sort', and he notes that Locke himself stresses that the word should be treated as 'a forensic term, appropriating actions and their merit'. As I read Locke's position, for X to be the same person as Y and accountable for Y's doings it is not (for all we know) essential that the same body should have survived, nor (for all we know) is it essential that the same substratum of thought should be present. What does matter is that two entities of whatever sort should be linked by consciousness, for then we have two entities perhaps but one person.[11]

There is nothing here to clear Locke of the charge of confusion, and Allison (whose main concern is to consider the possible influence of Locke's thinking on Leibniz and Kant) would not claim that there is. The basic confusion apparent throughout seems to be revealed with particular clarity in §13 where Locke refuses to rule out the conceptual possibility that 'one intellectual substance may not have represented to it, as done by itself, what it never did, and was perhaps done by some other agent', judging both that if this happened it would be a *false* representation ('without reality of matter of fact, as well as several representations in dreams are') *and* that if it did happen moral responsibility would have been transferred. Even here, however, he stresses that had we 'clearer views of the nature of thinking substances' we might be able to rule out the transfer of consciousness from substance to substance, recognizing, as he does in §27, that what he takes to be a conceptual possibility may be impossible *given the nature of things* or the way in which the world is in fact ordered. No doubt it is annoying, but it seems also to be true that Locke's firm belief that we have here entered an area where knowledge is impossible leads him to suppose that certain suppositions may (for all we know) be impossible in fact, this where the real question is whether they can be coherently described.

In conclusion I would suggest that to the extent that we can see Locke as offering not a rule for re-identifying a thing but rather a basis for ascriptions

[11] Thus far M. W. Hughes would probably agree. In his 'Personal Identity: a Defence of Locke' (see bibliography) he says: 'to Locke, personal identity was a relation that holds between different substances, which then form one being, but not one substance. Locke adopted this rather confusing but in some ways advantageous terminology because his view of the categories of substance seems to have been that any substance must be either spiritual . . . or material, and he did not wish to place the human person definitely in either category—questions about the personal and substantial categories were just what he wished to escape.' This comes from near the beginning of the paper and, as the title suggests, Hughes builds on to it something that approaches much closer to an attempted *vindication* of Locke than Allison would pretend to.

of moral responsibility and of praise or blame to things, it may be that *some* of the traditional criticisms of him can be seen to miss the mark. In particular, the objection derived from Reid will be much less powerful. One might indeed feel that X could be justly punished for his doings say ten years ago which he remembers clearly but not for his doings twenty years ago which he cannot recall at all, and there would be no *absurdity* here even if one added that ten years ago he could properly have been punished for the earlier doings which he then did remember. And we might even do better for Locke, for there is evidence that he may not require any more than that I can be brought to associate myself with doings which I may not at first think I remember. The objections now will be these. First, that even in forensic contexts none of us would think it appropriate to apply any such simple rule as might be derived from Locke (cf. Allison on Molyneux's drunkard and on Leibniz on rights). Secondly, that Locke will have failed completely to elucidate that sense of 'same person' in which as a conscious being I can be said to be the same person as the small child whose doings I may have forgotten beyond recall, but whose experiences in part explain the character I have as a person now. And, finally, he will not have solved the problem of personal identity in a way which will enable anyone to decide whether Y's doings can properly be referred to X at time two as *his* earlier doings. X may with some degree of ease be brought to represent to himself those doings as his, but the representation may be false. For X to be accountable for Y's doings those apparent memories (if they are relevant) must be actual memories, and memories of what *he* did. Locke has no answer to it, but the problem of what relationship must hold between X and Y if X's apparent memories of Y's doings are to be judged actual memories raises once more the problem of personal identity as traditionally conceived.

VI

Martin and Armstrong were not able to include anything on Locke's polemic against innatism in their collection, so it is fortunate that it is possible to include two papers on this topic here. Indeed this was one area where it was particularly difficult to decide which of a number of worthwhile papers should go in. It was to be expected that if there was a general increase of interest in the *Essay* this would extend to Book I, but of course there is an additional factor explaining the revival of interest here.

In the course of his brief treatment of Book I in his *John Locke* (originally published by Penguin Books in 1952) O'Connor observes that the theory Locke attacks 'seems to us at the present day grotesque and absurd' and that this is so because 'Locke's empirical outlook has become part of an intellectual background which we tend to accept without reflection'. Whether the 'crude' version of innatism attacked by Locke was ever accepted by any respectable thinker he judges to be 'an historical matter, and for our purposes unimportant'. Much more surprisingly we find Mabbott saying in his book, published as recently as 1973, that there has been 'no trace' of innate ideas in recent thought.

This is false, for the claim that we do indeed have innate knowledge is prominent in the extremely influential work of the linguist Noam Chomsky. As John Searle points out:

The most spectacular conclusion about the nature of the human mind that Chomsky derives from his work in linguistics is that his results vindicate the claims of the seventeenth-century rationalist philosophers, Descartes, Leibniz, and others, that there are innate ideas in the mind. . . . For empiricists all knowledge comes from experience, for rationalists some knowledge is implanted innately and prior to experience. In his bluntest moods, Chomsky claims to have refuted the empiricists and vindicated the rationalists.[12]

Basically Chomsky's view is that the facts of language-learning show that the mind is not simply a blank tablet receiving data from without, but that it must be stocked with complex *principles*, *schematisms* or *structures*—an innate and universal *grammar*—in accordance with which it organizes the data to master whatever natural language it is learning. The claim is an exciting one, and it means that Locke scholars have an additional reason for wanting to look again at Locke's attack on innatism in Book I.

When selecting papers for this collection I decided not to include anything where the main concern was Chomsky's philosophical reflections and in which Locke played a subordinate role. Instead I looked for papers where Locke was prominent, and from a number of these I selected one short piece by Grenville Wall in which Chomsky is not mentioned at all, and one by John Harris which is broadly sympathetic to Chomsky but which is of interest primarily because it looks at the relationship between Locke and Leibniz on this issue. As Searle points out, Leibniz is one of the rationalists whom Chomsky claims to be vindicating. Indeed Chomsky sometimes cites the famous passage to which Harris draws attention in which truths are said to be innate in us in the way in which the figure of Hercules might be said to be innate in a block of marble 'if there were veins in the block which should indicate the figure of Hercules rather than other figures'. In the same passage Leibniz tells us that 'ideas and truths are for us innate, as inclinations, dispositions, habits, or natural potentialities, and not as actions; although these potentialities are always accompanied by some actions, often insensible, which correspond to them'.

---

[12] The quotation comes from 'Chomsky's Revolution in Linguistics' which will be found (reprinted from *The New York Review of Books*) in the book edited by Harman which I have listed in the bibliography. It might be helpful if I refer here to the paper by Nagel contained in Harman's collection. Readers wondering whether Chomsky establishes the existence of innate *knowledge* should find this paper stimulating.

Wall, in his paper, is concerned to bring out and account for the surprising fact that Locke, who is concerned with human *knowledge*, fails to note that he could confront the innatist with the observation that even if the mind were stocked with innate principles it would not follow that we had any more than innate *beliefs*. Upgrading the beliefs to the status of knowledge could not be achieved simply by stressing that they formed part of the mind's original furniture. 'In other words, *how* we come to be acquainted with these principles is beside the point. Even if some principles are innate this is no guarantee of their truth.' That Locke does not make this point is explained by his assumption that if there were innate beliefs they would be implanted in our minds by God and so would, surely, be true. 'Thus, although it is Locke's theological convictions and his concern for religious toleration which inspire his attack on the doctrine of innate knowledge, it is his theological convictions which prevent him from using what would strike us as the most direct epistemological refutation of it.' We can compare here Leibniz's observation (quoted in part by Harris) that innate notions are 'luminous flashes, concealed within us', indicating 'something divine and eternal which appears especially in the necessary truths'.

Harris's paper provides us with a thorough study of Leibniz and Locke on innate knowledge. I shall not attempt to summarize all his findings here, though it is worth noting that the two emerge as having different ways of looking at the mind and that Chomsky is introduced not as supporting Leibniz but as having 'a third way of looking at the mind, which seems to me more reasonable than that of either of the two protagonists'. This is of course 'that there is an innate human faculty concerned with the learning of language, based on a "language acquisition device" which contains information relevant to, and even necessary for, the process of collecting data from the perception of speech, and incorporating it into a grammar of the language being learned'. Harris does not, then, see Chomsky as *vindicating* Leibniz, but he does see him as going much further than Locke in substituting extremely specific dispositions for the very general natural capacities that Locke was prepared to attribute to the human mind.

One point I should perhaps make on this is that not all philosophers would agree with Harris's observation that 'whether we choose to call this a theory about innate ideas and knowledge seems not to be important'.[13] For some would want to stress that, even if Chomsky has located very specific dis-

---

[13] As Jonathan Barnes points out in his paper (see bibliography), 'in one mood' Chomsky does himself say this sort of thing: claiming that 'the terminological question . . . seems hardly worth pursuing'. But Barnes goes on to stress that 'in other moods, and more frequently, Chomsky takes the question of innate knowledge seriously'. Given this, *we* can hardly treat the terminological question as unimportant, because there is a real issue involved, viz. what Chomsky's innatism amounts to.

positions, he has not shown that the language learner has what we can recognize as innate ideas, beliefs, or *knowledge* of the operative principles. This is clearly something that needs to be looked at, but here I can only refer to a long and detailed study of Locke's polemic in a paper by Jonathan Barnes (listed in the bibliography) in which the observation that Chomsky does not succeed in establishing more than innate dispositions to order data in certain ways has its role to play in supporting the conclusion 'first, that Chomsky is not, in any very direct fashion, the philosophical heir of Leibniz and his crew; and secondly, that he does not make good his claim to have revived innate ideas or innate knowledge'.

LOCKE'S ATTACK ON INNATE KNOWLEDGE

GRENVILLE WALL

MOST of the standard commentaries on Locke's *Essay* are inadequate in their treatment of Book I for one or more of a variety of reasons. Gibson's evaluation[1] of Locke's actual arguments is confined to one section. Lamprecht's paper[2] was of importance in drawing attention to the theological significance of Locke's attack on the doctrine of innate knowledge—a view which has been substantiated by the more recent work of Yolton.[3] However, neither of these authors examines Locke's arguments in any detail. Aaron[4] examines them in a sympathetic and fairly detailed manner, though he failed to notice what I shall argue is a notable omission from Locke's attack. O'Connor's discussion[5] of it is compressed into less than two pages. No doubt his view that the doctrine was 'grotesque and absurd' led him to believe that Locke's attack on it hardly merited attention. The purpose of this note is not to provide a thorough review of the arguments, but first, to point to a curious omission in them, and second, to try to explain it.

I

Despite Locke's dislike of the epistemological purposes for which the doctrine of innate knowledge was being used by his contemporaries, his specifically epistemological comments are oblique rather than direct. For the purpose of the attack Locke treats the doctrine primarily as if it were an empirical hypothesis about how we come to possess certain items of knowledge rather than as an epistemological thesis about why certain principles *are* items of knowledge.

From *Philosophy*, 49 (1974), pp. 414–19. Reprinted, with minor changes and corrections, by permission of the author and the publisher, Cambridge University Press.

[1] J. Gibson, *Locke's Theory of Knowledge* (Cambridge University Press, 1917), Ch. II, §6.

[2] S. L. Lamprecht, 'Locke's Attack on Innate Ideas', *Phil. Rev.*, 36 (2), Mar. 1927.

[3] J. W. Yolton, *John Locke and the Way of Ideas* (Oxford University Press, 1956).

[4] R. I. Aaron, *John Locke* (Oxford University Press, 2nd edition, 1955).

[5] D. J. O'Connor, *John Locke* (Dover Books, 1967), pp. 39–40.

That Locke treats the doctrine in this way is sufficiently evidenced by noting the sorts of arguments he deploys against it. These arguments are often fairly subtle, especially when he is dealing with the defensive manoeuvres which his opponents might make in response to his criticisms. But in essence his argument is directed towards showing that there are no adequate grounds for believing the hypothesis that there are any principles which are innate. The burden of his case is borne by Chapter ii of Book I in which he argues against the existence of innate speculative principles.[6] His attack rests on a series of critical points directed against the argument from universal assent. I shall not discuss them in detail, but confine myself to illustrating the sorts of points he makes.

The first is that even if there were propositions which commanded universal assent, this would not prove them to be innate unless all other explanations of such uniformity of belief could be confidently ruled out.[7] The second is that even for the most promising candidates, universal assent does not exist.[8] Thirdly, children and idiots do not possess such propositional knowledge.[9] All defensive moves against the last objection involve either modifying the doctrine to the true but trivial claim that we have an innate capacity to know, which if represented as a doctrine of innate knowledge is 'a very improper way of speaking',[10] or, alternatively, they involve the supposition that children do possess this knowledge, but with the qualification that it remains latent until a later date—for example, until they come to the age of reason. But this line of defence presupposes that it is possible for someone to know a proposition of which he has never been aware. Locke pronounces this to be 'near a contradiction'.[11] The remainder of Chapter ii consists of an examination of a number of variants on the theme that children do have innate knowledge of which they remain unaware until a later date. In some cases, when pressed into an extreme defensive posture, the doctrine becomes redundant or impossible to distinguish from other views, for example, the view that we can acquire knowledge by the exercise of reason.

In Chapter iii Locke points out that there is even less agreement over practical principles than there is over speculative ones.[12] Therefore the

---

[6] No doubt Locke chose to develop his criticisms against such principles first, before applying them to moral and religious principles, (a) because they seemed to be particularly good candidates for innateness, (b) because his criticisms might be more impartially considered when deployed against abstract principles.

[7] *Essay*, I, ii, 3. All references are to the Everyman edition, edited by J. W. Yolton. All italics are reproduced from the text.

[8] I, ii, 4.

[9] I, ii, 5.

[10] I, ii, 5.

[11] I, ii, 5.

[12] I, iii, 1–2.

argument from universal assent is even weaker in the sphere of morality. Furthermore the fact that whole nations break certain moral principles and yet show no remorse can hardly be made to square with the view that knowledge of such principles is innate.[13] Finally in Chapter iv, Locke points out that if principles are supposed to be innate, then the ideas which are involved in them must also be supposed to be innate. Once again, he argues, the evidence in no way supports such a conclusion.[14]

II

Nearly all the arguments which Locke deploys against the doctrine suggest that for the purposes of his attack he regarded it primarily as a psycho-genetic account of how we come to possess certain items of knowledge. There are one or two arguments which are suggestive of a more direct philosophical attack on it. For example, when he deals with the view that children become aware of their innate knowledge when they come to the age of reason, he points out that on one interpretation, this could mean that 'reason assists them in the discovery of these principles'.[15] But this can hardly count as a doctrine of innate knowledge any longer. Such an appeal to reason in order to account for the 'discovery' of such principles makes the doctrine redundant, not only psychologically, but also, one might add, epistemologically. Similarly, towards the end of Chapter iii, echoing his remarks on what were claimed by enthusiasts (fanatics) to be 'revelations',[16] Locke asks how 'genuine innate principles may be distinguished from others, that so, amidst the great variety of pretenders, I may be kept from mistakes in so material a point as this'.[17] It is only a small step from posing this problem to rejecting innateness as a criterion of truth altogether. Nevertheless he treats the doctrine primarily as an hypothesis which stands or falls according to the empirical evidence. But its primary use amongst Locke's contemporaries was epistemological. The mass of evidence accumulated in Yolton's book shows that it was constantly being appealed to in some form or other as a means of guaranteeing the truth of the fundamental principles of religion and morality.[18] Furthermore, some of Locke's critics argued that his attack on the doctrine was tantamount to an attempt to undermine belief in these fundamental principles.[19] It is also clear that Locke's own attitude towards the doctrine

[13] I, iii, 9–13.
[14] I, iv, 1–8.
[15] I, ii, 7.
[16] IV, xix. See also IV, xvi, 14.
[17] I, iii, 27.
[18] Op. cit., Ch. II.
[19] See for example Yolton's quotation from William Sherlock's *Digression Concerning Connate Ideas* (1704), ibid., p. 61.

was prompted by the epistemological uses which were made of it, as is sufficiently revealed by a quotation:

When men have found some general propositions that could not be doubted of, as soon as understood, it was, I know, *a short and easy way to conclude them innate*. This being once received, it eased the lazy from the pains of search and stopped the inquiry of the doubtful concerning all that was once styled innate; and it was of no small advantage, to those who affected to be masters and teachers, to make this the principle of *principles*: that principles must not be questioned. For having once established this tenet, that there are innate principles, it put their followers upon a necessity of receiving some doctrines as such; which was to take them off from the use of their own reason and judgment and put them upon believing and taking them upon trust, without further examination: in which posture of blind credulity, they might be more easily governed by and made useful to some sort of men, who had the skill and office to principle and guide them.[20]

Locke clearly felt that the doctrine was being used as a pseudo-epistemological device to buttress obscurantism and as an instrument of intellectual oppression. Nevertheless, his primary intent is to question its empirical foundation. True enough, if it can be shown to be empirically unfounded, it cannot be appealed to for epistemological purposes. But why was Locke content with this kind of attack when its epistemological pretensions had been charmingly exposed and decisively refuted by Samuel Parker twenty-four years before the publication of the *Essay*? Yolton quotes the relevant passage from Parker's *Free and Impartial Censure of the Platonick Philosophie* (1666):

But suppose that we were born with these congenite Anticipations, and that they take Root in our very Faculties, yet how can I be certain of their Truth and Veracity? For 'tis not impossible but the seeds of Error might have been the natural Results of my Faculties, as Weeds are the first and natural Issues of the best Soyles, how then shall we be sure that these spontaneous Notions are not false and spurious?[21]

In other words, *how* we come to be acquainted with these principles is beside the point. Even if some principles are innate this is no guarantee of their truth. What is so remarkable about Book I of the *Essay* is that Locke does not make use of this sort of attack. It is even more remarkable when we reflect on his insistence that we can usually establish the truth of many of the principles which are claimed to be innate by other means.[22] It is only a short step from this position to the conclusion that innateness cannot by itself be used as a criterion of truth.

III

Having remarked upon Locke's notable omission, we must now try to

---

[20] I, iv, 25.
[21] Yolton, op. cit., p. 44.
[22] See for example I, ii, 16.

explain it. One possible approach is to suggest that it just never occurred to him because of his psycho-genetic preoccupations in Book II. Therefore the kind of criticism of innate knowledge which would naturally suggest itself to him would have been an attack on it as a rival hypothesis about the source or origin of some of our beliefs, and therefore some of our ideas, rather than an attack on it as an account of why those beliefs should be taken to be true.

However, I wish to propose a more radical explanation. It is that Locke shared with his opponents the view that *if* there were any innate principles then they *would* be true. There is a significant passage in Chapter iii in which Locke argues against the view that there are any innate moral principles. He says:

Another reason that makes me doubt of any innate practical principles is that I think *there cannot any one moral rule be proposed whereof a man may not justly demand a reason*: which would be perfectly ridiculous and absurd if they were innate, or so much as self-evident, which every innate principle must needs be, and not need any proof to ascertain its truth, nor want any reason to gain it approbation.[23]

Even if we side-step the problem of deciding what precisely Locke means by 'self-evident' and how self-evidence would make itself manifest in innate principles, it is clear that Locke commits himself to the view that *if* there were any innate principles they *would* be self-evident and therefore true. If this is so, then it is hardly surprising that he did not avail himself of Samuel Parker's argument.

Now we face another puzzling question. Why was Locke committed to this view? One possible explanation is that he took it uncritically from his opponents.[24] After all the assumption was widespread. But a more definite and interesting answer can be given to this question. At the beginning of Chapter ii Locke says:

For I imagine anyone will easily grant that it would be impertinent to suppose the *ideas* of colours innate in a creature to whom God has given sight, and a power to receive them by the eyes, from external objects; and no less unreasonable would it be to attribute several truths to the impressions of nature and innate characters, when we may observe in ourselves faculties, fit to attain as easy and certain knowledge of them, as if they were originally imprinted on the mind.[25]

There is in this passage not only the explicit statement that God has given us our faculties, a point repeated elsewhere in Book I,[26] but an implied statement that if there were any innate principles, these would also have been

---

[23] I, iii, 4.
[24] See for example, I, iii, 13 and 14, and I, iv, 12.
[25] I, ii, 1.
[26] See I, i, 5, and I, iv, 12 and 23.

imprinted by God.[27] But fortunately we do not have to rely on speculations about what Locke might or might not have implied by these remarks. In Chapter iv he is more explicit:

I grant that *if* there were *any ideas* to be found *imprinted* on the minds of men, we have reason to expect *it should be the notion of his maker*, as a mark God set on his own workmanship, to mind man of his dependence and duty. . . .[28]

I think that these two passages point fairly clearly to the view that if there were any innate principles Locke could only explain them by supposing that they were imprinted by God. Further, Locke could not even countenance a God-deceiver problem. For example, revelations, if they are genuine (i.e. if they come from God) are trustworthy because 'we may as well doubt of our own being as we can whether any revelation from God be true'.[29] Therefore, if there were any innate principles imprinted on our minds by God, they would have to be taken as true. Thus, although it is Locke's theological convictions and his concern for religious toleration which inspire his attack on the doctrine of innate knowledge, it is his theological convictions which prevent him from using what would strike us as the most direct epistemological refutation of it.

[27] See also I, iv, 12 and 22.

[28] I, iv, 13.

[29] IV, xvi, 14. The problem here, of course, is how to distinguish genuine revelations from spurious ones.

II

LEIBNIZ AND LOCKE ON INNATE IDEAS*

JOHN HARRIS

'The question of the origin of our ideas and of our maxims is not preliminary in Philosophy, and we must have made great progress in order to solve it successfully.'

G. W. LEIBNIZ

INTRODUCTION

THE recent work of Chomsky and his colleagues on the nature and acquisition of language has brought innate ideas once again into the forefront of philosophical discussion. Since Chomsky has explicitly related his views on this issue to those of the seventeenth-century Rationalists, interest in their opinions and those of their opponents has also been revived, and I would like to take advantage of this renewed interest to examine the controversy over innate ideas as reflected in the work of Leibniz and Locke.

Locke's attack on the doctrine of innate ideas in the first book of *An Essay Concerning Human Understanding* is justly famous; but Leibniz's counter-attack and re-affirmation of the doctrine in his *New Essays Concerning Human Understanding*, a commentary on Locke's *Essay*, is less well known. As a result, Leibniz's views on innate ideas, which receive their fullest expression in the *New Essays*, are seldom discussed in the detail they deserve, and one of the aims of my paper is to remedy this. But my main aim is to make precise the nature of the differences between Locke and Leibniz over this issue, and I hope that this will prove valuable not only to students of the history of philosophy, but also to those who take an interest in the present debate concerning innate ideas. I discuss the views of the two philosophers on the mode of existence and the development of innate ideas and knowledge in the

From *Ratio*, 16 (1974), pp. 226–42. Reprinted, with very minor changes, by permission of the author and the publisher, Basil Blackwell and Mott Ltd.

* References to both Locke's *Essay* and Leibniz's *New Essays* give Chapter, Book, and Para-graph numbers, where all are available. I have used the edition of the *New Essays* translated by A. G. Langley (London, 1896) and the references here add the page numbers of this edition, referred to as 'Langley'. I would like to thank Colin McGinn and Desmond Henry for their helpful comments on an earlier draft of this paper.

mind, agreeing with Locke against Leibniz that they have substantially different theories. I then suggest an alternative to both and briefly argue its advantages. Finally I look at Leibniz's reasons for postulating innate necessary truths, and conclude that they are inadequate because they conflate logical and psychological issues; one possible reason for this conflation is mentioned.

Before we begin, one possible difficulty should be mentioned. Leibniz is famous as the author of the *Monadology*, and at a quick glance it might seem as though any views that he held about the origin of knowledge must be overshadowed by the metaphysics he expounds in this and other works. If, as Leibniz argues, persons are monads, self-contained and 'windowless' souls, then the contrast between knowledge which is derived from experience by sensation or reflection and that which has its source in the mind is lost; yet this contrast is central to arguments about the origin of ideas. In consequence, it is not easy to see how Leibniz can take part in an argument about innate ideas with a philosopher such as Locke who would reject his metaphysics completely.

Surprisingly enough, Leibniz does not see this as a difficulty. He tells us that for the moment we may forget the theory of monads and conduct the discussion using 'the received expressions':

since in fact they are good and tenable, and one can say in a certain sense that the external senses are in part causes of our thoughts, I shall consider how in my opinion one must say even in the common system . . . that there are some ideas and some principles which do not come to us from the senses, and which we find in ourselves without forming them, although the senses give us occasion to perceive them.[1]

In talking according to the common system Leibniz thinks that he is following the example of the Copernicans, who still speak, harmlessly enough, of the sun rising and moving across the sky. What they say, and what Leibniz says about innate ideas, is, like much colloquial speech, subject to translation into a more scientifically or metaphysically precise terminology. I do not myself share Leibniz's equanimity about this process, which in his case surely involves more than a mere translation from one terminology into another, but since I do not want to involve myself in a discussion about metaphysics and ordinary language which would be irrelevant to my purpose, I shall accept Leibniz's offer and treat his views on innatism as distinct from his monadology. They remain valid and interesting even if it should turn out to be impossible to reconcile them with other parts of his system.

Leibniz was a great admirer of Locke's *Essay*, describing it as 'one of the most beautiful and esteemed works of this period'. But his admiration did not prevent him being in basic disagreement with its empiricist standpoint.

---

[1] *New Essays*, 1/1/1 (Langley, p. 70).

'Our systems', Leibniz says, 'are very different. His has more relation to Aristotle, mine to Plato.'[2] With regard to the question of the origin of knowledge, he sees the issue as being between those like Locke and Aristotle who see the soul as entirely empty at birth, like a tablet on which nothing has been written; and those like Plato and himself who think that the soul contains the principles of many ideas and doctrines, which can be called to mind in certain circumstances.

These remarks support the commonly held view that Leibniz and Locke are completely opposed on this issue. Locke denies the existence of both innate propositional knowledge and innate concepts or ideas; Leibniz asserts that all kinds of innate knowledge exist—for example, all necessary truths are held to be innate—and many innate ideas, including those of God, identity, possibility, and geometrical figures such as triangles. But the position is complicated by Leibniz's occasional suggestions that there is really little difference between his views and those of Locke, if the latter are correctly understood and their consequences drawn out. These apparently conflicting claims will be evaluated later.

MODELS OF THE MIND

One thing which stands out clearly in even a brief survey of the seventeenth-century debates on innate ideas is the widespread use of picturesque models and metaphors to describe the mind and its contents. Locke, after denying the existence of innate principles and ideas in the first book of the *Essay*, begins the second by comparing the mind to 'white paper void of all characters'. More precisely it is the understanding, the faculty of the mind specially concerned with ideas and knowledge, which is empty at birth, before experience can begin to fill it through the channels of sensation and reflection. We should perhaps add something that Locke thought too obvious to mention explicitly in the *Essay*; that he nowhere denies the existence of natural faculties such as perception, understanding and memory, and innate mental powers like those of abstraction, comparison and discernment. The 'white paper' metaphor is meant to indicate that the understanding (and hence the mind) is originally empty of *objects* of thought like ideas; but it has whatever apparatus is necessary to acquire them through experience, and then to derive knowledge by comparing and contrasting them with each other.

Leibniz is fond of metaphors himself, but he objects to this one. One reason for this is his belief in the identity of indiscernibles, which makes the idea of blank-paper minds, presumably differing only *solo numero*, repugnant to him. But another reason for his objection is that he thinks the metaphor is inadequate as it stands, and so he offers one of his own:

[2] Preface to *New Essays* (Langley, p. 42).

I have made use also of the comparison of a block of marble which has veins, rather than that of a block of marble wholly even, or of blank tablets. . . . For if the soul resembled these blank tablets, truths would be in us as the figure of Hercules is in the marble, when the marble is wholly indifferent to the reception of this figure or some other. But if there were veins in the block which should indicate the figure of Hercules rather than other figures, this block would be more determined thereto, and Hercules would be in it as in some sense innate, although it would be needful to labour to discover these veins, to clear them by polishing, and by cutting away what prevents them from appearing. Thus it is that ideas and truths are for us innate, as inclinations, dispositions, habits, or natural potentialities, and not as actions.[3]

This suggests that innate truths, and presumably ideas as well, exist ready formed in the mind, and need only to be brought to light.

In another interesting passage Leibniz again replaces a model of Locke's with an elaborated version of his own. Locke in the *Essay* compares the understanding to a room, with small openings through which data from the senses can come and be ordered so that it is available when needed.[4] Leibniz says[5] that in order to make the resemblance greater we should suppose that in the room there was a canvas to receive the images from outside, not even, but diversified by folds; these would then represent the different kinds of innate knowledge. This canvas should also be seen as having certain natural powers and dispositions, such as elasticity, and an action of its own, which can be likened to the vibrations and oscillations of a plucked string. Thus, Leibniz says, the canvas which represents our brain is necessarily active and elastic; as for the mind, it represents these properties of the brain without extension.

Leibniz seems to want here to distinguish between innateness in the brain and in the mind; he turns Locke's model of the understanding into one of the brain; but it is not clear why he chooses to do this. In one place he criticizes Locke for using physical models like this to describe the mind ('Has the soul windows, does it resemble tablets, is it like wax? It is plain that all who so regard the soul, represent it as at bottom corporeal'[6]); but Leibniz himself is as guilty of this error, if it is one, as Locke. But whatever Leibniz's motivation, the point that he is making about the active and organizing nature of the brain seems a good one, and it is one that I think Locke would have agreed with. The comparison of the brain with an elastic canvas seems a little strange to us in the twentieth century; but it is only to be expected that our knowledge of its natural mode of operation and capacities of storage and computation should have increased far beyond that of Leibniz.

---

[3] Ibid. (Langley, pp. 45–6).
[4] *Essay*, II, xi, 17.
[5] *New Essays*, 2/12 (Langley, p. 147).
[6] Ibid. 2/1/2 (Langley, pp. 110–11).

But let us leave these speculations about the brain, and return to discuss innate ideas with reference to the mind, as Leibniz and Locke do most of the time. Both the revised metaphor of the block of marble with veins and the model of the brain as 'active and elastic' indicate that Leibniz wishes to stress the dispositional or virtual nature of innate ideas and knowledge. We can now pursue this notion a little further, with particular reference to innate propositional knowledge, around which much of the discussion centres.

Locke's attack on innate principles (and innate ideas as well) is two-pronged. He attempts to show first, that theories of innatism of varying sophistication are either unintelligible, false, or, if modified, trivially true; and second, that they are all irrelevant and unnecessary since we have no need of innate ideas to explain how the mind equips itself. I will be dealing with this second line of argument, and also with Leibniz's reply, in the last part of the paper.

What, Locke asks, can be meant by those who say that there are some principles stamped on the mind of man, 'constant impressions which the souls of men receive in their first beings, and which they bring into the world with them, as necessarily and really as they do any of their inherent faculties'?[7] This claim seems to imply that all who possess such principles *know* them; can state them or at least assent to them when they see and understand them. But this is not the case. Leibniz (and no doubt most other proponents of innate ideas) would have agreed that Locke was right about this. Innate knowledge is *potential* in all, but only actual in some, and so the facts are in accordance with this. Locke was very sceptical about the notion of innate potential knowledge; and sometimes it is just the idea of non-conscious knowledge that worries him. He thinks that it is 'near a contradiction to say that there are truths imprinted on the soul which it perceives or understands not: imprinting, if it signify anything, being nothing else but the making certain truths to be perceived'. And again, 'to imprint anything on the mind, without the mind's perceiving it, seems to me hardly intelligible'.[8] This, Leibniz quickly points out, must at least be an overstatement. If the notion of non-conscious knowledge is unintelligible, then what, in Locke's opinion, does memory consist in?

But sometimes it seems that it is not the idea of non-conscious knowledge *per se* that Locke dislikes—he allows the *un*conscious propositional knowledge of memory—but that of knowledge which is not only unconscious, but which has never at any time been conscious (which I shall now refer to exclusively as non-conscious knowledge). 'No proposition can be said to be in the mind, which it never yet knew, which it was never yet conscious of.'[9] Locke expands

---

[7] *Essay*, I, ii, 2.   [8] Ibid. I, ii, 5.   [9] Ibid.

this view later in the *Essay*,[10] where he claims that if there are any innate ideas in the mind which the mind does not actually think on, they must be lodged in the memory. But ideas stored in the memory are brought from there by remembrance and must be known when recalled to have been in the mind before, 'unless remembrance can be without remembrance'. But this is not possible for innate knowledge, that which by definition does not come from normal sources; hence innate knowledge cannot exist in the memory; and so, according to what was premissed, it does not exist in the mind at all.

This weak reasoning is soundly refuted by Leibniz.[11] First, it is not true that all memories are known as such in the mind; we frequently recall things yet are unaware of doing so, like the man who 'believed he had composed a new verse, which it turned out he read word for word a long time previous in some ancient poet'.[12] And second, what is at issue is the intelligibility of the notion of non-conscious knowledge; but if Locke allows that there can be unconscious knowledge, that stored in the memory, this concedes the central point. If acquired knowledge can be stored unconsciously in the mind, then why shouldn't there be a store of original or innate knowledge existing non-consciously? Why need all knowledge have been 'present to consciousness' at some time?

Leibniz has had much the better of the argument so far, but the matter is not as simple as it seems, and Locke has something of a rejoinder; or at least there is one that we can construct for him, and which I think is in sympathy with his general position. I think that Locke would have objected to the use of the word 'knowledge' to describe the contents of a non-conscious store such as Leibniz proposes; how can that which we have never openly considered and understood be called knowledge—or even belief, for that matter? As Locke says in one of his more modern-sounding passages: 'if these words (*to be in the understanding*) have any propriety, they signify to be understood'.[13] Knowledge must be *known* by the person who possesses it. This objection to the idea of non-conscious knowledge is identical to that which the opponents of Chomsky have urged against his claim that every user of a natural language non-consciously knows the rules which constitute the grammar of the language, in all their splendid (and to most people's conscious minds, incomprehensible) detail.[14] The reply is the same, too; that if the objector wishes we will not call this knowledge (or belief) until it becomes conscious—if this happens at all, since both Chomsky and Leibniz insist that it may not. Thus the mind contains non-conscious knowledge in the same sense that a library

---

[10] Ibid. I, iv, 21.
[11] See, e.g., Preface to *New Essays* (Langley, p. 46).
[12] *New Essays*, 1/3/20 (Langley, p. 106).
[13] *Essay*, I ii, 5.
[14] See, e.g., the debate in *Language and Philosophy*, ed. S. Hook (N.Y., 1969).

contains knowledge; a sense that does not imply that the knowledge is known to that which houses it.

Leibniz has other reasons, drawn from the murkier depths of his meta-physics, for not rejecting various notions of the unconscious. In particular he mentions the 'petites perceptions' which, taken singly, are below the sensory threshold and hence unnoticed by the conscious mind, but which rise above it when they are combined with others in a normal perceptual experience. In general Leibniz thinks that '*the insensible perceptions* are as eminently useful in Pneumatology as are the insensible corpuscles in Physics, and it is equally unreasonable to reject the one or the other under the pretext that they are out of reach of our senses'.[15] He even takes this admirable maxim to the doubtful extreme of claiming that 'we have an infinite amount of knowledge of which we are not always conscious, not even when we need it',[16] but this seems to be a reference to the nature of monadic perception, rather than a claim about innateness in 'the common system'.

THE DEVELOPMENT OF INNATE IDEAS IN THE MIND

In the *Essay* Locke considers theories of innatism of varying sophistication (though this is not the word he would have used!); hence the criticism some-times levelled against him that he chooses only the simplest is unfair. One suggestion[17] he examines is that knowledge of certain maxims is innate in the sense that the mind has a natural capacity to assent to them when it has under-stood them. Locke rejects this not because it is false, but because it is trivially true, and does not amount to a theory of innate *knowledge*. Thus if I under-stand or know any proposition then it follows that I must have had the capacity to do this, and so acceptance of their theory of innatism would mean that all the truths we come to know are innate, 'and this great point will amount to no more, but only to a very improper way of speaking; which, whilst it pretends to assert the contrary, says nothing different from those who deny innate principles'.[18] The latter persons, who include Locke, are quite willing to allow that there exist natural capacities to acquire knowledge and ideas, which the mind has in virtue of its natural endowment of faculties and powers; but these capacities are general in nature, and do not favour particular truths or concepts.

Leibniz denies that his theory, at least, states no more than that the mind has such natural general capacities for acquiring knowledge; the mind, he thinks, is not only capable of knowing innate truths, but has the further power

---

[15] *New Essays*, Preface (Langley, p. 50).
[16] Ibid. 1/1/5 (Langley, p. 77).
[17] *Essay*, I, ii, 5.
[18] Ibid.

of finding them in itself.[19] We can here profitably recall the difference between Locke's comparison of the mind at birth to a blank sheet of paper, on which any truth can be written and which therefore favours none in particular, and Leibniz's use of the model of a block of marble in which the figure of Hercules is marked out by veins, and only awaits uncovering. To sum up their differences on this point: Locke envisages the understanding *acquiring* all its knowledge and ideas by the exercise of its natural and unspecific faculties and powers, but Leibniz sees it as *possessing* some knowledge and ideas which can be extracted ready formed. Now in the *Essay* Locke goes into considerable detail as to how knowledge and ideas are acquired; what has Leibniz to tell us about the process of extracting at least some of them from the mind?

There seem to be two main causal factors involved: sense experience, which serves as the occasion or indirect cause of the emergence of innate knowledge into consciousness, and which Leibniz implies is a necessary condition of this process; and reflection and thought, 'attention to what is in us'[20] as Leibniz sometimes describes it, which is the direct cause and also necessary. Together these causes are usually sufficient. We can see how they work by recalling a famous example which Leibniz quotes with approval:[21] Plato's description in the *Meno* of a slave boy drawing principles and concepts of geometry from his mind under the expert guidance of Socrates. Here the diagrams drawn in the dust, and presumably also Socrates' expert instruction, serve as the occasion of the extraction; and its immediate or direct cause is the reflection and thought of the slave boy.

My hesitation as to what precisely Leibniz's view on extraction is comes about because he nowhere describes what it involves in detail. For example, the distinction between occasional and direct causes is used, but not mentioned in the *New Essays*; but fortunately it is both used and examined by Descartes in his *Notes Against A Certain Programme*, and I think we can assume that their views on its use are similar. Descartes, in discussing the innate knowledge we have of God, claims that in its extraction from the mind both tradition (explicit teaching) and observation are remote or indirect causes, 'inviting us to bethink ourselves of the idea which we may have of God, and to present it vividly to our thought'[22] and hence are not alone sufficient to give us this idea. They must be backed up by a clear and perhaps prolonged reflection on the idea of God (like that of Descartes in the *Meditations*) and it is this which is mainly responsible for the emergence of the idea and the knowledge of God associated with it into the conscious mind. This distinction

[19] *New Essays*, 1/1/5 (Langley, p. 80).
[20] Ibid., Preface (Langley, p. 45).
[21] Ibid. 1/1/5 (Langley, p. 78).
[22] Haldane and Ross, I, p. 444.

between the occasional and direct causes of an event seems to correspond roughly to the modern one between enabling conditions which provide a state of readiness for the occurrence of an event, and stimulus conditions which actually bring it about in those circumstances.[23] The idea that some aspects of individual development may require both enabling conditions, which affect only the onset of the changes and possibly also their continuation, but not their form; and stimulus conditions which guide and control the development, is well established in modern biology and psychology.

But there is one obvious objection that can be raised against Leibniz's claim that sense-experience is only the occasion of the development of innate knowledge and ideas in the mind. If we think of Socrates and the slave boy it is natural to suppose that the conditions which are on both Locke's and Leibniz's accounts necessary for the boy to learn geometry were also sufficient for this to happen. No hypothesis of innateness (apart from the minimal one which allows us natural faculties and the ability to use them) is required. This objection would, of course, be urged by Locke against Leibniz; Locke believes that we may attain to all the knowledge we have simply by use of our natural faculties, without the help of innate impressions. The difficulty here is to decide between the two positions: how are we to demonstrate that sense-experience and teaching plus normal intelligence are or are not sufficient to acquire knowledge of, say, geometry? Leibniz in fact backs up his claim that they are not enough by arguing that there is some knowledge and some ideas that just could not be acquired in this fashion, and I will be examining his argument later. But if this *a priori* argument fails we are back where we started, and we will have to find some experimental means of deciding the case; perhaps, in the end, we will have to turn to neurophysiology and a direct examination of the brain for the answer to this key question, which recurs again and again in arguments about innateness.

That we have this difficulty in demonstrating innateness is not, as some seem to think, an argument against the coherence of the innatists' position. We can imagine beings for which the existence of innate knowledge could be quite simply demonstrated: suppose we discover on another planet a race like humans in all but this respect; at a certain level of maturity the young display, either spontaneously or with some coaching, knowledge of certain facts of their planet's history—that a certain battle was fought on one date, or that a great leader died on another. I choose these facts deliberately, because they are the sort of facts that could not be conveyed by the kind of coaching Socrates gives the slave boy, or be deduced from normal sense-experience as the fact that 'sour is not sweet' can. As I remarked, in the case of Socrates and the slave boy, we are inclined to say that the knowledge of geometry the

[23] See *The Refutation of Determinism* by M. R. Ayers (London, 1968).

boy acquires is not innate, but simply acquired because the truths are self-evident—given a little prodding, a directing of attention to relevant features. This is what Locke suggests; and we might also agree with his belief that in other cases a concept or a truth can be acquired from normal sense-experience, without postulating innateness. In these cases, an alternative explanation is available, and one that we have independent reasons (perhaps based on Occam's Razor as applied to scientific hypotheses) for preferring—it is simply less extravagant than the innatist hypothesis. But no such alternative seems available in the case described above, where the truths are not self-evident, and cannot be arrived at by reason or experience. No amount of directing of attention to the question 'When did Napoleon die?', or no amount of scientific or everyday observation by him can produce the correct answer from a schoolboy who has not learned it at school. or overheard it in conversation etc., and so if it were the case that schoolboys, regardless of whether they have been exposed to the correct answer, could nevertheless give it if asked the question, we would have extremely good, not to say conclusive evidence that knowledge of this fact was innate. This may seem a fantastic situation to opponents of innatism, but it is a logically possible one, and this should be remembered. The substantial questions about innateness are the factual ones, those which are experimentally (and I don't mean armchair experimentally) decidable ones, and insofar as Leibniz (and Chomsky, for that matter) seek to show this, they succeed. *A priori* arguments, whether for or against innateness, seem to me to fail—and I hope to demonstrate this claim in a short while with regard to the arguments Leibniz uses *for* the innateness of certain truths.

Leibniz's view that sense-experience is only the occasion of the extraction of innate knowledge from the mind enables him to answer one of Locke's main arguments: that based on the lack of universal consent to the supposed innate maxims. The sense-experience of children, idiots and savages, who Locke claims do not understand or assent to principles such as 'whatever is, is', may not be of the right kind; or, more likely, they lack the requisite concentration. As Leibniz says:

Innate maxims appear only through the attention which is given to them; but these persons have little of it, or have it for entirely different things. Their thoughts are mostly confined to the needs of the body; and it is reasonable that pure and detached thoughts be the reward of cares more noble.[24]

Locke, of course, would, as a good democrat, have thought it extremely *un*reasonable that speculative and practical maxims should perhaps be unknown to those who needed their guidance.

[24] *New Essays*, 1/2/27 (Langley, p. 85).

INNATE IDEAS; AND A SUGGESTED ALTERNATIVE TO BOTH THEORIES

So far I have been concentrating on the views of Leibniz and Locke on the existence of innate propositional knowledge; though much of what has been said applies to innate ideas or concepts as well. I now turn my attention to innate ideas in particular; that is, to innate concepts.

Leibniz sometimes claims that Locke's theory of the acquisition of certain ideas by reflection is, in effect, a theory of innate ideas:

[Locke,] after having employed the whole of his first book in rejecting innate intelligence, taken in a certain sense, he nevertheless, at the beginning of the second and in the sequel, admits that ideas, which do not originate in sensation, come from reflection. Now reflection is nothing else than attention to what is in us, and the senses do not give us what we already carry with us. That being so, can it be denied that there is much that is innate in our mind, since we are innate, so to speak, in ourselves? and that there is in us: being, unity, substance, duration, change, action, perception, pleasure, and a thousand other objects of our intellectual ideas? And these objects being immediate to our understanding and always present (although they cannot always be perceived by reason of our distractions and needs), what wonder that we say that these ideas with all depending on them are innate in us?[25]

But elsewhere he does recognize a difference—though he perhaps did not see it as substantial—between his views and those of Locke. According to Locke's account, reflection is limited to perception of the operations of the mind; but Leibniz thinks that it extends to the mind itself—presumably to its contents, the 'objects' mentioned in the passage above. Leibniz's position is still ambiguous, though, for he might mean that the ideas themselves were innate, or that we can by reflection obtain data from which they can be formed. To take a concrete example, does Leibniz think that my idea of substance is extracted from my mind, or does introspection provide me with material I can use to acquire this idea, possibly by using one of the mental powers described by Locke? Leibniz almost certainly holds the former view; in which case his position is less like Locke's than he claims. There is no account in the *New Essays* of how we acquire innate ideas; the emphasis is always on how they are extracted, fully formed, from the mind. In particular, we find in the commentary on Book II of the *Essay* remarks like this one, on ideas of reflection in general: 'All these ideas, and particularly that of God, are in us originally, and we only make ourselves take notice of them.'[26] So it is clear that Leibniz believes that both innate knowledge and ideas are extracted from the mind, and that therefore his position differs substantially from that of Locke, who holds that the mind has only general capacities to acquire

[25] Ibid., Preface (Langley, p. 45).
[26] Ibid. 2/23/33 (Langley, p. 234).

all knowledge and ideas which do not favour any principles or concepts in particular.

There is in fact a third way of looking at the mind, which seems to me more reasonable than that of either of the two protagonists, and which is worth mentioning. Leibniz's views about the existence of preformed ideas and knowledge are too extreme for most modern rationalists, but the suggestion that there exist fairly specific natural capacities has found some favour. A great deal of evidence has been amassed to support the view that there is an innate human faculty concerned with the learning of language, based on a 'language acquisition device' which contains information relevant to, and even necessary for, the process of collecting data from the perception of speech, and incorporating it into a grammar of the language being learned.[27] This gives us a theory of innateness which is stronger than that of Locke; whether we choose to call this a theory about innate ideas and knowledge seems not to be important. Attributing such specific learning capacities is by no means a new idea; we frequently speak of someone inheriting their parents' talent for music or art, and Leibniz himself reminds us of the existence of mathematical prodigies, like 'that Swedish youth who, in cultivating his own [mind], went so far as to make great calculations immediately in his head without having learned the common method of computation, or even to read and write'.[28] The chances that a theory of mind such as Locke's could explain such phenomena seem slim.

One advantage of this modified theory is that it still leaves a place for learning; the capacities must be developed, and the relevant concepts and knowledge acquired. As we have seen, this is a process that Leibniz virtually ignores, and his account suffers in consequence; for the extraction of innate ideas, despite the various distinctions we noted earlier between occasional and direct causes, still seems suspiciously like drawing a rabbit out of a hat.

DO WE NEED INNATE IDEAS?

I would like finally to keep a promise made earlier to examine Leibniz's reasons for thinking that there is some knowledge and some ideas that cannot be obtained empirically, through experience and observation. Leibniz is here tackling Locke's second main argument against innateness, the claim that it is unnecessary.[29] Leibniz spends most time discussing innate propositional knowledge, and I shall follow him in this.

As I remarked earlier, Leibniz thinks that all necessary truths, or truths of reason, are innate. He sometimes distinguishes between a sub-set of these

[27] See N. Chomsky, *Aspects of the Theory of Syntax* (Cambridge, 1965).
[28] *New Essays*, 1/1/5 (Langley, p. 78).
[29] This argument is most clearly stated in *Essay*, I, ii, 1.

which are the axioms of the sciences, and of reasoning, and the rest, which derive from them. Since Leibniz believes that all truths of reason are derivable from the law of contradiction, it would seem most economical simply to regard this as innate, and this Leibniz sometimes explicitly claims.[30] But generally he does not commit himself as to whether one or all necessary truths are innate, probably thinking that it was not a very important point.

But why is Leibniz interested in necessary truths in the first place; why is the distinction between truths of fact and those of reason relevant to his psychological, rather than his logical theory? According to Leibniz, failing to appreciate this relevance is just where Locke errs: he 'has not sufficiently distinguished the origin of the necessary truths, whose source is the understanding, from that of the truths of fact, drawn from the experience of the senses'.[31] Leibniz offers several reasons for his belief that this is a mistake, and I will deal with them in turn.

Leibniz thinks that the laws of logic, and that of contradiction or identity (he treats them as the same) in particular, are innate:

The general principles enter into our thoughts, of which they form the soul and the connection. They are as necessary thereto as the muscles and sinews are for walking, although we do not at all think of them. The mind leans upon these principles every moment, but it does not come so easily to distinguish them and to represent them distinctly and separately, because that demands great attention to its acts, and the majority of people, little accustomed to think, has little of it.[32]

It is not important that we are not aware that we continually make use of these rules of thought, for 'at bottom everybody knows them, and makes use at every moment of the principle of contradiction (for example) without considering it distinctly; and there is no barbarian who, in an affair of any moment, is not offended by the conduct of a liar who contradicts himself'.[33]

Leibniz wishes to pass from an unexceptionable logical point, that all coherent discourses presupposes the law of contradiction, to a more debatable one, that all who discourse intelligibly know this law, and from this to the obscure thesis that the law is innate. The second thesis is not developed by Leibniz, and it would be premature to see it as an anticipation of later views on the relation between knowing how, and knowing that; or on tacit knowledge. Leibniz wishes to point out the distinction between explicit and formulated knowledge of logical principles, and implicit and unformulated knowledge of them. He would, to this extent, certainly have agreed with Ryle that

---

[30] 'On Locke's Essay on Human Understanding' (Langley, pp. 13–14).
[31] *New Essays*, 1/1/1 (Langley, p. 71).
[32] Ibid. 1/1/20 (Langley, p. 74).
[33] Ibid. 1/1/26 (Langley, p. 77).

Rules of correct reasoning were first extracted by Aristotle, yet men knew how to detect and avoid fallacies before they learned his lessons, just as men since Aristotle, and including Aristotle, ordinarily conduct their arguments without internal reference to his formulae.[34]

Leibniz's third claim, that necessary truths, or at least the principle of contradiction, are the very principles of our nature in some literal sense, is more difficult to understand, let alone agree with. Leibniz is plainly concerned with how we come to know necessary truths, and he may be anticipating Kant. Certainly Kant thought this, as this short extract from a note of his on Leibniz shows:

If it is taken too literally, a wrong interpretation is given to the view of Leibniz regarding the innateness of certain notions, by which he means a fundamental faculty to which the *a priori* principles of our knowledge are referable: he makes use of this idea merely as against Locke, who recognized no other than an empirical origin of these principles.[35]

But supposing that Leibniz was anticipating Kant does not help us at all, since the obscurity of Kant's doctrine of the *a priori* merely rubs off on Leibniz.

Leibniz might well have meant that the mind works according to the principle of contradiction because its natural powers of reasoning are logically consistent. Perhaps this can be best understood if we liken the brain to a computer, and consider its mode of operation in the collection and processing of data. If this operation is to be successful it must be consistent; for example, the grammar in a language acquisition device must have consistent rules if it is to be of any use. I am not sure whether this is true; but it is the only meaning I can give to Leibniz's claim that laws of logic are innate, and if Leibniz did not mean this, or would not have assented to it as a modern statement of what he meant, then his real meaning is unknown to me.

Leibniz's second reason for saying that the laws of reason are innate is based on what he sees as an important difference between rationalist and empiricist psychologies. He wishes to point out the contribution of the mind and its powers of reasoning to the formation of knowledge of necessary truths:

The senses, although necessary for all our actual knowledge, are not sufficient to give it all to us, since the senses never give us anything but examples, *i.e.* particular or individual truths.[36]

[34] *The Concept of Mind*, Ch. 2.
[35] *The Monadology*, translated by Latta (Oxford, 1898); Appendix E.
[36] *New Essays*, Preface (Langley, p. 43).

Again, human knowledge must be contrasted with that of brutes, for they are 'purely empirics and only guide themselves by examples; for, so far as we can judge of them, they never attain to the formation of necessary propositions; while men are capable of demonstrative sciences'.[37] From all this it follows that necessary truths 'do not come at all from the senses or from experience, and cannot be perfectly proved, but from the natural internal light, and this is what I mean in saying that they are innate'.[38]

Leibniz wishes to draw our attention to two things, though the above quotations show that he does not distinguish them as carefully as he should. The first is that human beings are capable of acquiring propositional knowledge, including knowledge of general truths; and the second is that we know some of this knowledge to be certain, and that this certainty is not derivable from observation and experience, which only gives us inductive generalizations. Both these observations are correct; but neither gives any support to the claim that necessary truths are innate. If knowledge can only be possessed by creatures which have a language in which to express it, then humans are indeed different in this respect to other animals; but what is the relevance of this observation here? It is also interesting and important that there is a logical difference between necessary and contingent truths; but unless Leibniz goes on to demonstrate that this difference shows that the latter but not the former can be learned, he has failed.

Leibniz's tendency to mix up psychological and logical issues is evident in some of the passages I have already quoted; but to press the point home here is another:

The original proof of the necessary truths comes from the understanding alone, and the other truths come from experience or from the observation of the senses. Our mind is capable of knowing both; but it is the source of the former, and, whatever number of particular experiences we may have of a universal truth, we could not be assured of it forever by induction without knowing its necessity through the reason.[39]

This conflation of separate issues is interesting because it highlights an important feature of seventeenth-century theories of innate ideas. The question of the origin of ideas which I have called psychological was not distinct from the logical one concerning their truth and validity primarily because innate ideas, in Leibniz's words, 'indicate something divine and eternal'.[40] They are, in the commonly used metaphors, the mark of the

---

[37] Ibid. (Langley, p. 44).
[38] 'Specimen of Thoughts upon the First Book of the Essay on Human Understanding' (Langley, p. 22).
[39] New Essays, 1/1/5 (Langley, p. 81).
[40] Ibid., Preface (Langley, p. 43).

workman on his work, seeds of knowledge that God has given us. And since God could not or would not deceive us, we can rely on them as infallible source of truth and guidance; they are special, privileged knowledge. This, then, is the reason for the link between 'innate' and 'necessarily true' that we find in the writings of Leibniz, and which would otherwise seem inexplicable.

III

LOCKE'S IDEA OF 'IDEA'

DOUGLAS GREENLEE

With a discussion by GUNNAR ASPELIN, *and a reply by* DOUGLAS GREENLEE

IT is not just by those who regard the history of philosophy as a sequence of more or less naïve philosophical blunders that Locke has the misfortune to be remembered as the propagator of a certain pernicious doctrine about the nature of ideas. Even by the most serious readers of his *An Essay on Human Understanding* this aspect of his reputation is seldom questioned. All sides grant that Locke regarded ideas as 'entities' of a very special sort, customarily called 'mental', that these entities are 'in the mind', that they are images, that they, rather than what they are images of, are what the mind 'directly' or 'immediately' knows, and hence that they serve as screens or barriers intervening between the mind and the world it is trying with a certain measured success to understand. But then this success, such as it is, is after all baffling, for the obvious reason that on such a view of knowing there is no way to explain how anything other than these mental objects can be known. Yet in employing what he called a 'historical, plain method' Locke makes it clear that he aimed to give an account of how *in fact* human understanding takes place.[1] No interpretation of 'idea' in the *Essay* could be more ironic then than the standard one, for Locke introduced 'idea' precisely in order to account for the fact of understanding, not to deny it and certainly not to set the stage, as he is so often accused of doing, for the scepticism of subsequent British empiricism. What I propose to do in the following pages is to raise again the question of what Locke meant by 'idea' and to review considerations which indicate that 'idea' can't be reduced to the standard interpretation without an irresponsible disregard for the complexity of his idea of 'idea'.

Ever since its appearance the *Essay* has caused puzzlement over what is to be understood by 'idea'. The earliest commentators felt uneasy about it.

From *Theoria*, 33 (1967), pp. 98–106. Aspelin's comments appeared in the same volume, pp. 278–83. They are reprinted by permission of their authors and the editor of the Journal. Greenlee's reply to Aspelin was written for this collection.

[1] *Essay*, I, i, 2.

The Bishop of Worcester (Edward Stillingfleet), for example, in his stuffy manner, complains about what he calls Locke's 'new way of ideas' and mutters that 'the world hath been strangely amused with ideas of late; and we have been told, that strange things might be done by the help of ideas . . .'[2] What troubled the Bishop were the sceptical religious implications, as he saw them, of such doctrines in the *Essay* as those on substance and on idea. And as John W. Yolton has shown in his *John Locke and the Way of Ideas*,[3] by 1700, ten years after the publication of the *Essay*, the charges of scepticism, both religious and epistemological, were among the most frequent levelled against it. But it should be noticed that Locke's doctrine of idea as the immediate object of perception was not the only nor even necessarily the main occasion for the charge of scepticism. Thus Berkeley, in the 1710 introduction to his *Treatise Concerning the Principles of Human Knowledge*, is concerned not with a scepticism derived from the inexplicability of the relation between idea and thing the idea stands for, but rather with the sort of scepticism that Locke himself espoused. This is the scepticism of Locke's principle that the understanding is unable to penetrate into the 'unknown essences' and 'internal constitution' of things. Locke actually maintains in the fourth book of the *Essay* that a 'science of bodies' therefore lies beyond the reach of the understanding (IV, iii, 26). The best we can have is opinion, in the place of science.

While Berkeley did elsewhere recognize, and turn to his own uses, the latent scepticism of Locke's conception of ideas as the immediate objects of the understanding, Locke, of course, never acknowledged this kind of scepticism as a serious threat. Here we come across one of the great mysteries of the working of Locke's mind, for it is pretty obvious that if it is ideas that the understanding encounters rather than the things ideas are of, and if access to things is by way of ideas, then there is no means of getting outside the circle of ideas to inspect the reliability of their alleged service as proxy for things. Was it sheer philosophical naïveté, to put it charitably, that barred Locke from seeing the force of this obvious problem? (He does at least acknowledge it, before dismissing it, in the *Essay*, IV, iv, 3.) Those who like to read the history of British empiricism from Locke to Hume as a march towards philosophical clarity and acumen have always answered in the affirmative. Yet there is evidence that Locke was clearly aware of the difficulties of such an idea-thing dualism as is customarily attributed to him. In *An Examination of P. Malebranche's Opinion* Locke turns the argument for a scepticism derived from this dualism against Malebranche, thus unmistakably revealing an awareness of its implications. Locke's argument runs: 'The ideas of all things which are in God, he elsewhere tells us, are not at all different from God himself; and if

---

[2] Quoted by Locke in his second letter to the Bishop, *Works*, 11th ed., IV (London, 1812), 129.
[3] (Oxford, 1956).

God's penetrating our minds be the cause of our direct and immediate seeing God, we have a direct and immediate view of all that we see; for we see nothing but God and ideas; and it is impossible for us to know that there is any thing else in the universe; for since we see, and can see nothing but God and ideas, how can we know there is any thing else which we neither do nor see?'[4]

Although Locke typically describes ideas as 'perceived', he consistently avoids Malebranche's locution of 'seeing', 'hearing', etc., ideas. As often as not Locke's way of putting it is that ideas are 'had', the only objects being seen, heard, etc., being those the ideas are of. He speaks indifferently, however, of both ideas and the things ideas are of as 'perceived'. But, it is important to observe, Locke never says in so many words that in the perceptual act where the object of perception is neither an idea nor the self, there are *two objects* perceived, the idea of the object as well as the object itself. Different occasions show him speaking of one or the other as perceived. Yet if 'idea' designates an object intervening between the perceiver and the thing, why doesn't Locke give us this analysis in so many words? And why doesn't Locke speak as, for example, does Hume, of ideas as discrete mental existences? There are enough things about ideas left unsaid in the *Essay* to make one wonder, without considering the other puzzles that arise, just what is Locke's idea of 'idea'.

This question of what is Locke's idea of idea can be taken in two ways. It may mean, How does Locke define 'idea'? Or it may mean, What *kind* of idea, according to Locke's typology, is the idea of idea? Let us turn to the second question in preparation for an answer to the first.

Book II of the *Essay* offers several classifications of ideas, the most important for our purposes being the following: some ideas are simple and some complex (curiously Locke does not assert that *all* ideas are *either* simple *or* complex); simple ideas are from sensation, reflection, or from both; complex ideas may be of substances, modes or relations, and of modes, simple or mixed. It is a great lapse on Locke's part neither to have asked nor to have answered in the *Essay* questions about the idea of idea, its origin and its classificatory location. Presumably this idea, like that of the faculty of perception, is from reflection. But Locke does not even come out with this observation. The closest he comes is to discuss the idea of the faculty of perception, about which he says what he might well be expected to say of the idea of idea, that 'it is the first and simplest *idea* we have from reflection, and is by some called thinking in general' (II, ix, 1). Why shouldn't the idea of idea be 'the first and simplest idea we have from reflection'? According to Locke's account of the genetic order of acquisition of ideas, ideas first are

[4] Locke, *Works*, 11th ed., IX (London, 1812), paragraph 43. Cf. 20.

had from sensation, and then as the individual grows in self-consciousness, 'the understanding turns inwards upon itself, *reflects* on its own *operations*, and makes them the object of its own contemplation' (II, i, 8). Further, Locke maintains that there is no having an idea without a consciousness of having the idea, or in the words of the *Essay*, consciousness, 'the perception of what passes in a man's own mind' (II, i, 19), 'always accompanies thinking' (II, xxvii, 9). Presumably the consciousness that an idea is had is itself an idea, or involves one (Locke is untroubled by the regress this account leads to); hence sensation, from the beginning, it follows, would have to be accompanied by the minimal reflective operation of the perception of having the sensory ideas. The reflective idea of idea, then, being as old as the ideas of sensation, would be had earlier than the idea of the faculty of having ideas (the faculty of perception) and ought to be accounted the 'first and simplest idea we have from reflection'. In any case, the idea of the faculty of perception being simple, it is just to conclude that, on Locke's principle of simplicity, whatever this is, the idea of idea is (i) simple as well as (ii) from reflection.

Since, according to Locke, ideas of substances, modes and relations are complex only, the idea of idea cannot be the idea of a substance, mode, or relation. And if ideas are not substances it becomes more difficult than ever to make anything out of the conception of idea as mental entity, intervening between knower and known and constituting what is known 'directly'.

Let us turn back to the question of how Locke defines 'idea' and consider what he offers explicitly by way of a positive characterization. In the *Essay* there are at least two separate and independent definitions of 'idea', though Locke at no place acknowledges that his use of 'idea' is equivocal. Quite early in the *Essay* 'idea' is introduced with the words: 'It being that term which, I think, serves best to stand for whatsoever is the object of the understanding when a man thinks, I have used it to express whatever is meant by *phantasm, notion, species,* or whatever it is which the mind can be employed about in thinking . . .' (I, i, 8). Notice that two alleged factors of Locke's conception of idea commonly taken for granted do not appear here. One is that all ideas are mental images. Apart from the fact that many of the examples of simple ideas, not to speak of other sorts of ideas, are examples of ideas that could not meaningfully be described as images and which Locke does not attempt to describe as images—such ideas as those of perception, willing, power, existence, and unity—Locke nowhere declares that all ideas are images and at most suggests something of the sort as in an off-hand and unelaborated remark near the end of Book II (xxix, 8). The emphasis on *any* object whatsoever may be intended precisely to avoid just this assumption that ideas are necessarily images. Secondly, the definition does not declare that ideas are mental entities. Perhaps Locke simply took it for granted that they are. Still, the fact is that he does not say that they are. Indeed, the direct realist, if willing to accept the definition as an arbitrary definition of 'idea'—and remember that 'idea' was not so familiar to philosophers before the publication of the *Essay* as it was afterward—could accept it unflinchingly, understanding by 'whatsoever is the object of the understanding' whatsoever is in fact such an object, a table when a table is being examined, a concept when a concept is being understood, a society when a society is being studied. Admittedly the remark following the introduction of 'idea' does appear, at first glance, to rule out a direct realism. Locke, adds, 'I presume it will be easily granted me that there are such *ideas* in men's minds . . .' About the perception of a table surely no philosopher is going to say that the table perceived is *in* a mind. Yet the wary pursuer of Locke's intentions will do well to be cautious at this point. What does it mean to say that an idea is 'in' the mind? Ideas can't literally be said to be in something the way, for example, picture postcards are in a box. Perhaps again the answer should be found in Locke's apparent naïveté and stupidly blunt common sensism. In a little-noticed paragraph in Book I, however, Locke expresses a critical and circumspect awareness of 'in the mind', about which he explains: 'For if these words (*to be in the understanding*) have any propriety, they signify to be understood. So that to be in the understanding and not to be understood, to be in the mind and never to be perceived, is all one as to say: anything is and is not in the mind or understanding' (I, ii, 5).[5] To say that an idea is in the mind need not, then, imply, as is so often supposed, anything about the ontology of ideas. Or as Charles Peirce put it, probably with Locke in mind, 'to say that an object is in the mind is only a metaphorical way of saying that it stands to the intellect in the relation of known to knower'.[6] Since as often as not Locke refers to ideas as had rather than as 'in the mind', there is not necessarily a distinction to be made between the location of an idea and who has it. Location may mean merely possession. And so far, therefore, there is nothing to 'idea' which excludes the possibility that an idea in the mind may be an 'outside' thing as understood. Indeed, a close reading of the *Essay* reveals Locke using 'idea' to designate the object of perception when it is clear that the object in question *is* the 'outside' thing (as in II, viii, 8).

According to the second definition of 'idea', idea and perceptual act are equated. Thus: 'To ask *at what time a man has first any* ideas is to ask when he begins to perceive: having *ideas* and perception being the same thing' (II, i, 9). And again, discussing memory: 'But, our *ideas* being nothing but

[5] I am indebted to Justus Buchler, who introduced me to Locke, for having pointed out this paragraph, as well as for raising the question this paper deals with and some of the considerations I am discussing. His 'Act and Object in Locke' (*Philosophical Review*, 46, 1937, 528–35) is well worth consulting.

[6] *Collected Papers*, VIII (Cambridge, Mass., 1958), 21.

actual perceptions in the mind, which cease to be anything when there is no perception of them, this *laying up* of our *ideas* in the repository of the memory signifies no more but this: that the mind has a power in many cases to revive perceptions which it has once had . . . And in this sense it is that our *ideas* are said to be in our memories, when indeed they are actually nowhere; but only there is an ability in the mind when it will to revive them again . . .' (II, x, 2. Cf. II, viii, 7 and *An Examination of P. Malebranche's Opinion*, paragraphs 8 and 15.) 'Perception' does not mean necessarily 'sense perception', it should be understood, even when 'sensation' covers internal as well as external sense. Here the two uses of 'perception' in the *Essay* should be kept in mind. In one use it designates the act (and also the faculty) of thinking or having ideas, no matter of what sort (II, ix, 1); in the other it designates merely the act (also the faculty) of acquiring the 'materials' of experience in either sensation or reflection, external or internal sense. Or, in other words, there are two conceptions of 'perceptual act', one as act of understanding, the other as (internal or external) sense-perceptual act. The conception of 'idea' as act of perception is based on the broader sense of perception. Clearly this conception of idea not only suggests that the equation of it with sensory image is too limited but furthermore rules out a meaningful categorization of ideas as substantial entities (unless acts be considered entities). If analogies help, ideas would be better likened to motions of material objects rather than to those objects themselves. But with or without this analogy, it is clear that to conceive 'idea' as act of understanding is not to conceive it as an entity blocking off the knower from what is known.

Are we, then, to interpret the perceptual (or thinking) situation in Locke's terms as composed of perceiver and act of perception, with no third factor of a representative thought-entity 'standing for' some other object? The elimination of the third factor would seem to ignore Locke's principle that ideas constitute one of the two chief classes of signs, the other being words, which are signs of ideas. Thus, 'since the things the mind contemplates are none of them, besides itself, present to the understanding, it is necessary that something else, as a sign or representation of the thing it considers, should be present to it: and these are *ideas*' (IV, xxi, 4). What does it mean to say that the mind can contemplate an object not 'present' to it—or to its faculty or understanding? Whatever this means, two points can be decided: (i) Locke does not, even here, say that ideas are substances, nor does he deny that they are perceptions; and yet (ii) the distinction between idea and thing signified is a distinction between two different things, one which serves as a sign and the other as what is signified by the sign. An idea is a sign and a sign is something. What kind of thing is the sign which is an idea?

Since Locke does not deal with this question, no certain answer is available.

Perhaps 'idea' means, after all, 'mental entity' in the usual sense, with all its vagueness and difficulties. Still, the answer could be 'perceptual act', even though in Book IV, on such a topic as the 'reality' of knowledge, we find that 'it is evident the mind knows not things immediately, but only by the intervention of the *ideas* it has of them'. And a little further: 'How shall the mind, when it perceives nothing but its own *ideas*, know that they agree with things themselves?' (iv, 3). Here Locke, declaring that ideas only are 'perceived', has gone further than he generally goes. Yet even here that which 'intervenes' permits interpretation as perceptual act, so that what the mind immediately perceives may be its perceptual act. And as Locke goes on to answer his question as to how the conformity of idea to thing can be known, giving a causal account of ideas such that ideas, as effects of the operations of objects on the mind, serve as reliable indices of those objects, it is 'idea' as perceptual act which is unequivocally identified as the sign-vehicle. Thus, of the two sorts of ideas which reliably agree with things, 'the first are simple ideas which, since the mind, as has been shown, can by no means make to itself, must necessarily be the product of things operating on the mind in a natural way and producing therein those *perceptions* which by the wisdom and will of our Maker they are ordained and adapted to' (iv, 4; italics mine).

What, finally, can be concluded about Locke's conception of 'idea'? It should be inescapably evident by now that this question allows of no simple answer. What I have been trying to show is, in order of importance, first, that Locke must have had more than one conception of 'idea' in mind as he worked through his *Essay*, and, second, that the interpretation of Locke's 'idea' which reduces it to 'imaged mental entity', or merely even 'mental entity', is hopelessly inadequate to his complex conception (or conceptions). Other than this we can conclude that in different contexts any of two different conceptions, and possibly a third, will be found to obtain: (i) 'idea' as any object of the understanding, where 'object' is to be construed in the broadest sense and (ii) 'idea' as perceptual act. Finally, there are passages in which it is by no means clear that 'idea' in a third sense, as 'mental entity', is not the prevailing sense. The second conception, however, I have found to be the most frequently occurring one.

DISCUSSION

'Idea' and 'perception' in Locke's *Essay*

Gunnar Aspelin

In his essay 'Locke's Idea of "Idea"', published in the last number of *Theoria*, Mr. Douglas Greenlee gives an interpretation of the term 'idea' in the *Essay on Human Understanding*. He justly accentuates the ambiguity of this concept;

it can't be 'reduced to the standard interpretation without an irresponsible disregard for the complexity of his (Locke's) idea of "idea"'. The difficulties, dependent on the use of vague and undetermined notions in the *Essay*, are presumably familiar to every student of this classical work.

The author distinguishes between two different meanings of the term at issue:

(1) idea as any object of the understanding,
(2) idea as perceptual act

and he asserts—unfortunately without any statistical proof—that the second sense is 'the most frequently occurring one'.

There are also, he adds, 'passages in which it is by no means clear that "idea" in a third sense, as "mental entity", is not the prevailing sense'.

In connection with this analysis of the term, I want to bring on a discussion of three principal questions:

(1) Is it possible to show any other essential moment of Locke's conception of 'idea'?
(2) Are we in the right, when we identify 'idea' and 'object of the understanding' without any further specification of the second concept?
(3) Are there good reasons for asserting with the author, that Locke 'most frequently' applies the term 'idea' in the sense of 'perceptual act'?

(1) As to the first question, we must pay regard to the well-known tendency of Locke to combine two different lines of thought. In part, he regards his subject from a *psychological* point of view, describing the mental appearances according to 'the historical, plain method', applied by his friends Boyle and Sydenham on the physical and medical fields of research. In part—and above all—he argues from an *epistemological* point of departure. He will, as he says in the introduction to the *Essay*, 'inquire into the original, certainty, and extent of human knowledge, together with the grounds and degrees of belief, opinion, and assent'. (To be sure, Locke never makes an explicit distinction between the two points of view.)

From a psychological starting point, 'idea' may be translated into 'object of the understanding'. Yet, this translation seems to be incomplete, as I will attempt to prove in the following discussion of the subject. But, from the epistemological point of view, an idea is not only the *object* of a given act of perceiving, but also the starting-point and the *material* of following operations, forming part of the procedure, by which the mind attains intuitive, demonstrative and sensitive knowledge. The simple ideas are the materials of thinking (II, i, 2). Our complex ideas are made by 'the mind' out of simple ones, and they function as materials of other intellectual operations, by which we arrive to true propositions. For example, to demonstrative propositions in mathematics and ethics.

(2) There are many passages in the *Essay* where Locke is speaking of 'idea' and 'object of perception', 'object of understanding', 'object of thinking', as interchangeable terms. However, in his search for a precise definition of the concept at issue, he makes an important addition. The passage runs thus: 'Whatsoever the mind perceives in itself, or is the immediate object of perception, thought, or understanding, that I call *idea*' (II, viii, 8). The expression '*immediate* object' deserves to be observed, just as the synonymous phrase 'whatsoever the mind perceives *in itself*'. It is of importance for a discussion of Mr. Greenlee's interesting article. There is, according to him, 'nothing to "idea" which excludes the possibility that an idea in the mind may be an "outside" thing as understood'. Certainly nothing, but for the expressions 'immediately' and 'in itself'. Of course, it may be possible to find passages in the *Essay* at variance with Locke's own definition. But the decisive question is: (a) has Mr. Greenlee's interpretation any basis in the text? and further: (b) is it impossible, by close reading, to find any statements, disproving the interpretation?

(a) I must confess, that I can't be convinced by the passage, to which the author refers in his article. He writes as follows: 'Indeed, a close reading of the *Essay* reveals Locke using "idea" to designate the object of perception when it is clear that the object in question *is* the "outside" thing (as in II, viii, 8).' It seems to me, that the passage in view fails to confirm his assertion.

What does Locke really mean? After the before quoted definition of 'idea', Locke defines 'quality' as 'power to produce any *idea* in our mind'. If he speaks of ideas 'as in the things themselves', he denotes by this expression 'those qualities in the objects which produce them [the ideas] in us'. Thus he says *expressis verbis*, that he makes an inadequate use of the term when he speaks of the qualities of things as ideas.[1]

(b) There are also statements in the *Essay*, quite inconsistent with the supposed interchangeability of 'idea' and 'outside thing as understood'. By way of example I take the following passage: 'It is evident the mind knows not things immediately, but only by the intervention of the *ideas* it has of them. *Our knowledge*, therefore, is *real* only so far as there is a conformity between

---

[1] This passage goes back to the first draft of the *Essay* from 1671 (*An early draft of Locke's Essay*, edited by R. I. Aaron and Jocelyn Gibb, Oxford, 1936). There, Locke speaks of 'these simple Ideas or qualitys' (p. 4), of 'that kind of idea or quality' (p. 4), and of 'other qualitys or simple ideas' (p. 14); dealing with 'simple idea' and 'quality' as with terms of the same signification. But at the end of the draft, he accentuates the ambiguity of the word. 'Idea when it is spoken of as being in our understanding is the very perception or thought we have here, when it is spoken of as existing without is yet cause of that perception, and is supposed to be resembled by it, and this also I call quality' (p. 73).

our *ideas* and the reality of things. But what shall be here the criterion? How shall the mind, when it perceives nothing but its own *ideas*, know that they agree with things themselves?' (IV, iv, 3).

Locke often makes use of vague terms, capable of manifold interpretation. But here he declares *clare et distincte* that the mind never knows external things immediately, but only by the intervention of 'its own ideas'. We can easily find many other statements, expressing the same opinion, and I doubt whether we can meet with a single negative instance. For my part, I have been unsuccessful in this undertaking.

I think, we must distinguish between:

(a) external things as transcendent realities, 'things themselves',
(b) external things as understood, viz. by the intervention of our ideas,
(c) ideas or immediate objects of the understanding.

If external things are to be understood, we must suppose a conformity between ideas 'in the mind' and qualities of the things themselves. From Locke's dualistical point of departure, the central task of epistemology is to find a criterion of the supposed conformity.

(3) We may begin the discussion of this point by quoting a statement in the article: 'According to the second definition of "idea", idea and perceptual act are equated' [p. 45 above]. This interpretation is founded on certain passages in the *Essay*, in which Locke asserts the equality of 'having ideas' and 'perception', and speaks of our ideas as being nothing but actual perceptions. But the question is: are we allowed to regard 'perception' as an unambiguous term, always able to be substituted for 'perceptual act'. I am afraid that this assumption will not be confirmed by an exegetical examination.

(a) In many passages, 'perception' seems to denote something like 'what the mind perceives' or 'the content of a perceptual act', as in the following instances:

several distinct perceptions of things (II, i, 3),
ideas of sensible qualities, which are all those different perceptions they [the sensible qualities] produce in us (II, i, 5),
ideas or perceptions in our minds (II, viii, 7),
as they [the sensible qualities] are sensations or perceptions in our understandings, I call them ideas (II, viii, 8),
qualities of light and warmth, which are perceptions in me (II, viii, 24).

(b) In other passages, 'perception' is applied in the sense of 'act of perceiving', 'perceptual act', by which the understanding obtains an idea. 'Idea' and 'perception' in this sense are never synonymous but correlative terms.

For example:

> [idea] is the immediate object of perception, thought, or understanding (II, viii, 8),
> what perception is, everyone will know . . . by reflecting on what he does himself, when he sees, hears, feels, etc., or thinks (II, ix, 2),
> wherever there is sense or perception, there some idea is actually produced, and present in the understanding (II, ix, 4).

According to Locke's theory, ideas are conditioned either by impulses from external things or by mental actions. Perception (= the perceptual act) is an action of the mind, and causes in the mind a corresponding idea. 'The mind . . . when it turns its view inward upon itself and observes its own actions about those *ideas* it has, takes from thence other *ideas*, which are as capable to be the objects of its contemplation as any of those it received from foreign things.'

In other words: Locke makes a clear distinction between:

(1) ideas or immediate objects of the mind, often called perceptions in the sense of perceptual contents,
(2) perceptual acts or actions of the understanding.

When the mind 'turns its view inward upon itself', the perceptual acts become immediate objects of other perceptual acts. Thus, we gain a new class of ideas, in Locke's terminology 'the ideas by reflection'.

REPLY

Idea and object in the Essay

Douglas Greenlee

Perhaps it is misleading to speak of Locke's *idea* of 'idea'. The foremost point I have tried to make about Locke's philosophy of understanding is that several ideas of 'idea' are at work throughout the *Essay*. Aspelin offers a valuable observation when he notes that one of these is 'idea' as the content of a perception. What remains to be explained is just what is Locke's conception (or conceptions) of such a content.

For the answer we need to return directly to the texts Locke produced and to try to give them a fresh reading, one free in particular of assumptions about Locke as a Cartesian or as a dualist. Aspelin assumes that 'Locke's point of departure' is 'dualistical'. With this assumption guiding the reading of Locke, it is inevitable that 'idea' in the sense either of object or content of perceptual act will be read as 'mental entity'. Given dualism (of the sort pertinent to this discussion), the two alternatives for the ontological status of idea are mental or material. Since ideas are 'in' the mind and are its 'immediate' objects, the only plausible option left is to take them as mental. Locke, however, is neither Cartesian nor dualist, not only because he rejects the doctrine of innate ideas, not only because he rejects both the possibility of and concern with certain or infallible physics, but also because he refuses to be convinced that thinking requires a special sort of substance different from that of bodies (IV, iii, 6). Locke shunned both dualism and the ontology of ideas as mental entities. He was quite aware of the position he was taking (cf. II, xiv, 13), although he was not aware of the number of senses he gave to 'idea' in the *Essay*.

Locke's non-dualism does not render him a monist, pluralist, materialist, or idealist. His concern is 'to consider the discerning faculties of a man, as they are employed about the objects which they have to do with' (I, i, 2). These objects are what is perceived; it is they which comprise the 'contents' of perception. About *objects*, when stating his original motive in writing the *Essay*, Locke explains that he wanted to 'see what objects our understandings were, or were not, fitted to deal with' ('The Epistle to the Reader'). In these passages Locke can't be read as meaning what mental entities or representations our understandings are fitted to deal with. 'Object' is here used in a neutral sense. An object of the understanding might be mental, as when the mind reflects on its own ideas and operations, and it might not be, as when it pursues the science of bodies. Now objects, when they are objects of the understanding, that is, when they are not only such as the understanding is fit to deal with, but when they are actually its objects—discerned by it—are precisely that with which Locke equates ideas in the remarkable definition at the outset of the *Essay*: *'idea'* is the term which 'serves best to stand for whatsoever is the object of the understanding when a man thinks' (I, i, 8). The monstrous error of Lockean interpretation is always to read 'idea' as 'entity blocking off knower from what is known'. An idea, in the sense of content of perception, is the object-of-the-understanding; it is the object as known. This object is the 'immediate' object, 'in' the mind, as contrasted with the object itself, not so qualified.

I do not contend that Locke fully or consistently realized the character of the non-representational vein of thought in the *Essay*. A philosopher, in following out his thoughts and their implications, may not be fully aware of what positions he has been led to from others he has assumed. Certainly there are many passages, such as IV, iv, 3—which asks how can the mind, 'when it perceives nothing but its own *ideas*, know that they agree with things themselves?'—that strongly suggest the dualistic reading. But even here deduction of the dualism is unwarranted. To say that the mind perceives only its own ideas is to say that when it perceives and discerns an object, the object is an object discerned. The question of the agreement of ideas with 'things themselves' (notice that the passage does not say 'with their objects') may well be merely the question of how it is possible to determine whether the mind discerns correctly, i.e. whether it confuses the object (or content) with some other, as is done in the cases of dreams and hallucinations, or whether it takes the object to be what it really is. If this is the question Locke is posing, then it becomes less puzzling as to why he found scepticism with regard to the senses worthy of no serious study in his *Essay* (cf. I V, ii, 14) and of no momentous threat to his account of understanding.

Two further points need to be made: (i) Aspelin has misread the passage in which Locke explains what he means by speaking of ideas 'as in the things themselves' (II, viii, 8). Locke states; 'I . . . mean those qualities in the objects which produce them in us.' His point is not that he makes an inadequate use of 'idea' when equating it with quality, but rather that when he speaks of ideas as in the things, he means the qualities (or powers) which produce perceptions and are the objects of perceptions. The equation, with no apologies rendered, is of 'idea' with 'quality in the object'. (ii) Aspelin bends a genuine issue out of shape when he attributes to me a 'supposed interchangeability of "idea" and "outside thing as understood"'. No such claim is made. The issue is rather whether 'idea' is to be read as designating an entity standing between the perceiving mind and its object, or whether, in its use as other than act of perception, it means any of the objects which can be perceived, whether these be mental, as in dreams, physical, when physical objects are perceived, qualities, memories, or what not. Many passages are indeterminate with respect to this issue. Many others are probably best understood with the dualist reading. Still others flatly contradict it. Among these are the passages in which an idea—the object of perception—is treated as interchangeable with quality in the object. (It is to be noted that since secondary qualities are powers in the object, they are *in* the object, along with primary qualities.) When in II, xxi, i, Locke traces the idea of power to the mind's considering 'in one thing the possibility of having any of its simple *ideas* changed', he is treating ideas as qualities, not as thoughts, since things do not have thoughts. II, xxiii, 6, is more explicit; the observer of the sun will be 'more or less accurate in observing those sensible qualities, *ideas*, or properties, which are in that thing which he calls the *sun*'. Passages such as these are not to be dismissed as slips of the pen; they are too numerous, and reveal a deep-lying vein of direct realism in the *Essay*, quite opposed to the representationalism. This vein is evident in all of the following passages: II, ii, 1, the hardness felt *in the ice* is also an 'idea' in the mind; II, viii, 24, 'qualities of light and warmth' in the sun are also 'perception in me'; II, xiii, 1, simple modes are '*modifications of the same* idea, which the mind either finds in things existing, or is able to make within itself'; II, xxi, 1, the mind observes simple ideas 'in things without';

II, xxiii, 1, simple ideas are furnished to the mind as *they* 'are found in exterior things'; III, ix, 14, there is 'scarce any particular thing existing which, in some of its simple *ideas*, does not communicate with a greater, and in others with a less, number of particular beings'; IV, i, 7, in knowledge of real existence we know of an idea that 'it has a real existence without the mind'; IV, xi, 9, 'such collections of simple *ideas*, as we have observed by our senses to be united together, do really exist together'. In addition to such passages as these, and perhaps even more important to the issue at hand, are the many in which Locke *treats* the objects perceived and the ideas had interchangeably; as when, on the faculty of perception, he says that *it* 'is the first and simplest *idea* we have from reflection' (II, ix, 1). Much of II, xxi, on the idea of power, may equally well be read as on a certain idea, that of power, or on power itself. The treatment of the idea of solidity (II, iv) is equally a treatment of the quality of solidity. The chapter on the idea of space is also on the nature of space (so II, xiii, 13 concerns the separability both 'really' and 'mentally' of the parts of pure space). The chapters on duration (II, xiv), extension (II, xv), substances (II, xxiii), and identity (II, xxvii) contain a similar treatment of their topics.

IV

LOCKE, MALEBRANCHE AND THE REPRESENTATIVE THEORY

H. E. MATTHEWS

In the introduction to his Fontana Library abridgement of the *Essay* (London, Collins, 1964), Woozley argues against the traditional view that Locke held a representative theory of perception. Amongst the arguments which he uses in support of his interpretation is one based on a quotation from Locke's *Examination of P. Malebranche's Opinion* (Section 51). In this section, Locke criticizes Malebranche's view that the ideas of things are unchangeable by saying, '. . . for how can I know that the picture of anything is like that thing, when I never see that which it represents?'. This, according to Woozley (op. cit., p. 27), 'is as concise a statement of the objection to this kind of repre-sensationalism as one could wish'. Farther down the page, he goes on, 'It is scarcely credible both that Locke should be able to see and to state so clearly the fundamental objection to the picture-original theory of sense-perception, and that he should have held that theory himself.'

To be fair to Woozley, he intends this argument only to 'shake . . . our confidence' in the traditional interpretation, but it seems to me to be too weak even to achieve that modest end. It is surely perfectly credible that a philosopher should fail to see that the implications of some view of his own might be open to the same criticisms as the views of another philosopher. And in this particular case, it is even more credible, since the view which Locke is criticizing is not a 'picture-original theory of sense-perception' at all, but, as the full title of his work says, 'P. Malebranche's opinion of seeing all things in God'. As Locke himself points out in his *Examination*, it is not always entirely clear just what Malebranche meant by 'seeing things in God', but part at least of what he meant seems to have been that we see things as they really are by means of the intellect alone—that is, when we have freed ourselves from the distortions inherent in sense-perception. Like Locke, in other words,

From the *Locke Newsletter*, 2 (1971), pp. 12–21. Reprinted, with very minor changes, by permission of the author and the editor, Roland Hall.

Malebranche includes more under the heading of 'perception' than we might do nowadays: it covers intellectual insight as well as sense-perception. In *Recherche de la Vérité*, Book I, Chapter 1, for instance, he distinguishes between what he calls *'perceptions pures'*, which are acts of the understanding, and *'perceptions sensibles'*, in which we are aware of external objects by means of the sense-organs. When, as we should normally say, we perceive something with our senses, what happens is that a *'sensation'*, or *'modification de l'esprit'*, is produced in us on the occasion of our body's being affected in a certain way. There is no real causal influence of body on mind involved, only 'occasional' causation. Malebranche specifically denies (*Recherche*, Book III, Part II, Chapter 2) that material objects convey impressions to the mind by affecting our senses—a denial which Locke naturally contests (cf. *Examination*, section 9 ff.). Now we may have these 'sensations' even if the object which we think we are perceiving does not exist; and in so far as our sensations tend to suggest that matter has such properties as colour and smell as well as extension, they are always liable to deceive us. That is, the senses are not really sources of knowledge at all: they do not tell us what things are like in themselves, but only express certain relations between things and our bodies, which need to be taken account of for purposes of self-preservation. A sensation is not, strictly speaking, an 'idea' (though Malebranche sometimes talks as if it were), so much as a distorted representation of an idea. We have sensations in virtue of our union with the body, but ideas in virtue of our union with God. Sensations, as mentioned earlier, are *'modifications de l'esprit'*, but ideas are only (*Recherche*, Book III, Part II, Chapter 1) 'quelque chose qui est intimement unie à notre âme'.

Now there is a sense in which Malebranche may be said to have held a 'Representative theory of perception'. He says (*Recherche*, Book III, Part II, Chapter 1): 'Je crois que tout le monde tombe d'accord que nous n'apercevons point les objets qui sont hors de nous par eux-mêmes. . . . l'objet immédiat de notre esprit, lorsqu'il voit le soleil, par exemple, n'est pas le soleil, mais quelque chose qui est intimement unie à notre âme, et c'est ce que j'appelle "idée". Ainsi par ce mot "idée", je n'entends ici autre chose que ce qui est l'objet immédiat, ou le plus proche de l'esprit quand il aperçoit quelque objet.'[1] Elsewhere, Malebranche talks about ideas 'representing' objects. So what we actually perceive are never the objects themselves, but always ideas which represent them: it sounds very much like the kind of Representative theory which has traditionally been attributed to Locke. But there are a number of

---

[1] 'I think everyone agrees that we do not perceive objects outside ourselves in themselves . . . the immediate object of our mind, when it sees the sun, for instance, is not the sun but something which is intimately united to our soul, and that is what I call "idea". Thus, by this word "idea" I mean simply the immediate or proximate object of the mind when it perceives some object.'

significant differences. First, and most important, this is *not* a theory of sense-perception, but of intellectual awareness (and of sense-perception as corrected by the intellect). Secondly, the ideas which we are said actually to perceive are not sensations or mental contents: they are things existing externally to our minds, in the mind of God. Cf. *Recherche*, Book III, Part II, Chapter 6: 'Lorsque nous apercevons quelque chose de sensible, il se trouve dans notre perception, sentiment et idée pure. Le sentiment est une modification de notre âme, et c'est Dieu qui la cause en nous; . . . Pour l'idée qui se trouve jointe avec le sentiment, elle est en Dieu, et nous la voyons, parce qu'il lui plaît de nous la découvrir . . .'[2] The ideas which we perceive, in other words, exist 'in God', not in our own minds (hence the doctrine of 'seeing all things in God'). This suggests, thirdly, that the sense in which ideas 'represent' objects is different from the sense of that word as used in the classical Representative theory.

In short, whatever else Malebranche's theory was, it was not an example of a 'picture-original theory of sense-perception', as Woozley calls it. In attacking it, therefore, Locke was not attacking a theory of this type, and his ability to see objections to it does not imply any awareness of objections to the traditional type of Representative theory. What he is criticizing is not the view that the material object which causes our ideas is itself unknowable, but the view that our ordinary sense-perception does not even give us an *indirect* acquaintance with material objects, since the sensations which we actually perceive are not even genuinely caused by the effect of material objects on our sense-organs. On Malebranche's view, we seem to have a threefold mystery: the mystery of the relation between sensations and material objects (which is not really solved by talk of 'occasional causes'); the mystery of the relation between sensations and 'pure ideas'; and the mystery of the relation between the ideas themselves (the 'pictures' in Locke's metaphor) and the things which they represent. It is this mystery, which Locke, as well he might, found baffling, which prompts the remark quoted by Woozley, '. . . how can I know that the picture of anything is like that thing, when I never see that which it represents?'

The difference between Locke and Malebranche is not, then, that Malebranche held a Representative theory of sense-perception to which Locke could see serious objections. It is rather in the sense which they give to the word 'idea'. To compare these different senses may throw some light on the more important question whether Locke held the Representative theory.

---

[2] 'When we perceive something sensible, there are present in our perception both sentiment and pure idea. The sentiment is a modification of our soul, and it is God who causes it in us . . . As for the idea which is found joined with the sentiment, it is in God, and we see it, because it pleases Him to disclose it to us . . .'

One must be clear from the outset, however, what question it is that one is considering. Locke certainly did not 'hold' the Representative theory in the sense that he consciously advocated it: most of the time he plainly takes it for granted that we directly perceive material objects. Nor did he 'hold' it in the sense that it was an important part of his philosophical purposes to establish it: Yolton is right to say (*Locke and the Compass of Human Understanding*, p. 14) that Locke's 'inquiry into the original, certainty and extent of knowledge is descriptive, not justificatory'. What Yolton means by this, in part at least, is that Locke did not *consciously* hold any philosophical (as opposed to scientific) 'theory of perception' at all, but was chiefly concerned to explore the ways in which ideas are built up into an experience of the world. Since this was his main purpose, any criticisms which might be made of his (alleged) representationalism do not seriously affect the value of his philosophy as a whole. The most that one could hope to show, therefore, is that the Representative theory is somehow *implicit* in Locke's thought, even though he was not aware of it. To use Wittgensteinian language, one could say that this theory was a 'picture' which 'held Locke captive'. To show even this adequately would require more space than is presently available, but I can try at least to make out the beginnings of a case.

Malebranche's view has already been described. He distinguishes, as we have seen, between *'sensations'* or *'sentiments'* and *'idées pures'*. 'Sensations' seem to be both modifications of the mind experienced during sense-perception and objects of sensory awareness, 'pure ideas' to be unambiguously *objects*, and objects of pure *thought*, i.e. concepts. On this view, even sense-perception becomes a confused awareness of concepts, and so Malebranche can justly be accused of the typical Rationalist error, described by Kant (*Critique of Pure Reason*, A271 = B327) as that of 'intellectualizing appearances'.

The nature of Locke's criticisms of Malebranche, in the *Examination*, makes it easy to see why Kant should have accused the Empiricists (loc. cit.) of the opposite mistake of 'sensualising concepts of the understanding'. Locke rejects (*Examination*, 38 ff.) Malebranche's distinction between sentiments and pure ideas. Colours, tastes, smells, and so on, which Malebranche calls 'sentiments', have, Locke argues, as much right to be called 'ideas' as the properties of extension and figure to which Malebranche reserves that title. Cf. *Examination*, 41: 'The making then the picture of any visible thing in my mind, as of a landscape I have seen, composed of figure and colour, the colour [on Malebranche's view] is not an idea, but the figure is an idea, and the colour a "sentiment". Every one I allow may use his words as he pleases, but if it be to instruct others, he must when he uses two words where others use but one, show some ground of the distinction. And I do not find but the colour of the marigold I now think of, is as much "the immediate object of my mind" as its figure, and so according to his definition is an "idea".' Locke does not mean by this so much that a 'sentiment' is an 'idea' in Malebranche's sense, as that an 'idea' in Malebranche's sense is no different from a 'sentiment'. To put it another way, Locke is not arguing that our perception of a colour is a perception of a quality really existing externally to our minds, as Malebranche's 'ideas' did, but that our perception of a figure is a perception of something in our minds which Locke would call an 'idea', but Malebranche a 'sentiment'. In Section 18 of the *Examination*, Locke says that he finds it unintelligible that an idea should be a 'real being', that is, something existing externally to the human mind; and in *Essay* II, viii, 7 he draws a careful distinction between '*ideas* or perceptions in our minds' and 'modifications of matter in the bodies that cause such perceptions in us', or qualities.

This assimilation of ideas to sensations is in line with the main theme of Locke's attack on Malebranche in the earlier part of the *Examination*. Locke there criticizes Malebranche for failing to make sense-perception intelligible, or rather for failing to give a *more* intelligible account of perception than the corpuscular hypothesis. To say that we 'see ideas in God' because of the 'intimate union of our souls with God' can throw no light on how we see unless it is explained what the nature of this 'intimate union' between two spirits could be. If, as Locke suspects, no intelligible account of its nature could be given, then it is in no better case than the union of soul and body. But Malebranche had claimed that his theory of 'seeing all things in God' made perception *more* intelligible than any theory which relied on postulating causal connections between body and mind. Locke therefore feels entitled to conclude (*Examination*, 8), 'And if I should say, that it is possible God has made our souls so, and so united them to our bodies, that, upon certain motions made in our bodies by external objects, the soul should have such and such perceptions or ideas, though in a way inconceivable to us; this perhaps would appear as true and as instructive a proposition as what is so positively laid down.'

Locke thus wants to postulate a certain causal mechanism for sense-perception, the final result of which is an 'idea' in the mind. On the physical and physiological side various processes take place: light is reflected from the object and reaches the retina, forming a retinal image, then there are 'motions' in the nervous system and brain. Finally, in some utterly mysterious way, which we just have to accept as a brute fact, the leap is made from body to mind, and an idea is produced in the mind. Locke says (*Examination*, 11) that, in a sense, what we see is the retinal image. 'The change of bigness in the ideas of visible objects, by distance and optic-glasses . . . would persuade one that we see the figures and magnitudes of things rather in the bottom of our eyes than in God: the idea we have of them and their grandeur being still proportioned to the bigness of the area, on the bottom of our eyes, that is affected by the rays which paint the image there; and we may be said to see the picture in the retina, as, when it is pricked, we are truly said to feel the pain in our finger.' The most natural way to read this is to take the 'idea' to be the mental counterpart of the retinal image, since it is proportioned to it.

All this suggests that an 'idea', for Locke, is a mental content, an entity existing in the mind as the retinal image exists in the body. In this connection, cf. Locke's description of ideas in *Essay* IV, xvii, 8 as 'particular existences'. At the level of sense-perception, an 'idea' is, fairly clearly, a 'sensation' in the Malebranchean sense. It is 'in the mind' in the same straightforward sense that a sensation is: that is, it is what goes on in the mind when our sense-organs are affected in a certain way. At the level of memory and imagination, an 'idea' seems to mean a mental image, a reliving of some sense-experience without external stimulation. Here too, it is easy to understand what is meant by saying an 'idea' is 'in the mind'. It is only when Locke uses 'idea' to mean 'concept' that it becomes difficult to see how an idea can be said to be 'in the mind'. The temptation is then to take this phrase to mean that ideas (concepts) are 'present to' the mind, as the concept 'horse' might be said to be present to my mind when I am thinking about horses. But since Locke uses the same word 'idea' to refer to sensations, mental images, and concepts, one suspects that he means the same by the phrase 'in the mind' in all three cases, and this suspicion is to some extent confirmed by Locke's remark to Stillingfleet that ideas are 'whatever is present in [not merely "to"] a man's mind when he thinks'.

Thus, Woozley's claim (op. cit., p. 31) that Locke is saying 'My idea of a horse is . . . what I mean by the word "horse"' is both true and misleading. It is misleading in two ways. First, because my idea of a horse is not always or necessarily what I mean by the word 'horse': often it is what is in my mind when I am perceiving a horse. Secondly, because even when my idea of a horse is my concept of a horse, it is treated by Locke as some kind of a mental entity such that my idea of a horse is peculiar to me and cannot be directly communicated to others. It may be possible to give an account of Locke's 'way of ideas' based on the assumption that an 'idea' is a concept in the modern sense of that term, that is, the shareable meaning of a word, but it is implausible to suggest that that is what Locke really meant all along.

To say that an idea is a mental content is not, in itself, to say that Locke held a Representative theory of the classical kind. What one must also show is that Locke held that these mental contents are the *objects* of sense-perception, what we actually perceive. The evidence in the text on this point is, as Yolton says (op. cit., p. 41), inconclusive. Often, especially in the *Examination*,

Locke talks as if an 'idea' were a perception, in the sense of being an operation of perceiving. Cf. *Examination*, 47: 'Perceiving, or having the idea of, the figure'; 'The thinking on, or the idea of the figure'. Or *Essay*, II, i, 9: 'Having *ideas* and perception being the same thing'. The stress in such passages is on the *activity*, the *having* of ideas. But equally often Locke explicitly treats ideas as the *objects* of perception: cf. *Essay*, II, viii, 8, 'Whatsoever the mind perceives in itself, or is the immediate object of perception, thought, or understanding, that I call *idea*'. If one asks what it is which can both be a mental content, something 'in the mind', and also in some sense be perceived, then the most plausible candidate is a mental image or picture. So that, in these passages at least, Locke is implying that what we actually perceive is a mental picture, caused in our minds by the action of external objects on our sense-organs: in other words, a 'picture-original theory of sense-perception'.

It is not surprising that the textual evidence on this point should be inconclusive, if one takes the Representative theory, not as an explicitly advocated doctrine, but as an assumption made by Locke, something which he took so much for granted that he would not think of questioning it. One can see how a philosopher could come to be gripped by such a picture at that time, in the attempt to combine a scientific theory of the mechanism of sense-perception with a Cartesian account of the mind–body relationship. To say that Locke held a Representative theory is not, as I said earlier, to criticize his philosophy at any very crucial point; but it is to say something in defence of his later critics, from Berkeley onwards. Their criticisms were not, as Woozley suggests, based on a total misreading of Locke, but are justifiable in terms of a tenable interpretation of his text. They did, after all, live in the same intellectual atmosphere as Locke, and took the same things for granted. It is more likely, therefore, that they would interpret him correctly than that his perhaps over-subtle modern defenders should do so.

V

BOYLE AND LOCKE ON PRIMARY AND SECONDARY QUALITIES*

PETER ALEXANDER

I. INTRODUCTORY

LOCKE has been seriously misrepresented in various respects ever since Berkeley set critics off on the wrong foot. I wish to discuss just one central view the misunderstanding of which has been particularly gross, namely, the distinction between primary and secondary qualities and, especially, the alleged arguments for this distinction in *Essay* II, viii, 16–21. Robert Boyle is often mentioned in connection with Locke but the extent and importance of his influence on Locke has seldom been realized.[1] If the arguments of II, viii were intended, as is usually thought, following Berkeley, to *establish* the distinction between primary and secondary qualities then Locke was both foolish and incompetent; a study of Boyle can help us to see that he was neither of these things by making it clear what he was driving at.

Misunderstanding of Locke begins very early, with the passage in the Epistle to the Reader about master-builders and under-labourers. Locke says:

The commonwealth of learning is not at this time without master-builders, whose mighty designs, in advancing the sciences, will leave lasting monuments to the admiration of posterity; but everyone must not hope to be a *Boyle* or a *Sydenham*; and in an age that produces such masters as the great *Huygenius* and the incomparable Mr. *Newton*, with some others of that strain, it is ambition enough to be employed as an under-labourer in clearing ground a little, and removing some of the rubbish that

From *Ratio*, 16 (1974), pp. 51–67. Reprinted, in substantially its original form, by permission of the author and the publisher, Basil Blackwell and Mott Ltd.

* This is a revised version of a paper read at the Universities of Maryland and Bowling Green, Ohio during 1971 and to the Annual Conference of the British Society of the Philosophy of Science in 1972.

[1] There are honourable exceptions, e.g., John W. Yolton in *Locke and the Compass of Human Understanding* (Cambridge, 1970) and Maurice Mandelbaum in *Philosophy, Science and Sense Perception* (Baltimore, 1964) but, in my view, neither of them gets the matter quite right. An excellent account of one aspect is to be found in L. Laudan, 'The Nature and Sources of Locke's Views on Hypotheses', *J. Hist. Ideas*, 28, 1967, pp. 211–23. See also G. A. J. Rogers, 'Boyle, Locke and Reason', *J. Hist. Ideas*, 27, 1966, pp. 205–16.

lies in the way of knowledge; which certainly had been very much more advanced in the world, if the endeavours of ingenious and industrious men had not been much cumbered with the learned but frivolous use of uncouth, affected, or unintelligible terms, introduced into the sciences [n.b. old sense], and there made an art of, to that degree that philosophy [i.e. natural, as well as metaphysical, philosophy], which is nothing but the true knowledge of things, was thought unfit or incapable to be brought into well-bred company and polite conversation.[2]

It has been held, rightly, I think, that one task of the under-labourer is the removal of conceptual muddles but I believe that this is not the only task Locke had in mind. Locke actually worked in Boyle's laboratory on relatively routine tasks, such as recording weather conditions, and from time to time he commented on Boyle's manuscripts before their publication;[3] in a literal sense he worked as an under-labourer. A more important task is clearly indicated in the above passage: that of making philosophy, the true knowledge of things, fit and capable 'to be brought into well-bred company and polite conversation'. I believe he saw himself as bringing the language and the findings of the master-builders, the 'new philosophers', to the intelligent layman and so clearing the ground and removing the rubbish of scholastic jargon, standing in the way of *his*, the layman's knowledge of the world.

This involved an even more fundamental task, the clue to which lies in his treatment of innate ideas. Having put forward direct arguments against innate ideas in Book I, Locke then, in effect, says that if anyone is unconvinced by these he should read the rest of the *Essay*; it is based on the hypothesis that there are *no* innate ideas and will, he hopes, show that a plausible account of our knowledge and understanding of the world can be given on this basis, thus giving *indirect* support to the hypothesis. For example, he says:

I know it is a received doctrine that men have native *ideas* and original characters stamped upon their minds in their very first being. This opinion I have at large examined already; and, I suppose, what I have said in the foregoing book will be much more easily admitted when I have shown whence the understanding may get all the *ideas* it has, and by what ways and degrees they may come into the mind; for which I shall appeal to everyone's own observation and experience.[4]

This I take to be of the form of the hypothetical argument of modern science, to the development of which Boyle was so significantly contributing. I believe it is also the form of argument in which Locke was using the corpuscular hypothesis: if he could base a convincing and adequate account of

[2] p. xxxv. All references are to the Everyman edition. Remarks in square brackets, here and later, are mine.

[3] See Boyle, *Works*, New Edition (London, 1772), Vol. V, pp. 655–83. All references to the *Works* will be to this edition. Also M. B. Hall, *Robert Boyle on Natural Philosophy* (Bloomington, 1966), pp. 107 and 110 and R. I. Aaron, *John Locke*, 2nd edition (Oxford, 1955), pp. 12–14.

[4] *Essay*, II, i, 1. See also I, iv, 26 and 'Epistle to the Reader', p. xxxvi.

our everyday experience and description of the world on the best available scientific hypothesis then this would provide powerful indirect support for the hypothesis.

A sympathetic reading of the *Essay* as a whole, in conjunction with the relevant works of Boyle, seems to me to put it beyond argument that the 'lasting monument' of the master-builders which most impressed Locke was the corpuscular philosophy; over and over again he uses it in his explanation of phenomena. Whatever he thought about hypotheses in medicine and whatever other Fellows of the Royal Society thought,[5] in the *Essay*, at least, Locke clearly agrees with Boyle in regarding it as a powerful explanatory hypothesis. Boyle is often said to be a Baconian and Bacon is said to have been hostile to the use of hypotheses; so Locke, strongly influenced by Boyle, is often said to have been hostile to the use of hypotheses. Most of this is based on misunderstandings.

It must not be thought, however, that Locke or Boyle regarded the hypothesis as finally established; for both it was the best available. This appears in many places but Locke's attitude to the hypothesis is perhaps made clearest when he says:

I have here instanced in the corpuscularian hypothesis, as that which is thought to go furthest in an intelligible explication of the qualities of bodies; and I fear the weakness of human understanding is scarce able to substitute another which will afford us a fuller and clearer discovery of the necessary connexion and *co-existence* of the powers which are to be observed united in several sorts of them. This at least is certain: that whichever hypothesis be clearest and truest (for of that it is not my business to determine), our knowledge concerning corporeal substances will be very little advanced by any of them, till we are made to see what qualities and powers of bodies have a *necessary connexion or repugnancy* one with another; which in the present state of philosophy I think we know but to a very small degree.[6]

Locke is, I believe, partly exploring the implications of this hypothesis and partly considering in general the nature and place of hypothesis in natural philosophy.

Boyle's main account of the corpuscular philosophy is *The Origin of Forms and Qualities* (1666). It is divided into two parts: The Theoretical Part, which comes *first*, and the Historical Part. In the first part he sets out to explain 'the doctrine (or rather the hypothesis) which is to be collated with, and to be either confirmed or disproved by the historical [i.e. experimental] truths that will be delivered concerning particular qualities (and forms). . . .'[7] I believe that just

[5] See J. W. Yolton, *Locke and the Compass of Human Understanding* (1970), pp. 58, 63, 76. But compare L. Laudan, op. cit.

[6] *Essay*, IV, iii, 16. If the bracketed portion appears to conflict with part of my interpretation, Locke may be taken to be saying that his purpose is not to compare various available hypotheses but to explain the consequences of this one.

[7] Robert Boyle, *The Origin of Forms and Qualities* (O.F.Q.), *Works*, Vol. III, p. 14.

as Boyle sought to establish or refute the hypothesis by experiment, Locke sought to give some support to it in the *Essay* by applying it to familiar, everyday phenomena. This makes many of Locke's arguments, and especially those about primary and secondary qualities more intelligible and more plausible than they have usually been supposed to be.

I do not wish to argue that this was all Locke was doing; he was clearly interested in the clarification of concepts used in the description and explanation of natural phenomena and in the consequences of Boyle's hypothesis for perception and epistemology. It is worth noting, however, that Boyle regarded the corpuscular philosophy as affording a better explanation of perception than the scholastic notion of 'sensible species'. In a passage in *Experiments and Considerations Touching Colours* he gives an account of perception on the corpuscular hypothesis which is explicitly directed against 'the schools' and 'some Modern Atomists'.[8]

II. THE DISTINCTION

For Locke, ideas, all of them, are in the mind, and qualities, all of them, are in objects. Experience is capable of showing us primary qualities as they are in objects; our ideas of primary qualities may be accurate representations of those qualities. Our ideas of secondary qualities are representations, but never accurate representations of those qualities; what we see as, for example, different colours are, in objects, different textures.[9] Body is defined in terms of the primary qualities, shape, size and motion/rest, to use Boyle's usual list. These are qualities both of sensible objects and of the insensible particles of which they are composed; colours and tastes are ideas representing the secondary qualities of objects, that is, different textures consisting of different combinations of the primary qualities of the superficial insensible particles of objects. Colour words, for example, should be thought of as the names of ideas, not of qualities; the 'names' of the corresponding qualities would have to be more complex descriptions of textures. Our *ideas* of primary and secondary qualities are caused, respectively, by the primary and secondary qualities of objects. Objects also have powers to act not on our organs of sense but upon other objects; these, also, are explained in terms of the arrangements of their insensible particles.[10]

Objects act upon our senses and upon other objects by the movements of their insensible particles, and the insensible particles of light, by producing changes in the insensible particles of our bodies and of other objects. The

[8] Robert Boyle, *Experiments and Considerations Touching Colours (E.C.T.C.)*, *Works*, Vol. I, p. 671. Also facsimile of 1664 edition, ed. M. B. Hall (New York, 1964), pp. 10–11. Quotations from this work are from this facsimile edition.

[9] 'Textures' is a technical term of Boyle's, which Locke sometimes adopts. See *O.F.Q.*, *Works*, Vol. III, p. 22; *Essay*, II, xxiii, 11 and III, vi, 9.

[10] *Essay*: heading to II, viii, 7; II, viii, 1–26.

explanation of this interaction is entirely mechanical, that is, it is in terms of shape, size and motion/rest.

III. BOYLE

The first edition of Locke's *Essay* was published in 1690 and he was probably working on it throughout the 1670s. During the 1660s Boyle published *The Sceptical Chymist* (1661),[11] *Experiments and Considerations Touching Colours* (1664) and *The Origin of Forms and Qualities* (1666), which were all devoted to the experimental establishment of the corpuscular hypothesis and in 1674 he published a short work entitled *Of the Excellency and Grounds of the Corpuscular or Mechanical Philosophy*,[12] which shows very clearly the importance he attached to it.

Boyle's distinction between the primary and secondary qualities is part of his corpuscular hypothesis. His distinction is the same as Locke's. What strikes me most forcibly in reading these works of Boyle is that many passages might have been written by Locke and that most of Locke's examples concern phenomena on which Boyle had experimented.

Boyle refers to 'one catholic and universal matter common to all bodies by which I mean a substance extended, divisible and impenetrable' and to matter as divided into parts, each part having its own magnitude and shape, these parts being 'too small to be singly sensible'. He talks of size and shape as 'primary affections of bodies' and distinguishes them from 'those *less simple qualities* (as colours, tastes and odours) that belong to bodies on their account'.[13] This distinction is crucial to Boyle because he is putting forward a hypothesis which will allow mechanical *explanations* of natural phenomena and *mechanical* explanations are in terms of shape, size and motion/rest.

Boyle was arguing against explanations of natural phenomena in terms of the real and occult qualities and substantial forms of the scholastics, the alchemists and others. He was looking for explanations of as many phenomena as possible in terms of as few basic concepts as possible, those concepts to be derived as directly as possible from sense-experience. Locke, in putting forward an empiricist basis for knowledge, was codifying the principles of the experimental natural philosophy which Boyle was championing against speculative natural philosophy. Both had to insist on empiricism because it was as relatively novel in natural science as it was in philosophy. The method and the hypothesis went hand-in-hand.

In his Preface to *The Origin of Forms and Qualities* Boyle says:

[11] Robert Boyle, *The Sceptical Chymist* in *Works*, Vol. I.

[12] 'Of the Excellency and Grounds of the Corpuscular or Mechanical Philosophy', in M. B. Hall, *Robert Boyle on Natural Philosophy* (Bloomington, 1966), pp. 187–209 from *Works*, Vol. IV, pp. 68–78.

[13] *O.F.Q., Works*, Vol. III, pp. 15–16.

For the knowledge we have of the bodies without us, being for the most part fetched from the information the mind receives by the senses, we scarce know any thing else in bodies, upon whose account they can work upon our senses, save their qualities: ...

and

... as it is by their qualities that bodies act immediately upon our senses, so it is by virtue of those attributes likewise that they act upon other bodies. ...[14]

Later he continues:

That then which I chiefly aim at, is to make it probable to you by experiments (...) that almost all sorts of qualities, most of which have been by the schools either left unexplicated, or generally referred to I know not what incomprehensible substantial forms, may be produced mechanically; I mean by such corporeal agents, as do not appear ... to work otherwise than by virtue of motion, size, figure, and contrivance of their own parts (which attributes I call the mechanical affections of matter, because to them men willingly refer the various operations of mechanical engines): ...[15]

A type of experiment very frequently conducted by Boyle is one in which the colour of an object is changed by changing the texture of its surface. He says:

... after all I have said of Colour, as it is modified Light, and immediately affects the Sensory, I shall now re-mind you that I did not deny, but that Colour might in some sense be considered as a Quality residing in the body that is said to be Colour'd, and indeed the greatest part of the following Experiments referr to Colour principally under that Notion, for there is in the bodyes we call Coloured, and chiefly in their superficiall parts, a certain disposition, whereby they do so trouble the Light that comes from them to our Eye, as that it there makes the distinct Impression, upon whose Account we say, that the Seen body is either White or Black, or Red or Yellow, or of any one determinate Colour. ... we shall (God permitting) ... shew, that the changes, and consequently in divers places the Production and the appearance of Colours depends upon the continuing or alter'd Texture of the Object. ...[16]

It should be noted, and remembered when we are considering Locke, that Boyle, in *O.F.Q.* refers to the secondary qualities as 'less simple' than the primary qualities; this could hardly be an *experienced* contrast, and it refers, I think, to the complexity of the account or *explanation* of the secondary qualities.

In *Of the Excellency and Grounds of the Corpuscular or Mechanical Philosophy* (1674)[17] Boyle summarized the hypothesis and listed its advantages. At this stage he believed that his earlier experiments had established the main features of the hypothesis and here he lists five reasons for regarding it as a

[14] *O.F.Q.*, *Works*, Vol. III, p. 11.

[15] *O.F.Q.*, *Works*, Vol. III, p. 13.

[16] *E.C.T.C.*, ed. Hall, p. 21; *Works*, Vol. I, p. 674.

It has been pointed out to me by Dr. R. S. Woolhouse that Boyle here, and in the passage quoted in fn. 24, refers to colour as modified light, which Locke does not do. However, Boyle considers several ways of accounting for colours, of which this is but one; the account he appears to favour is, I believe, the same as Locke's.

[17] See esp. Hall, pp. 189–93; *Works*, Vol. IV, pp. 69–70.

powerful one. They are that it allows clear and intelligible explanations which
are simple, economical and comprehensive and based upon the most primary
principles we can conceive, i.e. matter and motion. It is of great importance
that these features all concern the *explanatory power* of the hypothesis.

I think we may summarize Boyle's aims and attitudes in the following way.
He is a believer in the experimental philosophy, that is, the basing of science
on close attention to the phenomena met with in sensation. He believes that,
as Locke said, it is in experience that 'all our knowledge is founded and from
it that it ultimately derives itself' and that sensation and reflection supply 'our
understandings with all the materials of thinking'. Observation shows us
objects, with various qualities, acting upon one another and upon ourselves,
to change the qualities of things and produce ideas in us. Boyle, in the scientific
spirit, wishes to explain as much of this as possible in terms of as little as
possible.[18] He wants simple, intelligible, economical and comprehensive
accounts of phenomena in terms of concepts which are directly derived from
experience.

Our experience leads us to believe in the independent existence of bodies;
this belief may be questioned but why should we reject it unless the super-
structure, the total account of the world we erect on it, shows some weakness?
Take it as a working assumption and see where it leads. Sense experience
apparently shows us various different qualities of bodies. Is there any way of
separating these qualities into two groups, one as small as possible and the
other as large as possible, such that the smaller group can plausibly be made
the basis for the explanation of the larger? This is a central question and it
is a question addressed to the understanding rather than to the senses; *it
concerns conceivable explanations rather than qualitative differences in our
sensations.* The clearest explanations we have are mechanical explanations of
such contrivances as watches and they depend upon the specifications of the
character and arrangements of component parts which are solid and which
move one another. The colours, tastes and odours of these parts do not figure
in the explanation.

Perhaps we can extend this technique and explain the different behaviour
of two solid lumps of matter, say gold and silver, in terms of their component
parts. Consider the qualities that bodies appear to have; does our very conception of body involve some of them and not necessarily others? Well, many
bodies have no odour or taste and we can discover the presence of a body
without the help of colours, but can we even conceive of a body without some
shape and size and some ability to be moved? Perhaps, then, we could even
explain the difference in colour of gold and silver by reference to uncoloured
component parts. And so on.

[18] In Hall, pp. 208–9; *Works*, Vol. IV, pp. 77–8.

This leads to a more fundamental question about explanation. We can conceive of an explanation of colour in terms of shape, size and motion/rest. We know that light is reflected in different ways and many of Boyle's experiments had shown that by roughening, or otherwise changing the texture of, a surface you could change its colour; if light is corpuscular, such changes could be explained by the different ways in which its corpuscles are reflected from, or absorbed by, different textures, that is, different arrangements of the superficial corpuscles of bodies. But can we even *conceive* of the explanation of, say, the shape of a body in terms of colours, tastes or odours? Could we even understand the instruction *to operate* on the colour of an object in such a way as to change its shape or size?[19]

The assumptions, if I am right, are realist and empiricist. Bodies exist and experience shows them to be divisible. Their observable properties can perhaps be explained by reference to the properties of their insensible parts. How may an empiricist talk about 'insensible parts'? He must attribute to these parts only properties which are like those properties of ordinary middle-sized bodies of which experience gives us accurate ideas. If knowledge of the world depends ultimately upon sense-experience, there must be some aspects of sense-experience which do not mislead us, some ideas of sensation which accurately represent the reality and give us accurate ideas of their causes. So let us try the working hypothesis that among our ideas of shape, size and motion/rest are accurate ideas and that large and middle-sized bodies can be regarded as made up of insensible particles having just these properties; and let us then see if the hypothesis can be used to construct a plausible and complete account of the natural world and its appearance to us.

Boyle, in fact, has an argument which moves from the character of observed primary qualities to the character of the qualities of the corpuscles. He says:

And since experience shows us (especially that which is afforded us by chymical operations, in many of which matter is divided into parts too small to be singly sensible) that this division of matter is frequently made into insensible corpuscles or particles, we may conclude that the minutest fragments, as well as the biggest masses of the universal matter, are likewise endowed each with its peculiar bulk and shape.[20]

Resemblance is important here. The qualities of the insensible particles are of the same *kind* as the primary qualities of observable bodies; and of these

---

[19] Locke appears to have some such notion as this in mind when he says: 'That the size, figure, and motion of one body should cause a change in the size, figure, and motion of another body is not beyond our conception, . . .' *Essay*, IV, iii, 13.

[20] Boyle, *O.F.Q.*, *Works*, Vol. III, p. 16.

Unlike Mandelbaum, I think that this is a crucial step in the argument of Boyle and Locke; it is the empiricists' justification for attributing any properties to insensible particles. See Mandelbaum, op. cit., pp. 26–7.

experience gives us accurate ideas. This is why we understand what we are saying when we attribute properties to insensible particles. This is all part of the hypothesis which is to be tested by means of the feasibility of giving, on its basis, plausible explanations.

IV. LOCKE

My main thesis is that Locke was not attempting to *make* the primary/secondary quality distinction but was accepting it, ready-made, from Boyle as an essential part of the corpuscular hypothesis, which was already well on the way to being established. The distinction was made on theoretical grounds in relation to possibilities of explanation. I do not believe that Locke thought that it could be made from within sense-experience on the basis of differences between the *ideas* of the various qualities of bodies. It follows that the arguments of sections 16–21 of Book II, Chapter viii of the *Essay*, about manna, porphyry, the pounding of almonds, heat from a fire and the felt temperature of water, are not, as they are usually thought to be, intended to *establish* the distinction. They are *applications* and *explanations* of the distinction. What underlies them is the belief that all the phenomena mentioned can be explained, simply and economically, in terms of the corpuscular hypothesis. It is often not noticed that *the hypothesis is actually mentioned in each of these sections*. Thus, if these are arguments at all, they are parts of the grand argument for the corpuscular hypothesis and mechanical explanation. Locke was reporting scientific findings to the layman and showing how we could make sense of some superficially puzzling features of our everyday experience and our everyday descriptions of the world.

It is part of the hypothesis that our ideas of sensation are ultimately caused by complex arrangements of minute particles having only primary qualities disposed in a potentially infinite variety of ways. We cannot observe the causes themselves, and that is why Locke is doubtful of our ever *knowing*, in his strict sense, the specific texture responsible for a given idea,[21] but we postulate causal relations between corpuscles and groups of corpuscles on the pattern of observed causal transactions between observed bodies. In terms of matter and motion, Boyle's two grand principles, we can explain the effect of bodies upon one another, and upon us to produce ideas. None of this involves occult qualities, for although the explanations involve many things and qualities we do not observe, they do not involve anything of a *kind* we do not observe. Locke holds that *analogy* is the method by which we can regard hypotheses which go beyond the senses as probable.[22] I should now like to consider, in the light of this interpretation, the examples of Book II, Chapter viii.

[21] See *Essay*, IV, iii, 13.
[22] *Essay*, IV, xvi, 12.

The first (II, viii, 16) concerns the effects of fire, at different distances, on my hand. If I hold my hand at some little distance from the fire I feel heat but if I move it closer I begin to feel pain. I think of the heat as in the fire and of the pain as in me. This, according to Locke, is a mistake; but do my sensations show it to be a mistake? Nothing in the sensations shows the heat to be in the fire and the pain in me but, equally, nothing in the sensations shows them to be both in me or both in the fire. However, I do *feel* both; the ideas (or sensations) are both in me. Now these can both be explained by the communication of motion to the particles of my hand by particles set in motion by the particles of the fire. Since this is so, it seems sensible to say that, as ideas, heat and pain are both in me, which is obvious, but that they have correlates and causes in the fire. Moreover, their causes are of the same general sort since they are both motions of particles, differing mainly in speed. The paragraph ends thus: 'Why are whiteness and coldness in snow, and pain not, when it produces the one and the other idea in us; *and can do neither, but by the bulk, figure, number, and motion of its solid parts?*' (My italics).[23]

The manna example in II, viii, 18 is similar but the porphyry example in II, viii, 19 is rather different. Under normal conditions porphyry looks red and white. But, Locke says:

Hinder light but from striking on it, and its colours vanish: it no longer produces any such *ideas* in us; upon the return of light it produces these appearances on us again. Can anyone think any real alterations are made in the *porphyry* by the presence or absence of light; and that those *ideas* of whiteness and redness are really in *porphyry* in the light, when it is plain *it has no colour in the dark?* It has, indeed, such a configuration of particles, both night and day, as are apt, by the rays of light rebounding from some parts of that hard stone, to produce in us the *idea* of redness, and from others the *idea* of whiteness; but whiteness or redness are not in it at any time, but such a texture that hath the power to produce such a sensation in us.[24]

Could this be intended to make the primary–secondary quality distinction, by pointing to differences in our ideas of them? In the first place, white and red are treated as ideas from the beginning, whereas textures are treated as undoubted qualities of the porphyry. The notion of a configuration of particles clearly does not come directly from experience; what place could this theoretical notion occupy in a mere comparison of different *experiences*? If this passage were intended as it is usually taken, is it likely that Locke would not have

[23] It is noteworthy that the theory of heat accepted here was proposed by Francis Bacon in *Novum Organum*, 1620.

[24] Compare Boyle, *E.C.T.C.*, ed. Hall, pp. 74–5; *Works*, Vol. I, p. 690: '. . . if colour be indeed . . . but Light Modified, how can we conceive that it can Subsist in the Dark, that is, where it must be supposed that there is no Light; but on the other side, if Colour be consider'd as a certain Constant Disposition of the Superficial parts of the Object . . . there seems no just reason to deny, but that in this Sense, Bodies retain their Colour as well in the Night as Day . . . it may be said that Bodies are Potentially Colour'd in the Dark and Actually in the Light.'

mentioned the very obvious fact that extension remains when we remove the light, because we can still feel it? He does not do so because, I suggest, what he is supporting is his belief that the appearance to sight of both the colour and the extension in the light, the appearance to touch of extension in the dark and the failure of sight to show us colour in the dark, can *all* be explained in terms of the action upon us of configurations of particles, a theoretical notion, postulated for explanatory purposes.

The next example, in II, viii, 20, concerns the result of pounding an almond in a mortar. The section reads:

Pound an almond, and the clear white *colour* will be altered into a dirty one, and the sweet *taste* into an oily one. What real alteration can the beating of the pestle make in any body, but an alteration of the *texture* of it?

Pestles and mortars are size- and shape-changing devices, not colour- or flavour-changing devices. Sometimes their use to change size and shape also results in a change of colour, sometimes not. It is plausible to explain changes in colour, if they occur, in terms of the particular way in which the substance is broken up, the particular change in its texture. Can we conceive of either the colour of the pestle and mortar causing the change of texture *or* the primary qualities of the pestle and mortar operating directly, that is, not *via* textures, on colours to change them? Perhaps we could, but the explanation would have to be very much more complex. I think that Locke is issuing a challenge: show me how the pounding could produce a change of colour *except through* changes of texture.

The final example occurs in II, viii, 21 and this seems to me to show clearly that my interpretation is not wildly out. Locke there says:

Ideas being thus [i.e. 'in this way', *not* 'by these arguments'] distinguished and understood, we may be able to *give an account* [i.e. explain] how the same water, at the same time, may *produce* the idea of cold by one hand and of heat by the other, whereas it is impossible that the same water, *if those ideas were really in it*, should at the same time *be* both hot and cold. [My italics and glosses.]

This shows that Locke was using the distinction between primary and secondary qualities as central in a manner of explanation. We can explain how the ideas of heat and cold may be set up in us by something that is, properly speaking, neither hot nor cold. The corpuscles of the water are moving at a certain speed which is greater than the speed of the corpuscles of the cold hand and less than the speed of the corpuscles of the warm hand; the consequent increase in speed of the corpuscles of one hand and decrease in speed of the corpuscles of the other produce in us respectively the ideas of heat and cold.

My interpretation is, I believe, supported by II, viii, 22 where Locke says he has just 'engaged in physical inquiries a little further than perhaps I intended' for the purpose of making clear (not *making*) 'the difference between the *qualities* in bodies, and the *ideas* produced by them in the mind'. He says 'I hope I shall be pardoned this little excursion into natural philosophy' (i.e. physical science, in our terms). It was necessary to engage in physical inquiries because that is where the basis for the distinction lies; more precisely, it lies in the theoretical requirements of mechanical explanation by means of corpuscles rather than in observationally detected differences between the qualities.

Those who know their Locke will have noticed my avoidance of a statement which appears to present difficulties for my interpretation. In II, viii, 21 Locke says that by his explanation

. . . we may understand how it is possible that the same water may at the same time produce the sensation of heat in one hand and cold in the other; which yet figure never does, that never producing the *idea* of a square by one hand which has produced the *idea* of a globe by another.

This *suggests* that primary qualities never produce illusions in the way that secondary qualities do, a suggestion which Berkeley was quick to seize upon, but it does not entail it and Locke cannot have thought it did.

There is more than one possible interpretation of this but here I mention the one which is probably the simplest. It relies upon Locke's well-known lack of clarity of expression. He may have been just mistaken about a matter of fact in a particular case and still the intended argument may go like this: if we think of heat and cold as qualities of the water we should be led into saying that the same water is hot and cold at the same time and this would be as *contradictory as saying* that an object is square and spherical at the same time, but we avoid this if we say that heat and cold are, *as experienced*, merely ideas in us. My interpretation allows Locke to explain illusions of shape and size in a similar way because it in no way commits him to thinking that we are never misled about shapes and sizes.

V. CRITICISMS OF LOCKE

If I am correct, some orthodox criticisms of Locke miss the mark. In particular, any criticism which seeks to show that Locke in II, viii, 16–21 has failed to provide an adequate philosophical justification of the primary/secondary quality distinction is misplaced if this is not what he was trying to do.

1. Locke is often taken to be arguing for the distinction on the basis of the invariability and freedom from illusion of our perceptions of primary

qualities, in contrast to our perceptions of secondary qualities. But Locke could not have missed *either* the fact that the shape and size of an object may appear differently from different points of view *or* the significance of this fact for his argument. He mentions illusions about primary qualities at II, ix, 8, II, xiv, 6 and II, xxi, 63. His claim, I suggest, is that our ideas of both primary and secondary qualities, and of the variations in them may all be explained in terms of the corpuscles. If pressed, I think he would have said that having an accurate idea of something does not mean, and must not mean, having the *same* perception of it under every condition; for a visible thing to be of a given size *just is*, in part, for it to 'look smaller' at 50 feet than it does at 10 feet.

2. Another alleged objection is that an empiricist cannot hold that ideas of sensation represent, and are caused by, unperceived external objects such as the corpuscles. *Ex hypothesi* there can be no direct perceptual evidence for them and how could their existence be established by reason? However, Locke does not claim *knowledge* of these external objects through either sense-experience or reason.[25] Their existence is a hypothesis adopted by the natural philosopher as a basis for explanation. It would be indirectly supported, eventually, if it allowed a plausible account of the world and our experience. As I have said, this is precisely the pattern of Locke's clinching argument against innate ideas; it is plausible to suppose that he is using that pattern here.

3. Whether Locke was being consistent as an empiricist or not depends upon the kind of empiricist he was trying to be. Locke's empiricism does not include the principle that nothing must figure in our account of the world unless it has been, or could be, the subject of experience. He wants to show 'whence the understanding may get all the *ideas* it has';[26] that it is in experience that 'all our knowledge is *founded*, and from that it *ultimately* derives itself'; and that sensation and reflection together supply 'our understandings with all the *materials* of thinking'.[27] This implies that the understanding is able to work on these materials. He nowhere appears to be committed to the slogan 'Nothing in the mind which was not first in the senses'. At most he is committed to some such more moderate slogan as 'Nothing in the mind that is not somehow connected with the senses'. He does not aspire to membership of the Vienna Circle. The account I have given is consistent with this. The only qualities attributed to objects, whether sensible or insensible, are based upon ideas gained through experience; no reference is necessary to qualities *of a kind* of which experience never could give us accurate ideas. This is the

[25] *Essay*, IV, ii, esp. §13.
[26] *Essay*, II, i, 1.
[27] *Essay*, II, i, 2, my italics.

empiricism of the *natural* philosopher and is perfectly respectable if we recognize as Locke clearly did, that natural philosophy may not give us know-ledge, in the strict sense, but may give us something valuable, namely, probable 'conjecture'.[28]

4. A serious criticism concerns the alleged resemblance between primary qualities and our ideas of them. Locke surely did not suppose that my idea of extension is itself extended, that my idea of a foot-rule is twelve inches long. His use of the words 'resemblance' and 'likeness' may mislead us about what he was groping for. There may be a connection here with his views on abstract general ideas; in spite of Berkeley, Locke did not think that an abstract idea of 'triangle' has some indeterminate and unspecifiable shape any more than he thought that an idea of extension has extension. Nor did he need this. What he did need was an account of an *accurate* idea; we in fact talk of accurate ideas of things without committing ourselves to resemblances between ideas and objects. Locke needed to be able to say that ideas of primary qualities are accurate ideas of those qualities, whereas ideas of secondary qualities are not.

It may be possible to explain why Locke talked about resemblances in groping for the necessary account. He was interested in language and the relations between our descriptions of the world and what they describe. He seldom, if ever, uses 'idea' in the way in which more recent empiricists use, or ought to use, 'sense-datum'; for him, an idea is, nearly always, an idea *of* something. What follows 'of' is a description and, in a sense, it is descriptive of the idea. We describe an idea by saying that it is an idea of red or of an extension of one foot. This is how, in speech, we distinguish our ideas. Now primary qualities are such that the words we use in describing our ideas of them are also the appropriate words for describing the qualities; secondary qualities are such that the words we use in describing our ideas of them will not do for describing the qualities. The description of an idea of a primary quality is of the form 'of x' and the description of the object having the quality is 'has x' or 'is x'; the resemblance is in the description. Similarly, the abstract idea of triangularity is of 'a plane figure bounded by three straight lines' and this is accurate if anything that is a triangle *is* a plane figure bounded by three straight lines; there is no need for the idea and the triangle to resemble one another in shape.

5. Finally, perhaps the most difficult objection for Locke to meet is an argument about causality put by Berkeley, who says that shape, size and motion/rest are ideas and, as such, 'perfectly inert' and incapable of causing anything; 'there is no other agent or efficient cause than *spirit*'.[29] Locke

[28] *Essay*, IV, xvi, 12.
[29] Berkeley, *The Principles of Human Knowledge*, §102.

would, of course, deny this but Berkeley is quite right when he goes on to develop his earlier remark that no philosopher even pretends to explain 'how matter should operate on a spirit'.[30] In other words, Locke's account involves him in the mind/body problem and he has failed to solve it. Locke, of course, realized this but thought, in the first place, that this problem could not be avoided and that the answer might always remain a secret hidden in the mind of God.[31] It is difficult for the natural philosopher to discover the necessary connections between bodies because our senses are not acute enough to discern the textures on which these depend.[32] If such knowledge is ever obtained then a partial explanation of sensation could be given by the natural philosopher but this must, logically, always remain incomplete because at the point at which mechanical motion gives way to sensation, mechanical explanation becomes inappropriate.[33]. Locke believes, as does Boyle, that the facts of experience force dualism upon us; the consequent problem is not scientific but philosophical and is therefore not particularly involved in the distinction between primary and secondary qualities.

I am aware that in this paper I have not dealt adequately with Berkeley's conclusion from his various arguments that the idea of matter is unintelligible. Nor have I been concerned to argue that Locke's view is, in the end, acceptable; that argument would involve me in a much fuller discussion of the 'resemblance' between ideas of primary qualities and the qualities themselves. I have simply hoped to give, of part of the *Essay*, an interpretation which seems to me to emerge from a careful reading of it in the light of the work of the natural philosopher who most strongly influenced Locke and to urge that the result is more coherent and intelligible, and depends less on the ready assumption that Locke was confused, than more orthodox interpretations.

[30] Berkeley, *Principles*, §50.
[31] See, e.g., *Essay*, IV, iii, 28 and IV, x, 19.
[32] See, e.g., *Essay*, IV, iii, 16 and 25.
[33] See, e.g., *Essay*, IV, iii, 10–13 and 28.

THE IDEAS OF POWER AND SUBSTANCE IN LOCKE'S PHILOSOPHY

M. R. AYERS

1. INTRODUCTION

THE concept of substance is at least as important in Locke's philosophy as the concept of an idea. Indeed, his doctrine of substance helps to constitute the end to which the general theory of ideas and knowledge is a means or preliminary: i.e. the mapping of the extent and limits of human understanding. Locke's philosophy of science rests on two great divisions. One division lies between, on the one hand, sciences like geometry and (as he thinks) ethics, in which certainty and *a priori* understanding can be achieved; and on the other hand theoretical natural science, in respect of which such certainty is beyond the reach of human beings: here we must be content at best with reasonable hypothesis and approximation and at worst with blank ignorance.[1] The other division lies between this unattainable explanatory science of nature on the one hand, and on the other hand the descriptive, practical 'natural history' of the Royal Society, which is concerned not with things and processes as they are in themselves, but with the *phenomena*, with things as we can regularly observe them to be and to behave. A full account of Locke's theory of substance would be an account of how he explains and expounds these divisions.

In this paper, however, I shall try only to settle a single question, the subject of what is probably the most important and radical difference of opinion still outstanding in the interpretation of Locke's philosophy. The question is this: does Locke think of the 'substance' or *'substratum'* of *observable* properties as an entity distinct from *all* its properties? He certainly draws a distinction between the underlying, intrinsic properties of a thing,

From *Philosophical Quarterly*, 25 (1975), pp. 1–27. The paper has been revised for this volume, and is reprinted by permission of the author and the editor of the journal.

[1] Corpuscularianism was such a conjecture. There were none in psychology (cf. *Essay*, IV, xii, 12).

its 'real essence' or constitution, and the phenomenal or observable properties by which we identify it as gold, lead, a diamond, a man or whatever—its 'nominal essence'. But is the unknown 'substance' or *'substratum'* nothing over and above the unknown 'real essence'? Or is it the case, as Pringle-Pattison says, that 'Locke plainly distinguishes the two, and teaches a two-fold ignorance' of real essence and of 'naked substance'?[2]

The importance of this issue should be obvious, for, if Locke does distinguish ontologically between substance and essence, we have next to ask what on earth he is up to—a question to which a variety of more or less ingenious answers have been given, largely dependent upon the philosophical proclivities of the commentator. Consequently there are quite different opinions current as to the *kind* of philosopher Locke is: not merely as to whether he is good or bad, highly confused or reasonably coherent, but as to his motivation—as to whether he is driven by an interest in 'logical' questions as well as in philosophy of science; and as to whether his pervasive agnosticism is to be ascribed to a transcendentalist tendency to postulate unknowables[3] rather than characterized as a sane and realistic estimate of the limited achievement and possibilities of contemporary science and scientific methodology. There is even room for disagreement over whether Locke is advancing a theory of *substratum* or attacking it, being serious or being ironical.

Now it seems to me that all these issues can be settled decisively, and that the party of Pringle-Pattison is in the wrong. There is a short way to this conclusion, although it is a circumstantial argument likely to be un-popular among philosophers. For it is improbable to the point of impossibility that Locke, who is an anti-Aristotelian corpuscularian of the school of Boyle, should himself, using the very term *substratum*, advance a view so analogous to what Berkeley describes as 'that antiquated and so much ridiculed notion of *materia prima* to be met with in Aristotle and his followers'.[4] Locke is only advancing the familiar party line when he himself deplores 'those obscure and unintelligible discourses and disputes which have filled the heads

---

[2] In his abridged edition of the *Essay* (Oxford, 1924): see his note on III, iii, 15. For other versions of this interpretation see, e.g., J. Gibson, *Locke's Theory of Knowledge* (Cambridge, 1917), Ch. 5; J. Bennett, *Locke, Berkeley, Hume* (Oxford, 1971), Ch. 3; G. Buchdahl, *Metaphysics and the Philosophy of Science* (Oxford, 1969), Ch. 4; R. S. Woolhouse, *Locke's Philosophy of Science and Knowledge* (Oxford, 1971), Chs. 4 and 7. For contrary views, closer to the interpretation adopted here, see, e.g., R. I. Aaron, *John Locke* (Oxford, 1955), Ch. 5; M. Mandelbaum, *Philosophy, Science, and Sense Perception* (Baltimore, 1964), Ch. 1; F. C. Copleston, *A History of Philosophy* (London, 1944–66), Vol. 5; J. W. Yolton, *Locke and the Compass of Human Understanding* (Cambridge, 1970), Ch. 2.

[3] For this standard empiricist polemical misreading cf. Berkeley, *Principles*, Introduction §§1–2 and I. §101.

[4] Op. cit., I. §11.

and books of philosophers concerning *materia prima*' (III, x, 15).[5] Whatever Locke's *substratum* is, if he wrote *compos mentis*, it cannot be an entity that is undifferentiated, or 'other than' its properties, in fact; although it might be said to be so from our point of view, in so far as it is in some sense 'other than' the phenomenal properties by which we know it. I put this objection with some vehemence since it may illustrate the sort of reasons why a number of scholarly commentators have neglected the task of producing detailed, point by point arguments against the Pringle-Pattison interpretation. Someone who offered an ingenious interpretation of passages in St. Thomas as expressions of atheism might expect similarly short shrift.

There is, however, a further strategy available for the defence of the theory that Locke would distinguish ontologically between substance and real essence. For we might understand him to do so with the purpose of discarding the one from his system while retaining the other. On this view, Locke is being ironical whenever he seems to be admitting the intellectual necessity of postulating a 'common subject' or support for observable qualities to exist in: he is merely describing a manoeuvre which he himself regards as meaningless or unjustifiable. Now such an interpretation avoids the historical objection, but requires us to discount far too many apparently serious and straightforward discussions, as well, indeed, as some vigorous and unambiguous pronouncements. The single passage most favourable to the ascription of ironical intent occurs in the discussion of space at II, xiii, 16–20, which is derisively polemical and *capable* of interpretation as if it were part of an all-out attack on the very notion of substance. Yet even *prima facie* it can equally well be read as no more than an attack on the belief that talk of 'substance' expresses *knowledge* of something ultimate: in particular, knowledge enough to afford certainty that 'there . . . could be, nothing but solid beings which could not think, and thinking beings that were not extended', a view which leaves no ontological room for empty space. The explicit conclusion of the argument, as it relates to substance, is merely that 'of *substance*, we have no *idea* of what it is, but only a confused, obscure

[5] Locke here attributes the doctrine to their mistaking a distinction between ideas for an ontological or real one: i.e. the distinction between the idea of *solid* substance and the idea of a *solid and extended* substance. There is no real difference, since whatever is solid is extended. The substance/attribute distinction is not involved, but Locke's argument well illustrates his scorn for a multiplication of entities on the basis of merely logical distinctions. Moreover, Descartes's point that the substance/attribute distinction itself is merely logical must have been well known to him. Indeed, we shall see that Locke goes further: for, if we knew its essence, there would be no difference between our idea of a general substance such as matter and our idea of its essence, and so not even a logical distinction could be drawn. (But there *is* a logical distinction between the general substance and a determinate, specific 'essence'.) For an attempt to explore further the relationship between Locke's argument and Aristotelian and Cartesian logic, see my 'Substance, Substrate, Essence and Accident: Some Antecedents to Locke's *Essay*', forthcoming.

one of what it does'.[6] Among the many other passages that should help to settle the question, it is worth mentioning Locke's extended, indignant disclaimer in reply to Stillingfleet, who had complained that he seemed to 'deny or doubt that there is in the world any such thing as substance'. Yet every theorist can multiply epicycles, and if we are prepared to postulate enough insincerity, secret doctrine, ambivalence and confusion on Locke's part,[7] it is just possible to maintain that II, xiii, 16–20, understood as a scornful rejection of the whole notion of a substrate, represents Locke's true views about substance. To avoid the pursuit of such unrewarding complications, I shall now turn to a more positive line of argument.

2. THE IDEA OF POWER

The treatment of the idea of substance does not stand alone in the *Essay*. A good way of approaching it is through the analogous discussion of the idea of power. For the two are not only analogous, but are connected parts of a single theory, which we may call Locke's philosophy of science.

The idea of power is formed as follows:

The mind . . . concluding from what it has so constantly observed to have been, that the like changes will for the future be made in the same things, by like agents, and by the like ways—considers in one thing the possibility of having any of its simple *ideas* changed, and in another the possibility of making that change; and so comes by that *idea* which we call *power*. Thus we say fire has a *power* to melt gold . . . and gold has a *power* to be melted. . . . In which, and the like cases, the *power* we consider is in reference to the change of perceivable *ideas* [II, xxi, 1].

What is Locke saying, in this and in surrounding passages? As the last sentence quoted reminds us, he is concerned to show that the content of our idea of power—and of our ideas of particular powers—extends no further than we can observe. And yet the idea has reference to what we do not observe, a postulated something in agent and patient, lying behind the observed relationship between them. The idea of power is quite unlike the idea of yellow, in that, first, it is not acquired in a special experience and, secondly, it is used to refer to something beyond experience; but the corollary is that it has no positive content by itself, since its positive content in any particular case is supplied by the observable effect. It seems to me that

[6] Quoted by Locke himself in *The First Letter to the Bishop of Worcester*.

[7] Bennett (op. cit., p. 61), admitting that the *Letter* to Stillingfleet is not ironical, asks: '. . . but is Locke likely to have been less clear and candid in his magnum opus than in his letters to a touchy and not very intelligent bishop?'—a question which misrepresents both the facts and the issue. Since it is improbable that Locke would say what he did not mean in either work, we should prefer the interpretation that implies no conflict between them. The *Letter* was Locke's published response to a prominent critic, not private correspondence. Since one of its aims was clarification, it is not surprising if it is clear. Explanatory extracts from the *Letters* were inserted in the Fifth Edition of the *Essay*, possibly with Locke's approval: see Yolton's introduction to the Everyman edition of the *Essay*, p. xv; cf. Clarendon Edition (ed. P. H. Nidditch, Oxford, 1975), p. xxxii.

Locke sees it as operating in everyday thought as a sort of dummy concept, *faute de mieux.*

In other words, the function of the idea springs from the rationality of explaining observed interactions by underlying, unobserved properties of the things interacting. But from observation we know these properties only as whatever properties have such and such an effect in such and such conditions. In Russellian terms, our knowledge is knowledge by description. Thus it is entirely natural that, when he is assuming the atomic hypothesis, Locke should sometimes *identify* the power with the actual primary qualities supposed responsible for the effect: '. . . what is sweet, blue, or warm in *idea* is but the certain bulk, figure, and motion of the insensible parts in the bodies themselves, which we call so' (II, viii, 15).

It is not the observation of mere change, but of repeated, regular change, that is said to give us the idea of power. The idea is acquired or suggested to the mind by contact with things that always or nearly always behave observably in a given way in given observable circumstances. It is because we *regularly* observe the melting of gold *whenever* it comes into contact with fire that we cannot reasonably avoid thinking in terms of continuously existing but intermittently operative properties in each, which are independent of this relationship and reaction. Yet we come to see that the idea has universal application, so that 'whatever change is observed, the mind must collect a power somewhere able to make that change, as well as a possibility in the thing itself to receive it'(II, xxi, 4). Power becomes abstractly definable as 'the source from whence all action proceeds' (II, xxii, 11)—not just observably regular action.

As an account of the genesis of an idea purely from experience, this story may be unsatisfying. The suggestion that it is rational to take discontinuous but 'regular' observable behaviour as an indication of underlying, permanent, causally operative structure may be acceptable, but seems to presuppose, not only the concept of causality, but that there is a causal order—that events do not just happen, that experience is experience of, and within, a law-governed universe. It does not appear, however, that Locke saw the idea of causality as prior to the idea of power. On the contrary, the latter is treated first, and the ideas of cause and effect are discussed as if they are concepts of the same kind and on the same level as the concept of power. Let us look at that discussion.

In the notice that our senses take of the constant vicissitude of things, we cannot but observe that several particular, both qualities and substances, begin to exist, and that they receive this their existence from the due application and operation of some other being. From this observation we get our *ideas* of *cause* and *effect*. . . Thus, finding that, in that substance which we call wax, fluidity, which is a simple *idea* that was not in it before, is constantly produced by the application of a certain degree of heat, we call the simple *idea* of heat, in relation to fluidity in wax, the cause of it, and fluidity the effect [II, xxvi, 1].

Once again observed regularity is what prompts the idea, when experience of 'constant vicissitude' compels us to accept certain hypotheticals as reliable. Yet the idea has reference beyond what is observable, i.e. to the unobserved relation linking the terms: for the cause normally produces its effect 'working by insensible ways' (II, xxvi, 2).[8] Locke calls the unknown but rationally presumed connection between cause and effect the *'modus operandi'*, or 'manner of operation':

For to have the *idea* of *cause* and *effect*, it suffices to consider any simple *idea* or substance as beginning to exist by the operation of some other, without knowing the manner of that operation [II, xxvi, 2].

And again:

. . . *many words which seem to express some action* signify nothing of the action or *modus operandi* at all, *but* barely *the effect*, with some circumstances of the subject wrought on, or cause operating: v.g. creation, annihilation, contain in them no *idea* of the action or manner whereby they are produced, but barely of the cause and the thing done [II, xxii, 11].

We can approach the question of what it would be to know the *modus operandi* involved in some causal relationship through Locke's assertion that we have ideas of only two sorts of action: '. . . we can, I think, conceive [action], in intellectual agents, to be nothing else but modes of thinking and willing; in corporeal agents, nothing else but modifications of motion' (ibid.). These represent the limits of the intelligibility of what goes on, as far as human beings are concerned. Complicated exegetical issues are raised by the example of mental activity, but it is clear that the limitation of physical action to 'modifications of motion' is a result of the standard corpuscularian view, which appears more overtly elsewhere in the *Essay*, that the only intelligible physical change is mechanical change. Crudely, we do perceive and understand the manner in which clocks and billiard balls operate. It is true that Locke's acceptance of the intelligibility of clockwork is overlaid by certain doubts about the adequacy of our grasp even of mechanical operations, for example doubts about the intelligibility of physical coherence. Mechanical explanations assume *coherent*, *rigid* elements, such as the atoms

[8] Cf. IV, iii, 29: 'The things that, as far as our observation reaches, we constantly find to proceed regularly, we may conclude do act by a law set them, but yet by a law that we know not.' In certain cases the *modus operandi* is sensible: in II, xxvi, 2 Locke mentions *making*, when an object is 'produced by a sensible separation or *juxtaposition* of discernible parts'.

were presumed to be. If we emphasize only these doubts, as for example Gibson does, it is possible to argue that Locke believed that we never to any degree grasp the *modus operandi* involved in any interaction. Yet this would be to ignore his acceptance of the atomic theory, in all but the most agonistic passage of the *Essay*, as a good explanatory hypothesis, the best available. His favourite contrast between seeing the mechanism and seeing only the face of a clock implies that mechanical change is at least relatively intelligible.[9]

To sum up. Locke's treatment of the idea of power and related ideas is much more than an embarrassed attempt to bring some awkward abstract concepts under the principle that all our ideas come from experience. It is a positive contribution to a central theme of the *Essay*, i.e. the identification of an epistemological gap between the level of phenomena (objective, not subjective phenomena—*not* 'sense-data') and the unobservable level at which reality is in principle intelligible; between the everyday level at which human knowledge and conceptions of the world are mediated by our sensibility and powers of observation, and the level of things as they are in themselves and as they should be conceived of in theoretical, explanatory science. Locke is faced with the task of explaining how we acquire and use ordinary causal concepts, given that there is such a gap and that we lack innate knowledge of the second, deeper level. He argues that the idea of power and cause and effect arise simply as a rational response to the phenomena, to reality as we experience it. Consequently, while they carry implications of the unknown, they tell us nothing directly about it. Perhaps it follows that the concept of power would be dispensable for one who had knowledge of the intelligible level, or would serve a different function;[10] but such a conclusion is hardly alien to Rationalism.

Locke's critics may think that he has simply assumed an innate or, alternatively, a meaningless notion of intelligible causality; but then Locke is neither Leibniz nor Hume. I shall not offer to arbitrate between them, but it is not obvious that Locke's position is the least tenable, or most confused, of the three.

3. THE IDEA OF SUBSTANCE

Certain concepts are called by Locke 'ideas of substances'. What is he talking about? Although it may not seem very helpful to say so, substances

[9] See, e.g., III, vi, 3; cf. II, xxiii, 10–14.
[10] Even if we knew the intrinsic properties and general laws, it might still be informative to be told what powers flowed from them; as we can know the essence of a triangle without knowing all that it implies. To epistemology this would be a different function from that of being the concept through which we can think of *unknown* intrinsic properties. Such at least seems to be the point of view from which Locke explains the concept.

are 'things' in a narrow sense in which not everything that can be a subject of discourse is a *thing*. States, properties, events, processes and so on are non-things. 'Obligation, drunkenness, a lie, etc.' are cited by Locke as examples of 'mixed modes', one of his classes of non-things. Lead, water, men, leopards and watches are things.[11]

To the logically inclined such a distinction may look disgracefully rough and ready, and it is tempting to begin by trying to polish it up to one's own philosophical satisfaction in the hope of identifying precisely, from the outset, the distinction that Locke *must* have had in mind. But apart from being —unsurprisingly—very difficult, such a procedure tends to be a distraction from the historian's business of discovering how Locke himself conceived of the matter.

Much twentieth-century discussion of 'the problem of substance' sees it as having to do with particularity or individuation. The trite question 'Is a *thing* anything over and above its properties?' seems lacking in ontological bite unless the 'thing' is taken to be particular. But there is no evidence that Locke's thoughts on the idea of substance were ever directed towards any such question; although he would not, of course, deny that Plato, or this tree, is an individual substance. There is every indication in the *Essay* that he was prepared to deal with the status of particulars *vis-à-vis* universals in very traditional ways (and none the worse for that), since he assumes that all particulars have position in space and time, and that universals are creatures of the mind. But the role of the idea of *substance* is in explaining the idea of *man*, i.e. the concept of the Aristotelian 'secondary' substance, not the concept of the Aristotelian 'primary' substance, the idea of *this particular man*.[12]

Locke's explanation of 'ideas of substances' is that they are complex ideas formed on the basis of observation and aiming at a peculiar correspondence with what exists in nature: i.e. at bringing under a single complex idea the

---

[11] *Father, servant, islander*, etc., are not substance terms for Locke, but relational terms, a relation being 'something extraneous and superinduced'. Functional terms might well seem relational: whether something is a *watch* seems to depend on how *people* use it. Indeed, Boyle remarks that 'whether a bullet be silver, or brass, or lead, or cork, if it swing at the end of a string, 'tis enough to make it a *pendulum*' (*Origin of Forms and Qualities* (1667), p. 342). But both Boyle and Locke assimilate functions to powers: i.e. they mark no difference between defining a pendulum as something that *people use* as a swinging weight, and defining it as something that *can* or *would* swing at the end of a string. Consequently, in the service of their mechanism, they can exploit the analogy between natural substances and artificial machines unencumbered by complicating provisos. Our ideas of both are 'ideas of substances': cf. III, vi, 39, a passage concerned specifically with watches.

[12] The latter is hardly discussed in the *Essay*. Locke seems unconcerned by the gap between an idea's being determinate and its being the idea of a particular; or, rather, by the problem of how 'circumstances of time and place' are incorporated in the idea of a particular so as to explain its particularity in a non-circular way (time and place being, for Locke, relative). But certainly (1) it is unsurprising if he failed to resolve that difficult issue, and (2) his doctrine of substance has nothing to do with it.

ideas of properties that are combined as a genuine unity in nature. The character of this combination, as conceived of by Locke, is easily understood: the constituent properties are powers and sensible qualities, which are united in so far as they all depend upon a common structure. For example, *water*, as the human observer knows it, has the power to dissolve certain substances, to cause corrosion in some metals and to quench fire; the property of liquidity; a disposition to solidify in cold and to vaporize in heat; sensible transparency; a certain taste (or 'tastelessness') and so forth. All these known properties are reasonably presumed due to the same underlying structure: according to Locke this is more or less what we *mean* when we say that they all belong to one *thing* or when we define water as a *substance* having such and such observable properties. The nature of that thing or substance, however, is (in Locke's reasonable seventeenth-century view) unknown, except as 'something' that accounts for the combination of those properties. Thus, in order to mark the presumption of such a natural unity among the powers that we include under one complex idea on the basis of their observed 'co-existence', we add the idea of 'some *substratum* wherein they do subsist, and from which they do result'.

The concept of 'substance', *'substratum'*, or 'thing (having such and such properties)' is thus a concept by means of which we refer to what is unobserved and unknown—or known only through its effects and relatively to the level of observation. In other words, *substance* is a 'dummy' concept like *power*, and Locke's derision is directed against those who think of it as something more. His jokes about 'Indian philosophers' and 'children who, being questioned what such a thing is which they know not, readily give this satisfactory answer, that it is *something*' are jokes closely analogous in content and purpose to Molière's joke about the purported explanation of the effect of a drug in terms of its 'dormitive power': the target of both is the pretence of understanding what is not understood, and the implication of both is that there is more to be known. It is therefore hardly surprising that Locke reacted irritably to Stillingfleet's provocative suggestion that, having made so much fun of substance, he might as well have denied its existence.

Yet the persistence of the misunderstandings of Locke invites explanation. Certainly the fault lies partly in his terminology, if that is not too grand a term for what sometimes seems almost an affectedly imprecise and figurative way of expressing himself.[13] Yet the ambiguities can all be fairly easily ironed out by reference to the context, textual and historical.

[13] The pose of the amateur, innocent of the sophisticated pedantry of academic philosophers, may well have been a conscious affectation that pervades Locke's manner of exposition. (See, e.g., the Epistle or his footnote to II, xv, 9. And cf. R. Colie, 'The Essayist in his *Essay*', in Yolton, *John Locke: Problems and Perspectives* (Cambridge, 1969).) If so, the professionals are still exacting their revenge.

Some difficulties in interpretation may be illustrated by the opening
paragraph of the chapter on the idea of substances:

The mind being, as I have declared, furnished with a great number of the simple *ideas*
conveyed in by the *senses*, as they are found in exterior things, or by *reflection* on its
own operations, takes notice also that a certain number of these simple *ideas* go
constantly together; which, being presumed to belong to one thing, and words being
suited to common apprehensions and made use of for quick dispatch, are called, so
united in one subject, by one name; which, by inadvertency, we are apt afterward to
talk of and consider as one simple *idea*, which indeed is a complication of many *ideas*
together: because, as I have said, not imagining how these simple *ideas* can subsist
by themselves, we accustom ourselves to suppose some *substratum* wherein they do
subsist, and from which they do result; which therefore we call *substance* [II, xxiii, 1].

First, what does Locke mean by 'simple ideas conveyed in by the senses'
and 'go constantly together'? Even the normally shrewd Gibson takes them
to be 'elements of immediate experience' united in certain combinations, so
that 'the problem of substance centres . . . round their reference to something
which is not itself a simple idea or content of experience'.[14] On this view
'inherence' becomes the relation between patterns of *sensations* and their
external causes or objects (or between ideas of reflection and their objects).[15]
Bennett has more recently endorsed something like this interpretation of §1,
but makes the point that elsewhere Locke is clearly concerned with the
relation, not between sensations and physical objects, but between things
and their properties. The solution that he proposes is that Locke has conflated
two different philosophical problems: i.e. Locke is crudely confused.[16] Yet
there is no such confusion, for Gibson is wrong. In the earlier chapter on
power, Locke tells us, after due apology, that although the idea of power
is relative, he will treat it as a 'simple idea': it 'may well have a place amongst
other simple *ideas* and be considered as one of them, being one of those that

[14] Op. cit., p. 92.

[15] Berkeley, who denies the distinction between ideas and sensible qualities, is able to offer
some such polemical characterization of Locke's conception of material substance. He can then
ask how a sensation could 'inhere' in anything but a mind (see my 'Substance, Reality and the
Great, Dead Philosophers', *American Philosophical Quarterly*, 1970). But even one who accepts
Berkeley's unlikely premiss should be sensitive to the difference between polemical caricature
and serious interpretation of intent.

[16] Op. cit., pp. 78 ff. Bennett uses another argument for diagnosing gross confusion. Having
mislocated Locke's concern with the substance/property distinction in the 'purely logical' question,
'What is it for a quality to be instantiated by a particular?', he stigmatizes the phrases 'which
go constantly together' and 'from which they do result', for obvious reasons, as 'puzzling'. The
puzzles are then supposed to disappear when we recall that 'ideas can also be sensory states':
for the *patterns* among our sensations comprise our ground for thinking that there are physical
objects, and physical objects are taken by the realist to *cause* these sensations. Fortunately this
ridiculous mish-mash need not be attributed to Locke, who is simply saying that we acquire the
idea of substance when we are forced to refer co-existing powers and sensible qualities to a
common ground or explanation, 'the unknown cause of their union'. Experienced constant
concomitance of properties has the same sort of role in the acquisition of the idea of substance as
regularity has in the case of the ideas of power and cause and effect.

make a principal ingredient in our complex *ideas* of substances' (II, xxi, 3).
The real point is that ideas of specific powers can conveniently be regarded as
'simple ideas' by contrast with the complexity of ideas of substances. It is a
point, moreover, that is dealt with at considerable length in Chapter 23 itself:
sections vii–x supply a context that makes the reading of 'simple ideas' as
'elements of immediate experience' wholly gratuitous. In any case, Locke's
use of 'idea' for quality in the object as well as for immediate object of experience is well known.[17] His saying that some 'ideas' are 'conveyed in by the
senses as they are found in exterior things' means, alas, no more than that we
have knowledge and acquire concepts of such properties from observation of
the physical world.

Again, we may ask, who is being accused of 'inadvertency'? The ordinary
man? Does the word perhaps refer forward to 'accustom' with its overtones
of mindlessness? As Gibson correctly points out, other passages make it
quite clear that Locke believes that the idea of substance is one that we arrive
at rationally, and cannot in reason avoid. The word 'accustom' seems to
refer, not to the process by which we acquire and first apply the idea, but to
the condition we are in once we use it habitually. The 'inadvertency' which is
consequent upon this condition and upon our language habits, consists in
the failure of some people to recognize that our ideas of substances are complex. Here the allusion is to the doctrine that substances are simple unities
(which in a certain sense Locke would not deny)[18] and to *philosophers* who
mistakenly, if naturally, think that we have correspondingly simple, adequate
concepts of them. A classic text is Aristotle's *Metaphysics* VII, where the
substance-term 'man' is distinguished from compound terms such as 'athlete',
Aristotle's own example being the word 'himation' stipulatively defined as
'white man', a complex of substrate and accident. Locke's claim is that the
definition of all *our* substance-terms can be similarly broken down, the substrate being the unknown 'thing' which bears the accidents.

It is, I think, often supposed that Locke's 'one subject' is an individual and
the 'one name' a proper name; and that the observation of a number of
qualities 'going constantly together' which is said to give rise to our idea of
substance is the repeated observation of an individual, e.g. of the cat Peter.
Locke has in mind specific names, however, and the repeated observation of
types, i.e. cats, gold and so on. The observed qualities go together in individual
instances of course, but 'constantly' covers all occasions on which they

[17] See the much-quoted II, viii, 8, and, e.g., II, xxvi, 1, quoted above, in which the power of
fluidity is described as a 'simple idea' in wax of which 'the simple idea of heat' is the cause.
[18] See II, ii, 1: '. . . the qualities that affect our senses are, in the things themselves, so united
and blended that there is no separation, no distance between them . . .' Substances may be compounds of simpler substances, as a clock of its parts, but are not compounds of properties as
ideas of substances are compounds of ideas of properties.

co-exist, whether in my cat, in the neighbour's cat or in the College cat. Luckily Locke's repetitiveness comes to the exegete's rescue, and the point is reiterated in II, xxiii, 14: 'These *ideas* of substances, though they are commonly called simple apprehensions, and the names of them simple terms, yet in effect are complex and compounded.' The example is 'the *idea* which an *Englishman* signifies by the name *swan*', and reference is made to 'a man who has long observed this kind of birds'. Swans are of course individuals, but the name 'swan' and the idea of a *swan* are as indubitably general. The general idea of substance, or the 'one common subject', is not explicable as the logical concept of an individual, in this or in any other passage.

It may be helpful towards identifying certain other apparent difficulties for the present interpretation if I summarize as much of it as has been advanced so far. Locke interprets the substance/accident distinction in terms of the distinction upon which his whole philosophy of natural science is based: the distinction between the underlying realities and the phenomena conceived of objectively in terms of phenomenal or observable *properties*—which are relative to our sensibility but are not sensations or 'sense-data'. These observable properties include powers to act observably upon other things. They are not (as Aristotelians suppose) 'real beings',[19] i.e. absolute or ultimate properties of the substance in which they can be said to 'subsist' or 'inhere' as 'accidents', or by which they are 'supported'. Indeed talk of such a *support* or *thing having* phenomenal properties can only be interpreted intelligibly as alluding to this unknown intrinsic nature which is causally responsible for the relational,[20] phenomenal properties, i.e. for the effect of the substance upon us and on other things:

---

[19] If I may be excused a rather sloppy allusion to II, xiii, 19, which itself is an echo of Boyle's intricate attack on 'one thing the Modern Schools are wont to teach concerning Accidents . . . namely that there are in Natural Bodies store of *real Qualities*, and other *real Accidents*, which are not onely no Moods of Matter, but are real Entities distinct from it, and . . . may *exist separate* from all Matter whatsoever' (op. cit., p. 7). Boyle's point, very roughly, is that it is impossible to conceive of physical properties that are not either 'determined quantities' of Matter or else powers (including secondary qualities) which 'are not in the Bodies that are Endow'd with them any Real or Distinct Entities, or differing from the Matter its self, furnish'd with such a Determinate Bignesse, Shape, or other Mechanical Modifications' (op. cit., p. 13). Hence we can and need postulate no other physical substance than matter itself. Locke's approach in II, xiii, 19 is scientifically more agnostic and philosophically less clear, but he is evidently attacking any pretension that talk of accidents (i.e. powers and sensible qualities) inhering in a substance can offer an *ultimate* account of reality.

[20] For a strong statement that powers are relational, see II, xxiii, 37: '. . . most of the simple *ideas* that make up our complex *ideas* of substances, when truly considered, are only powers, however we are apt to take them for positive qualities . . . all which *ideas* are nothing else but so many relations to other substances, and are not really in the gold, considered barely in itself, though they depend on those real and primary qualities of its internal constitution, whereby it has a fitness differently to operate and be operated on by several other substances.' Cf. II, xxi, 3 *et al.*

when we speak of any sort of substance, we say it is a *thing* having such or such qualities: as body is a *thing* that is extended, figured, and capable of motion; a spirit, a *thing* capable of thinking; and so hardness, friability, and power to draw iron, we say, are qualities to be found in a loadstone. These and the like fashions of speaking intimate that the substance is supposed always *something* besides the extension, figure, solidity, motion, thinking or other observable *ideas*, though we know not what it is [II, xxiii, 3].

Thus we do, it seems, know that we do not know, and that implies that we have some notion of what it would be like to know the intrinsic nature of some substance. I have, I hope, already said enough to indicate that, for Locke, we could suppose that we knew the intrinsic nature of something only if its behaviour, including its effects upon our sensibility, was wholly 'intelligible'. It is to the unintelligibility of the concomitance of the observable properties of a 'horse or stone' to which Locke alludes, when he says that 'because we cannot conceive how they should subsist alone, *nor one in another*, we suppose them existing in and supported by some common subject' (II, xxiii, 4, my emphasis).

The difficulties mentioned earlier are chiefly two. First, the *primary* qualities of physical objects are not merely powers, but are said by Locke to be actually 'in the object'. Why then should he postulate an unknown nature lying behind them? The point is thrown into some relief by the two stages in one of Locke's arguments:

If anyone should be asked what is the subject wherein colour or weight inheres, he would have nothing to say but, the solid extended parts; and if he were demanded what is it that that solidity and extension adhere in, he would not be in a much better case than the *Indian* before mentioned . . . [II, xxiii, 2].

It might seem hard not to conclude that 'substance' is supposed to be an unknown something lying behind *all* properties, however actual or intrinsic.

The answer to this difficulty has already been suggested by Yolton, when he points out that the 'solidity and extension' here are *observable* solidity and extension.[21] On this interpretation the 'solid extended parts' are the parts we can perceive, not the 'minute parts'. For the discussion explicitly concerns the unknown support of that which is known by observation, i.e. of 'such qualities which are capable of producing simple *ideas* in us; which qualities are commonly called accidents'. Locke would seem to have two points here. The first is that it will not help to say that colour and weight inhere in the solid, extended parts, because that is non-explanatory: there is nothing in the *perceptible* solidity and extension which could explain why the thing also has

---

[21] Op. cit., p. 45. II, xxiii, 3 is even more explicit: '. . . the extension, figure, solidity, motion, thinking or other observable *ideas* . . .'. The passage is significantly misquoted by Buchdahl, who, by omitting 'other', promotes a contrast precisely opposed to Locke's intentions (op. cit., p. 217).

a certain colour and weight.[22] The second is that perceptible solidity and extension palpably require explanation in terms of an unperceived structure. Locke may have had in mind, for example, that the degree of sensible hardness or the perceptible shape of an object are evidently relative to the sensibility of the perceiver and are not ultimate;[23] or that the cohesion of the parts, which keeps the thing sensibly solid and extended, itself requires explanation;[24] or, more specifically, that we must suppose some internal principle that explains the particular enduring observable shape of, e.g., a man or a horse; or he may even have in mind that *all* sensible qualities can initially be regarded as mere powers to affect our senses 'immediately', and as needing speculative explanation in terms of intrinsic properties.[25] The second suggestion, relating to cohesion, is perhaps the most attractive, since it fits in very well with the later sections of Chapter xxiii and would be appropriate even if we think that Locke had the minute 'solid extended parts' in mind. The last suggestion ties in with sections 7 or 11. In any case there need be no difficulty about the *kind* of thing that Locke is saying, or the kind of reason he might have for denying that the solid, extended parts are 'that unknown common subject which inheres not in anything else', the 'cause of the union' of the observable properties by which we define a substance. Even if enduring shape is not a mere power (since even the perceived shape of a united group of atoms does roughly correspond to its actual shape), yet it is for the purposes of the argument analogous to a power. Just as much as a power it is one of the 'qualities and actions, or powers . . . perceived by the mind to be of themselves inconsistent with existence', having therefore a 'necessary connection with inherence or being supported': i.e. it falls among the properties which call out for explanation in terms of something more ultimate.[26]

4. SUBSTANCE IN GENERAL AND REAL ESSENCE

The second apparent difficulty for my interpretation requires much more discussion. It hinges on the relation between *substance* and *real essence*. The

[22] The point of II, xxiii, 4: '. . . we cannot conceive how they should subsist . . . one in another . . .'.

[23] See II, iv, 4 on the relativity of *hardness* ('a firm cohesion of the parts of matter making up masses of a sensible bulk') as opposed to *solidity*, which consists in absolute 'repletion' and admits of no degrees. In that case, *sensible* 'solidity' is presumably *hardness*, and there is a problem, of which Locke seems unaware, as to how we get an idea of *solidity* from sense-experience.

[24] Cf. II, xxiii, 23. 'If anyone says he knows not what it is thinks in him, he means he knows not what the substance is of that thinking thing; no more, say I, knows he what the substance is of that solid thing. Further, if he says he knows not how he thinks, I answer: neither knows he how he is extended, how the solid parts of body are united or cohere together to make extension.'

[25] Cf. IV, xi, 2 and II, viii, 8. But cf. II, xxiii, 9, which emphasizes that *perceptible* primary qualities are really in things.

[26] The phrases quoted are from the *First Letter*.

observable qualities of any 'particular sort of substance' are said to flow from the 'unknown essence of that substance'. If this is the same relationship as 'inherence in' substance, then it seems that the essence from which observable properties 'flow' and the substance 'from which they do result' must be the same thing. But Locke says much that points to a distinction between them.

First, the idea of substance that enters into our ideas of the sorts of substances is described by Locke as the 'notion of pure substance in general' and as 'an obscure and relative idea of substance in general'. He also talks of 'the secret and abstract nature of substance in general' and says that 'the general idea of substance is everywhere the same'.

It is clear, on the other hand, that 'real essences' are specific.[27] The real essence of lead must be presumed different from that of iron, simply because its observable qualities and powers are different. Locke's model for what it would be like to know a real essence is supplied, of course, by the atomic theory, despite his ambivalent attitude towards mechanical explanation. On the other hand, we might wonder what it would be like to know the 'secret and abstract nature' of substance. Is this perhaps an ironical way of saying that substance, as something underlying all properties, is unknowable in principle since it *has* no 'nature'? Or did Locke surprisingly fail to see that if something underlies *all* properties it cannot have a nature?[28]

The answer is, first, that the general *idea* of substance is 'everywhere the same', not because Locke thinks that there is a mysterious undifferentiated substrate, the same in everything, but because the *idea* is equally lacking in positive content whenever it occurs: the idea of 'something' is everywhere the same.[29] Secondly, and more importantly, when Locke writes, 'Whatever therefore be the secret and abstract nature of *substance* in general, all the ideas *we have of particular distinct sorts of substances* . . . (etc.)' (II, xxiii, 6), he is turning from a discussion of the general or determinable substances, spirit and body. These undoubtedly possess, in the dualist system of thought that Locke a little hesitantly shares with Descartes, an 'abstract', i.e. determinable,

---

[27] We need not here go into Locke's view that species are creatures of the understanding. (He holds that specific 'real essences' are relative to 'nominal essences', since there is no ontological distinction between specific and non-specific differences.) But we do need to be clear that, although Locke normally, perhaps exclusively, uses the term 'real essence' for *specific* natures, he also uses the term 'essence' in the way of Descartes for the general nature of matter or spirit (cf. II, i, 10: '. . . the perception of *ideas* being . . . to the soul what motion is to the body: not its essence, but one of its operations'). In *this* usage, knowledge of essence and knowledge of substance are one and the same.

[28] Cf. Pringle-Pattison on II, xxiii, 15.

[29] The point of the difficulty raised in II, xiii, 18. God, finite spirit and body are all in the same sense 'substances', not because they agree 'in the same common nature of *substance*' ('a very harsh doctrine'), but because we are equally ignorant of the natures of all, and the same word merely signals that ignorance.

nature. His point is that we identify and distinguish spirit and body, not by the essential nature of each, which we do not know, but by their phenomenal properties and operations: in the case of body by 'those many sensible qualities which affect our senses', and by 'thinking, knowing, doubting, and a power of moving, etc.' in the case of spirit. Hence

we have as clear a notion of the [nature, or] substance of spirit as we have of body: the one being supposed to be (without knowing what it is) the *substratum* to those simple *ideas* we have from without; and the other supposed (with a like ignorance of what it is) to be the *substratum* to those operations which we experiment in ourselves within [II, xxiii, 5: the words '*nature, or*' occur only in the First Edition].

Now questions about the abstract or determinable nature of substance in general (including the question whether there are two 'finite' general substances, spirit and body, each with its nature) are not the same as questions about the specific nature of the 'particular' substances, *man, horse, sun, water, iron*; but they are closely related. Both water and iron are matter, but they differ in structure. It is this determinate structure which is the 'real essence'. Indeed, Locke's word 'constitution', which is used everywhere in the *Essay* in explanation of the term 'real essence', is simply and obviously a synonym for 'structure'. Thus his usage of the term 'substance' for an unknown determinable *something* is (allowing for his fluctuating agnosticism) congruent with that of Descartes, or with that of Boyle when he says of the physical world that there is one substance, 'universal matter'. This substance is quantitatively 'constituted' in many ways, and so behaves and is perceived in many ways; hence the qualitative variety, at the level of observation, of the 'particular sorts of substances', in another usage of the word 'substance' which is more or less coextensive with the usage of the Aristotelians although vastly different in philosophical connotation.

Pringle-Pattison and others, however, have been greatly influenced by two passages that I have not yet mentioned, but which, as it should now be possible to see, they have seriously misconstrued. From the *First Letter to the Bishop of Worcester* Pringle-Pattison quotes:

I do not take [real essences] to flow from the substance in any created being, but to be in everything that internal constitution or frame or modification[30] of the substance, which God in his wisdom and good pleasure thinks fit to give to every particular creature, when he gives a being. . . [And such essences] may be changed all as easily, by that hand that made them, as the internal frame of a watch.

[30] The term 'modification' (i.e. 'mode' or 'mood') is here used in an accepted sense of determinate of a determinable attribute. Cf. Boyle, op. cit., p. 7: '. . . these Accidents [*determinate* sizes and shapes] may . . . conveniently enough be call'd the Moods or primary affections of Bodies, to distinguish them from those lesse simple Qualities (as Colours, Tastes, and Odours), that belong to Bodies upon their account'. The contrast between a difference in *substance* and a mere difference in *modification* (i.e. constitution, real essence) is very clearly drawn by Locke in II, xiii, 18.

Pringle-Pattison claims that the passage throws an instructive light on Locke's conception of 'naked substances' to which any kind of qualities may be arbitrarily 'annexed'.[31] Buchdahl appeals to the 'explicit' ontological distinction here between substance and real essence. Yet the passage, once approached from the right direction, is unambiguously concerned with the merely logical distinction between the general, 'abstract' substance, such as matter, and the various determinations of that substance in concrete things. There can be no suggestion in what Locke says that God could create a 'naked substance' and then 'annex' a 'constitution' or 'modification' to that substance any more than he could create something that possessed only *determinable* shape, and afterwards give it a *determinate* shape. The real essence does not 'flow' from the substance, on the corpuscularian hypothesis, because the laws of mechanics which comprise the general nature of matter do not determine that there should be atoms of any particular shape in any particular relationship. The point that real essences are mutable is simply the anti-Aristotelian assertion that species are not immutable relatively to the general laws of nature. The everyday example of changing the construction of a watch is not a merely human, physical analogy for some divine, transcendental annexing of new qualities to a metaphysical substrate, but literally an *example* of what is under discussion. Locke as a mechanist sees no difference in principle between changing the specific character of an animal and changing the specific character of a machine by modifying its structure. Boyle, in fact, makes a somewhat similar move, speculatively attributing the original creation of species to God's direct modification of matter:

the first and Universal, though not immediate cause of Forms is none other but God, who put Matter into motion (which belongs not to its Essence) . . . and also, according to my Opinion, guided it in divers cases at the beginning of Things [op. cit., p. 101].

Another passage, this time in the *Essay*, runs as follows (Locke is emphasizing the inadequacy of our ideas of substances):

And, after all, if we could have and actually had in our complex *idea* an exact collection of all the secondary qualities or powers of any substance, we should not yet thereby have an *idea* of the essence of that thing. For, since the powers or qualities that are observable by us are not the real essence of that substance but depend on it and flow from it, any collection whatsoever of these qualities cannot be the real essence of that thing. Whereby it is plain that our *ideas* of substances are not *adequate*. . . Besides, a man has no *idea* of substance in general, nor knows what substance is in itself [II, xxxi, 13].

It is this passage that stimulates Pringle-Pattison's comment, quoted with approval by both Buchdahl and Woolhouse, that Locke 'teaches a twofold ignorance—in the first place, of the essence . . . and in the second place, of the substance itself'. But the last sentence of the passage has been misconstrued.

[31] Op. cit., note on III, iii, 15.

The word 'besides' is appropriate, not because knowledge of substance would be *additional* to knowledge of real essence, but because the former is, in a sense, a *lesser* knowledge, comprised within the latter, as knowledge that something is a plane figure is comprised within knowledge that it is a triangle.[32] The whole sentence therefore means, 'What is more, human beings do not even know the *general* nature of substance, as it is in itself'. What underlies 'the powers or qualities that are observable by us' in anything is *a substance constituted* (or modified or determined) *in certain ways*. There are not two underlying levels, *first* the real essence, *then*, beneath it, the substance.

This reading seems put beyond doubt by a passage in the *First Letter*. Locke is arguing that we cannot have 'as clear and distinct an idea of the general substance, or nature, or essence of the species man, as we have of the particular colour and figure of a man when we look on him'. He continues:

Because the idea we have of the substance, wherein the properties of a man do inhere, is a very obscure idea: so in that part, our general idea of man is obscure and confused: as also, how that substance is differently modified in the different species of creatures, so as to have different properties and powers whereby they are distinguished, that also we have very obscure, or rather no distinct ideas of at all.

In this passage the 'twofold ignorance' is described in a more logical order than in the other, an order which makes it clearer that the distinction between two levels of knowledge—first, of the underlying general substance or determinable nature and, secondly, of its modifications or determinations—implies no distinction between entities or *ontological* levels, since it is founded on a merely logical distinction.

Now let us return to a more central and famous passage, which supplies one of Buchdahl's main arguments. This is the latter half of II, xxiii, 3, quoted above, in which Locke claims that our 'fashions of speaking intimate that the substance is supposed always *something* besides the extension, figure, solidity, motion, thinking or other observable *ideas*'. Locke is arguing that the observable properties by which we define a substance do not constitute the nature or essence of the substance, and that the *linguistic form of our definitions* betrays at least a dim awareness of this. There is no suggestion that he is talking about anything but our verbal definitions of kinds of substances, and their relation to our complex ideas of those substances. He betrays absolutely no interest, for example, in the linguistic or logical subject–predicate relationship in its other manifestations, and makes no general claim about it. His point is only that there is something in the verbal definition which corresponds to that general idea of substance (with, in the

---

[32] It could be said that *explicit* knowledge that something is a plane figure might come after knowledge that it is a triangle. But Locke does not seem to have had such a point in mind, and in any case the general point is unaffected.

case of specific substances, a 'real constitution or essence') that is, as he has told us, an ingredient of our complex idea of any substance.

That there is something wrong with Locke's appeal to language hardly needs to be said, and appears from the point (alluded to by Leibniz) that even if we knew the imperceptible essence of body, we should hardly alter the form of the definition: we would still define *body* as a substance having such and such properties. Buchdahl, like others, seizes upon this point, concluding that Locke is committed to a view of substance as intrinsically unknowable and underlying *all* properties. He remarks that 'It is a "logical" fact that where there is such a body, with such and such a constitution . . . the fact of such a body's existence may be construed in terms of the [sub-stance-]attribute logic'.[33] But Locke cared little for such 'logical facts'. It is true that he could not consistently maintain his suggestion that the form of the definition intimates ignorance without holding the implausible view that knowledge of essences would automatically bring a change in language such as *Buchdahl* would, doubtless rightly, regard as a change in 'logic'. But it seems that this is precisely the view that Locke did hold: not only from its being such an obvious consequence of what he says here, but also from less well-known passages in which a very similar (if not, indeed, the very same) appeal to language is made:

That *body* and *extension*, in common use, stand for two distinct *ideas* is plain to anyone that will but reflect a little. For were their signification precisely the same, it would be proper, and as intelligible, to say the *body of an extension*, as *the extension of a body* [III, x, 6].

Locke's point, of course, is that *extension* is not the essence of *body*, and the linguistic or logical difference is taken to reflect a difference in idea.[34] Thus if the discovery were made that the essence of S (hitherto defined by observ-able properties, O) is E, the terms S and E would become the same in meaning and interchangeable *because there would not be two distinct ideas*. The gram-matical difference corresponding to the inclusion in the idea of S of the general idea of *something* underlying O would simply not survive. Locke

[33] Op. cit., p. 223.

[34] In III, vi, 21 the same point is brought against both the Cartesian doctrine that extension is the essential attribute of body and the Aristotelian doctrine that (e.g.) rationality constitutes the real essence of man. Locke appeals to the principle that 'we can never mistake in putting the essence of anything for the thing itself': to do this with Cartesian or Aristotelian essences produces nonsense (e.g. 'no one will say that rationality is capable of conversation'). The ordinary *nominal* essences, however, do not suffer from the same defect (e.g. 'to say an extended solid thing moves or impels another is all one, and as intelligible, as to say *body* moves or impels') but this is precisely because the *nominal* essence, or our idea of it, includes, 'besides the several distinct simple *ideas* that make them up, the confused one of substance or of an unknown support and cause of their union'. The whole argument obviously requires that the inclusion of the idea of substance or or thing is the distinguishing mark of a nominal, as opposed to real, essence: i.e. it would drop out if our idea corresponded to the real essence.

evidently did not regard the substance–attribute relationship as profoundly 'logical'. That, perhaps, betrays the incapacity of the 'way of ideas' to deal adequately with a category difference, and with the fact that *substance* is a peculiar logical category; but it is safe to assume that Locke had no particular respect for the doctrine of categories and its logical distinctions, which he regarded as obscure and worthless, since of no use to science.[35] It was precisely such 'rubbish' that the 'way of ideas' was intended to sweep aside. Locke's positive purpose in philosophy was to introduce a conceptual scheme fit for the new science and his own agnostic rationalism: in this scheme the idea of 'substance', like the idea of 'power', is given a role at the level of observation, in experimental science or 'natural history'; but virtually denied one in the theoretical science that would be ours if reality were fully known and intelligible to us. Yet not all is new, for one suggestive aspect, at least, of the Aristotelian scheme is prominently retained, if appropriately and radically re-interpreted in the light of corpuscularian theory: that is, the close link between the notion of a specific substance and the notion of an enduring nature or essence in terms of which its behaviour and life-history can be explained.

5. THE NATURE OF LOCKE'S PHILOSOPHY

Now to turn to some wider, rather less manageable issues. Those who find in Locke an undifferentiated substrate, unknowable in principle, fall into two groups. One of these explains the doctrine as the initiation of an historical process, constituting an incoherent, transitional stage in the critique of 'traditional' metaphysics and in the construction of the Empiricist alternative; while the other sees it as a timelessly intelligible, if wrong-headed, reaction to some eternal logical problem. In my own view, both stories are exceedingly improbable, but I want to consider them here, partly because they raise further points of interpretation of the text, but also because they demonstrate how far preconceptions as to how philosophy comes to be written determine acceptance of this or that interpretative hypothesis.

The first approach is instantiated in the commentaries of Gibson, Pringle-Pattison and, most recently, of Buchdahl. Gibson represents Locke's treatment of substance as the stumbling of one still shackled to an unquestioned 'inheritance from Scholasticism'. To put it crudely, the doctrine that substance exists as an unknowable is ascribed to Locke as if it were well on the road to the view that 'substance' does not exist at all because the conception is incoherent or empty. Locke is allegedly half-aware that his halfway house is uninhabitable, which is why he finds it necessary to indulge in that uneasy mockery of 'the very great clearness there is in the doctrine of *substance* and *accidents*'.

[35] Cf. III, x, 14 and the attack in the *Port-Royal Logic* I, iii.

It is a doubtful convenience of such an interpretation that—since Locke is taken to be very much confused—it can accommodate almost any textual evidence whatsoever, even passages that would otherwise naturally be taken as unambiguous counter-evidence to the main contention that Locke's 'substance' is intrinsically unknowable. Thus Gibson notes that

the emptiness which (Locke) finds in *our* idea of substance is in the end to him only an indication that 'the ideas we can attain to by our faculties are very disproportionate to things themselves' (IV, iii, 23). But superior intelligences may be supposed to possess a primitive, clear, distinct idea of substance although this is 'concealed from us' [op. cit., pp. 192–3].

Presumably because of his readiness to see inconsistency in Locke, Gibson shows no surprise that the passage quoted implies a much closer ontological and epistemological relationship than he is in general prepared to allow between Locke's substance and real essences. It is thus by a stroke of poetic justice that Woolhouse reads Gibson's discussion here as evidence of confusion in Gibson's own thinking between the two conceptions. For Woolhouse comments that

It is adequately clear, . . . and not only from the passage which Gibson quotes, that what superior intelligences may be supposed to possess is not an idea of Substance but some idea of 'the nature and inmost constitution of things', i.e. of real essences [op. cit., p. 129].

Now this is careless, for the immediate context of Gibson's quotation includes

What faculties . . . other species of creatures have to penetrate into the nature and inmost constitutions of things, what *ideas* they may receive of them, far different from ours, we know not. . . And we may be convinced that the *ideas* we can attain to by our faculties are very disproportionate to things themselves, when a positive clear distinct one of substance itself, which is the foundation of all the rest, is concealed from us [IV, iii, 23].

Gibson is therefore right (or at least not clearly wrong) to argue that Locke conceives of the same remedy for ignorance of substance as for ignorance of real essence: i.e. better cognitive faculties (which for Locke can only be Sense and Reason, working together). It is gratuitous, however, to discount such close association of the two, as if it were the clear manifestation of nothing intellectually more respectable than an uneasiness about traditional doctrines combined with a diametrically opposed, blindly 'inherited' prejudice in their favour.

I do not believe that the thought of one man is ever to be explained in this fashion, by the postulation of diverse, historically conceived motives without any plausible account given of its aspect of coherence, reasonableness and truth to the man himself.[36] Moreover, Locke's *Essay* was not only

---

[36] I make no apology for echoing a theme of John Dunn's *The Political Thought of John Locke*, an outstanding book which should be read by every serious student of the history of philosophy for its historiographical good sense.

found intelligible, but was widely applauded as a classic expression of a philosophy of nature and our knowledge of it which had a great and beneficial influence at a particularly important time in human intellectual history. In case this seems no more than a feebly deferential appeal to Locke's 'greatness', it should be made clear that the problem for Gibson's view is not merely to account for Locke's high reputation or self-satisfaction, but to explain how half-doubts about the current rationalist concepts of substance —whether Aristotelian or Cartesian—could naturally or even conceivably find expression in an ontological and epistemological distinction between substance and essence, or in what is taken to be an emphatic, if ironical, commentary on the difficulties that attend such a distinction. Locke could hardly have supposed that the division had been explicitly postulated, since for both Aristotelian and Cartesian philosophy knowledge of the essence *constitutes* knowledge of the substance.

The criticism that Gibson himself advances against a generalized 'traditional' view is that substances were wrongly thought of as independent entities, with an 'absolute' or 'intrinsic' nature existing, and in principle capable of being comprehended, out of relation to other things.[37] Yet this is an objection to the notion of intrinsic properties, a notion which admittedly very much enters into Locke's belief that a thing's powers can always be explained in terms of its actual or intrinsic structure, and thus into his conception of real essences. This fundamental issue is beside our point. For it is difficult to see how an implicit uneasiness, however well-founded, about the notion of intrinsic properties could ever have led Locke to feel that there is some unknowable non-property underlying all properties, including intrinsic properties. If such a movement of 'thought' were known to have taken place, it would be entirely mystifying: hence it explains nothing to postulate one.

In the commentaries of Pringle-Pattison and Buchdahl[38] we find further attempts to make historical sense of Locke's alleged belief in 'naked substance'. The former sees it as leading up to a suggestion that God could,

---

[37] See, e.g., op. cit., p. 196; cf. Pringle-Pattison, op. cit., pp. 175 and 295. Both writers refer to IV, vi, 11, approvingly but as evidence of further Lockean inconsistency. Yet they misinterpret this passage too, reading it as criticism of the notion of intrinsic properties. But Locke is saying that the *observable* properties by which we distinguish substances are in general dependent upon surrounding circumstances: '. . . things, however absolute and entire they seem in themselves, are but retainers to other parts of nature *for that which they are most taken notice of by us*. Their *observable* qualities, actions, and powers are owing to something without them' (my emphasis). The anti-Aristotelian point is clearly in line with Locke's normal conception of an unknown intrinsic nature underlying observable interactions (cf. II, xxiii, 37, quoted in footnote 20 above); but the misinterpretation is typical of those upon which Locke's reputation for inconsistency chiefly rests.

[38] I cannot here discuss Buchdahl's long argument. He yokes his interpretation of Locke's alleged 'fascinating muddles' to a vision of the interplay of 'metaphysics' with the philosophy of science which is undeniably impressive but (in my view) not the way it was.

if he wished, arbitrarily annex any property or combination of properties whatsoever to any substance. Commenting on Locke's famous speculation on the possibility of thinking matter (IV, iii, 6), he asserts that Locke 'departs altogether from the Cartesian equation (as we may say) of a substance with its fundamental attribute':

> For Locke . . . substance is something purely indeterminate, and therefore finite substances have no intrinsic nature which they express in action. Any attributes or powers may be annexed to, or conferred upon any substance, according to 'the good pleasure' of their Maker. . . . There can be no 'repugnancy' . . . in the idea of the same substance acting as a support both of bodily and of mental phenomena. Locke's tendency, in reaction against dogmatic rationalism, to fall back on 'the arbitrary will and good pleasure of the Wise Architect' . . . contains in itself the germ of a scepticism which soon showed itself in the historical development.

Now a full discussion of 'thinking matter' must lie beyond the scope of this article, but if Pringle-Pattison's speculative interpretation could be upheld, we should be dealing with no ordinary inconsistency and might reasonably wonder whether the *Essay* was by a single hand. For if he let in the possibility that powers or phenomenal properties should belong to things as a matter of brute or miraculous fact not naturally intelligible, Locke's whole carefully constructed philosophy of science and his support for the corpuscularian case against the Aristotelians would collapse. In effect, he would be allowing the despised doctrine of 'real accidents', and foregoing all right to criticize the view that an analysis of the nature or essence of things could end with powers, as the Aristoleian analysis of the essence of man ends with rationality.

Fortunately there is nothing in Locke's discussion to suggest even an implicit appeal to a conception of 'naked substance'. Moreover, in IV, iii, 6 Locke is merely emphasizing our ignorance of the nature of matter and spirit. The burden of the passage is not (as even Leibniz *seems* to have supposed) that thought is naturally a property of immaterial substance but could by an arbitrary miracle be annexed to material substance. It is that, of the two hypotheses tenable by us, each equally involves something 'dark and intricate'. Dualism raises difficulties as great as materialism, with respect not only to the interaction of spirit and matter, but also to such a question as how spirits can have position, like all individual things, and yet lack extension. (The latter difficulty could hardly be resolved by a miracle.) And so far from concluding from the dilemma that there must be 'brute facts' of one sort or another, Locke merely inveighs against our tendency uncritically to accept one theory because of difficulties in the other, adding that he

> would fain know what substance exists that has not something in it which manifestly baffles our understandings. Other spirits, who see and know the nature and inward

constitution of things, how much must they exceed us in knowledge? To which if we add larger comprehension . . . we may guess at some part of the happiness of superior ranks of spirits.

All is intelligible, but not to us. Pringle-Pattison, like others before him, has mistaken an epistemological point for an ontological one. When Locke says of a causal power unintelligible to us that 'we are fain to quit our reason, go beyond our *ideas*, and attribute it wholly to the good pleasure of our Maker', he means, not that we have to postulate a miracle, 'arbitrary' in the modern sense and so unintelligible in principle to any intellect, but that we can say no more about it than what is true of every power whatsoever: its exercise is thanks to God. Since thought is an intermittent and accidental property, it is taken as a presupposition of the discussion that the power of thinking 'cannot be in *any* created being but merely by the good pleasure and bounty of the Creator'.[39]

When Locke says that matter 'is evidently in its own nature void of sense and thought', he means by this that thought is not an essential or original property of matter. Of this the existence of *some* unthinking matter is sufficient proof. We should remember that for Locke as for Boyle motion itself is a property of matter that 'belongs not to its essence':[40] hence (they believed) God not only created matter, but also put it in motion. To 'super-add' to matter the power of thought would naturally be a more complicated business: hence Locke envisages the possibility that God 'annexes' the power not to *any* body, but to 'some systems of matter, fitly disposed', or to bodies 'after a certain manner modified and moved'. His view is, then, that (1) we do not know enough to choose between a materialist and an immaterialist explanation of thought, (2) *we* can therefore conceive of material substance thinking, as readily as of immaterial substance thinking, and (3) if we conceive of the former, we must suppose that thought is the compound effect or operation of a complex material mechanism. Thus the warning to the dogmatic dualist is that an omnipotent God may be a cleverer maker of physical clocks, so to speak, than we are capable of comprehending: which hardly constitutes a retreat from mechanistic rationalism. All this deserves much fuller discussion, as does its relation to Locke's shaky argument for God's existence. But we can already be sure that Pringle-Pattison's speculation is entirely groundless.

The second group among recent commentators adopt an approach that is

---

[39] It needs stressing that for Locke no causal connections are *ontologically* brute facts (c.f., e.g., G. J. Warnock, 'Hume on Causality', in D. Pears, *David Hume: A Symposium*). Locke is not so crudely transitional between Descartes and Hume.

[40] Cf. II, i, 10: '. . . what motion is to the body: not its essence, but one of its operations'; and Locke's Journal entry for 20 Feb. 1682 (f.31): spirit and matter 'may both lye dead and unactive, i.e. the one without thought, the other without motion . . . which wholly depends upon the will and good pleasure of the first author'.

virtually a product of currently orthodox conceptions of philosophy. It has always been tempting to assume that the possible philosophical motives, insights and mistakes, like philosophical truth, are the same in every age; but the present emphasis on language and logic seems to supply a peculiar justification for dealing with the texts solely within the context of our own independent appreciation of the eternal problems calling for solution through analysis. And it is easy to see why Locke's unfortunate, explicit appeal to language should have come to be treated as the core of his doctrine of substance, as if it were intelligible independently of its position within the exposition of a complex and important philosophy of science.

Thus O'Connor finds it natural (or found it so in 1952) to attribute the doctrine to 'our ordinary language', which

distinguishes between 'nouns' on the one hand and 'verbs' and 'adjectives' on the other. . . This convenient syntactical device was fossilized in the traditional subject–predicate logic. . . Moreover, because . . . ordinary language is the medium in which most of our thinking is carried on, we come to regard the noun–adjective or noun–verb patterns as pictures of the way in which the world is constructed.[41]

A second muddle supposed to contribute to Locke's position is

an illegitimate extension or generalization of a perfectly genuine type of query. Some questions about uniform conjunctions of characteristics are quite proper and understandable. 'Why are cacti always found in dry conditions?' is an example. . . But 'why are qualities found in stable inter-relations?' is only superficially similar to questions of this type. In this case, we do not even know what sort of answer we should find acceptable. . . . And it is . . . silly to suggest that the unity of qualities in one subject has to be 'explained' in the way that the unity of sticks in a bundle is explained by the string that binds them. To reply that the qualities of a body must be united and supported by a sort of transcendental glue in which they inhere does not solve any problem, because there is no problem to solve.

It should hardly be necessary to point out that a speculative account of Locke's motives is here, in the crudest possible way, determined by a view of philosophy and of the origin of philosophical theories. No Freudian or Marxist could deal with a question of historical interpretation in a more doctrinaire or summary fashion. One aspect of the intellectual background to Locke's thought is indeed mentioned, but only in the vaguest terms, and is itself dismissed as 'fossilized syntax'. Such brutal linguistic positivism represents a temptation that is still with us. For Bennett reconstructs the 'line of thought' entertained by Locke as follows:

What concepts are involved in the subject of the statement that *The pen in my hand is valuable?* Certainly, the concepts of being a pen and of being in my hand; but these are not all, for the statement is about a *thing which* falls under these two concepts. What thing is this? It is the purple thing which I now see; but when I say that the purple thing I now see is a pen and is in my hand, I speak of a *thing which* is purple, etc.,

[41] D. J. O'Connor, *John Locke* (New York, 1967), pp. 81–2.

and so I have still failed to capture the whole concept of the subject in my original statement. . . What will be missing from any list of descriptive concepts is the concept of a 'thing which. . .' . . . This constituent of every subject-concept is the concept of a property-bearer, or of a possible subject of predication—let us call it the concept of a *substance*. So, if any existential or subject–predicate statement is true, then there are two sorts of item—substances, and properties or qualities [op. cit., pp. 59 ff.].

A lack of understanding of what Locke is about could not be more clearly demonstrated than in the various features of the example, 'The pen in my hand is valuable'. For the subject of this proposition (which is not a definition) is a particular or individual object, identified by a definite description, of which is predicated not a natural, but a conventional or 'institutional' property. Yet Locke's point is explicitly and always and necessarily made with reference to the definitions and ideas of *sorts* of substances, and the properties that are mentioned in such definitions are always natural powers and sensible qualities, which he classes together as 'observable ideas'. But perhaps the most curious aspect of Bennett's case is that, with the express purpose of 'showing how "substance in general" relates to "particular sorts of substances"', he quotes a lopped and disembowelled version of the long section II, xxiii, 3 which omits not only Locke's explicit and clear opposition between the 'substance' and *observable* properties (rather than all properties), but even Locke's statement that the defining properties of any sort, being found in combination 'by experience and observation of men's senses', 'are therefore supposed to flow from the particular internal constitution or unknown essence of that substance'.[42] Yet it is precisely this clause which conveys Locke's theory that the differences between physical species consist ultimately (and are commonly and reasonably supposed to consist) in differences in the quantitative determination of some determinable substance from which the defining observable qualities flow. His opponent, identified by the phrase 'whatever substantial forms he may talk of', is the Aristotelian, and the point comes virtually straight from Boyle. Boyle's argument was widely known among educated and interested Englishmen, and the closely parallel passages from the *Origin of Forms and Qualities* (containing, incidentally, the clause 'whatever men talk in Theory of substantial Formes') could hardly have failed to be before Locke's mind when he wrote, if not before his eyes.

Locke's point is admittedly very slightly obscured by his examples. The examples of 'the ideas of a man, horse, gold, water, etc.', 'iron' and 'a diamond',

---

[42] There is *some* room for doubt about the reference of the expression 'that substance' in this sentence. Locke could either mean 'that specific substance' or 'that substance in general of which we have an obscure idea'. Grammar points to the latter (since Locke has spoken of sorts of substances only in the plural) but the expressions 'internal' and 'unknown essence' require the former (which unfortunately on its own seems compatible with incorrect interpretations). Nevertheless, in context the meaning is clear and unaffected by this question.

entirely appropriate to a discussion of Aristotelian species, are followed by those of 'body' and 'a spirit', as well as 'a loadstone'. The explanation is that he has moved on from the point that observable specific differences 'are supposed' due to underlying quantitative differences in the determinate 'constitution' of a substance, to a more general point aimed at Descartes as well as the Aristotelians, that we ordinarily define both specific and general or determinable substances in terms of *observable* properties and powers. These properties will be, correspondingly, either specific, like the power to draw iron, or general, like the power of thought or observable shape (the determinable), but all of which we suppose dependent upon an unknown 'something besides'. Everything is sorted out in the next two sections. For §4 is restricted to 'any particular sort of corporeal substances, as *horse*, *stone*, etc.', while §5 spells out the point that the distinction between body and spirit is different from distinctions between physical species in that, although like them it is made in terms of 'observable ideas', unlike them it is taken by us to rest on an underlying difference in *substance*: i.e. not merely a difference in the particular constitution of a substance.

Woolhouse evinces a much superior appreciation of Locke's relation to contemporary science, yet also sees in the 'idea of substance in general' a confused response to a more or less purely 'logical' question which can be independently identified and solved (with the help of Professor Geach). He does state clearly that Locke is concerned with something narrower than predication in general, and that Locke's interest centres on a categorial concept of *thing* or *substance*. He also sees that Locke sometimes approaches the category from the point of view of philosophy of science, since it is important that substances have explanatory 'natures'. But he identifies these 'natures' with specific real essences, and so feels free to explain the doctrine of 'substance in general' as a theory not directly related to science but concerned with individuation. The problem for Locke is supposed to be: what makes instances of substance-concepts countable and/or re-identifiable? (*This cat* is countable and re-identifiable, while *the lead in this roof* is re-identifiable.) Just how the inclusion in sortal ideas of a general idea of substance was supposed by Locke to explain these logical properties Woolhouse leaves unclear (it was after all a bad theory!). Nor does he mention that the second and later editions of the *Essay* contain a chapter on the individuation of such things as cats and people in which Locke explicitly warns us that the identity and continuity of their *substance* is irrelevant.[43] Indeed, the only textual evidence offered for linking Locke's talk of 'substance' with individuation is

---

[43] By 'the same substance' Locke means, roughly, the same component stuff—whether it is corpuscularian matter or some other general substance. Only on the interpretation adopted here can sense be made of the complicated chapter on identity.

the sentence '.. . . the *ideas* of *substances* are such combinations of simple *ideas* as are taken to represent distinct particular things subsisting by themselves, in which the supposed or confused *idea* of substance, such as it is, is always the first and chief' (II, xii, 6). But, as the immediately following example of *lead* well enough illustrates, 'thing' here means '*sort of thing*' (embracing *stuff*), while the words 'distinct particular' look forward to II, xxiii itself and have the meaning *determinate* or *specific*, not *individual*. The relevant expressions in II, xxiii, 6 are 'particular distinct sorts of substances' and 'particular sorts of substances', but the words 'sorts of' were added in both cases to the Second Edition, a clarification Locke merely omitted to make in the case of II, xii, 6. Woolhouse, however, seems influenced not so much by the text—except in so far as that suggests *some* distinction between substance and real essence—as by his own philosophical belief that the topic of individuation and continuity best reveals the eternally significant logical features of substance terms or sortals, so that Locke's concern with them can be presumed to be at least a concern with individuation. As much as Bennett's, his reading requires that Locke flitted crazily from topic to topic even in mid-sentence.

If all this diagnosis of error seems unhelpfully moralistic or polemical, I must plead my belief that the history of philosophy is a department of history, and that we shall not read the philosophy of the past correctly if we do not bring ourselves to argue seriously and openly about the question of *how* to read it. Unless methodological preconceptions are aired and evaluated it seems unlikely that agreement on substantive interpretations will ever be reached. It is my hope that agreement will now prove possible on Locke's theory of substance.

VII

LOCKE'S THEORY OF PERSONAL IDENTITY: A RE-EXAMINATION

HENRY E. ALLISON

In Chapter xxvii of Book II of *An Essay concerning Human Understanding*, John Locke provided the earliest systematic treatment of the problem of personal identity in the history of modern philosophy. The historical significance of this treatment is best evidenced by David Hume's reflection, less than fifty years later, that personal identity 'has become so great a question in philosophy, especially of late years in England. . . .'[1] Locke's influence, however, was largely negative. He was the first to pose the problem, but his specific solution was generally repudiated.

Locke's early antagonists included such formidable thinkers as Leibniz, Berkeley, Hume, Butler, and Reid, and many of their objections, as well as those of a recent critic, Antony Flew,[2] are fatal to his theory. However, since these criticisms often treat the theory in abstraction from the context in which it was formulated, and which largely determined its nature, their very cogency tends to obscure its significance. Thus, this paper is an attempt to rectify an injustice. Its aim will be to suggest that although Locke's theory is untenable, yet, when viewed in relation to its historical context, it may be seen as an important contribution to the development of the philosophical concept of the self.

This paper is divided into four sections. The first suggests some of the factors which lead Locke to treat the problem. The second is devoted to an analysis of Locke's theory in the light of these factors. The third considers some of the criticisms raised against the theory, and the fourth contains a brief assessment of the theory's historical significance.

From *Journal of the History of Ideas*, 27 (1966), pp. 41–58. Reprinted, with changes, by permission of the author and the editor of the journal.

[1] Hume, *Treatise of Human Nature*, ed. L. A. Selby-Bigge (Oxford, 1951), 259.

[2] I am here referring to Flew's article: 'Locke and the Problem of Personal Identity' in *Philosophy*, 26 (1951), 53–68. [Reprinted in Martin/Armstrong.]

I

Since Locke was a pioneer, it is germane to inquire into the reasons which led him to treat the problem of personal identity. This is especially true in view of the fact that the chapter first appeared in the second edition of the *Essay*. The original stimulus was provided by Locke's friend, William Molyneux, who suggested that a discussion of the *principium individuationis* be included in the new edition.[3] This, however, is not sufficient to explain why Locke decided to concentrate upon this special, and until then neglected, aspect of that traditional problem. To answer this question we must examine the philosophical climate within which the *Essay* was written, and here the answer is not hard to find. It was nothing other than his fundamental opposition to the dominant philosophy of Descartes which posed the problem for Locke. For Descartes, the indivisibility of the self or thinking substance is a self-evident truth,[4] and from this rationalistic standpoint the problem of personal identity never really arose. However, Locke's empirical account of the origin of ideas, and his consequent scepticism in regard to the possibility of metaphysical knowledge, precluded such a view. The human mind, for Locke, is not furnished with any clear and distinct ideas of substance, and hence can have no intuitive knowledge of its nature. For, as Locke asserts, '. . . *our specific* ideas *of substances* are nothing else but *a collection of a certain number of simple* ideas, *considered as united in one thing.*'[5]

This is as true of our ideas of immaterial, as of material substance. The only difference is that the former is a collection of simple ideas of reflection, united with the idea of something in which they inhere, and the latter a collection of simple ideas of sensation, similarly united. From the former we derive our idea of spirit, and from the latter of body, but our idea of one is as indistinct as of the other. Thus Locke writes:

I think, we have as many and as clear *ideas* belonging to spirit as we have belonging to body, the substance of each being equally unknown to us, and the *idea* of thinking in spirit as clear as of extension in body; and the communication of motion by thought which we attribute to spirit is as evident as that by impulse, which we ascribe to body.[6]

Finally, on the basis of his analysis of the idea of thinking substance, Locke goes so far as to deny the possibility of knowledge of the immateriality, and hence of the immortality, of the soul: 'it being, in respect of our notions, not

---

[3] Letter of Molyneux to Locke, 2 Mar. 1693, *The Works of John Locke* (London, 1794), VIII, 310. See also Locke's letter to Molyneux of 23 Aug. 1693, ibid., 322–7, where in acknowledgement of Molyneux's request, he refers to the completed chapter on identity and diversity.

[4] Descartes, VIth Meditation, *Philosophical Works of Descartes*, translated by E. S. Haldane and G. R. T. Ross (New York, 1955), I, 196.

[5] *Essay*, II, xxiii, 14.

[6] II, xxiii, 28.

much more remote from our comprehension to conceive that God can, if he pleases, superadd to matter a faculty of thinking, than that he should superadd to it another substance with a faculty of thinking. . . .'[7] Thus, far from affirming, with Descartes, that the human understanding possesses an intuitive knowledge of the indivisibility of the soul, Locke even denies that we can *know* anything of its nature, and it is precisely this scepticism in regard to the nature of the soul which posed for Locke the problem of personal identity. For if we do not know that our soul is indivisible, how do we know that it persists through time? And if it does not persist, in what sense can we talk about the person remaining the same?

If, however, Locke's critique of Descartes called the problem to his attention, it was the recognition of its ethical significance which forced him to provide a solution. Here he could not rest content with the mere probability that the person remained the same. For it is morality and divinity which are 'those parts of knowledge that men are most concerned to be clear in',[8] and as he was well aware: 'In this *personal identity* is founded all the right and justice of reward and punishment.'[9] Thus it is the combination of his critique of Descartes with the recognition of the ethical importance of the concept of personal identity that provides the background of Locke's theory, a background which has generally been overlooked by its critics. Since Locke's main purpose, both in this chapter and the *Essay* as a whole, is the preservation of the 'great ends of morality and religion',[10] it becomes imperative to separate the concept of personal identity from that of substance. For if personal identity were linked with substantial identity, we would, on Lockean grounds, have no clear means of determining the limits of moral responsibility. This, I believe, is the problem which Locke faced, and it must be kept constantly in mind if a fair appraisal of his theory is to be possible.

II

Locke fits his discussion of personal identity into the framework of a general analysis of the concept of identity. His main point is that identity is an ambiguous term, its precise meaning depending upon that to which it is applied. Thus, the identity of a simple physical body, e.g. a pile of stones, depends upon the identity of its constituent parts. If one stone is removed, it is no longer the same pile. The identity of a living organism, however, does not depend upon the identity of its parts. We commonly consider an oak tree or a horse to remain the same, even though its ultimate material constituents are constantly changing. Here the identity is found to reside in the organization

[7] IV, iii, 6.
[8] *Essay*, 'Epistle to the Reader'.
[9] II, xxvii, 18.
[10] IV, iii, 6.

of the parts, or, in Lockean language, in the fact that they partake of the same life. Furthermore, Locke argues, a similar statement can be made about man. 'This also shows wherein the identity of the same *man* consists: viz. in nothing but a participation of the same continued life, by constantly fleeting particles of matter, in succession vitally united to the same organized body.' [11]

The main issue of this analysis is that the idea of man entails a certain determinate size and shape. Man cannot be adequately defined either in terms of his immortal soul or of his rationality. The first alternative, the location of the essence of man in his soul, renders conceivable the absurd consequence (Locke is here no doubt thinking of the doctrine of transmigration of souls, which was much discussed by the Cambridge Platonists[12]) that 'men living in distant ages, and of different tempers, may have been the same man'.[13] The second alternative is disposed of with the fantastic account of an allegedly rational parrot. Despite its intelligence, Locke argues,[14] such a creature could never be considered a man, because it is lacking the requisite physical appearance.

However, the idea of man, thus separated from the concept of soul or immaterial substance and defined in essentially corporeal terms, is obviously not adequate to account for personality or moral responsibility. Hence, Locke is led to posit a further distinction between the idea of man, and that of person, which he defines as 'a thinking intelligent being that has reason and reflection and can consider itself as itself, the same thinking thing in different times and places . . .', and it can do this 'by that consciousness which is inseparable from thinking and, as it seems to me, essential to it: . . .'[15]

Locke has here adopted the Cartesian conception of consciousness as necessarily entailing self-consciousness. We cannot, for both Locke and Descartes, feel, meditate, or will anything without knowing that we do so. Moreover, since it is by this immediate self-awareness that 'everyone is to himself that which he calls *self* . . .'[16] it follows that this self-consciousness constitutes the essence of personality, and consequently that the identity of the person is to be found in the identity of the consciousness.

For since consciousness always accompanies thinking, and it is that that makes everyone to be what he calls *self*, and thereby distinguishes himself from all other thinking things: in this alone consists *personal identity*, i.e. the sameness of a rational being. And as far as this consciousness can be extended backwards to any past action or thought, so far reaches the identity of that *person*: it is the same *self* now it was then, and it is by the same *self* with this present one that now reflects on it, that that action was done.[17]

---

[11] II, xxvii, 6.
[12] In this regard see the correspondence between Henry More, Francis van Helmont and Lady Conway in *Conway Letters*, ed. Marjorie H. Nicolson (New Haven, 1930).
[13] II, xxvii, 6.   [14] II, xxvii, 8.   [15] II, xxvii, 9.   [16] Ibid.   [17] Ibid.

Thus, Locke succeeds in distinguishing the idea of person and his identity, from the ideas of man and of substance. However, when this definition of personality in terms of consciousness is viewed in connection with the previous discussion it leads to the interesting result that the essentially Cartesian conception of consciousness is divorced from, and upheld independently of, the correlative doctrine of thinking substance, i.e. of that being to which consciousness necessarily pertains. This divorce, which is, as I have already stated, rooted in Locke's scepticism in regard to the knowledge of substance, is the source of many of the difficulties to which this theory leads. But it is also, as I shall later try to suggest, the ground of its philosophical significance. This distinction between personal and substantial identity immediately raises two further questions: (1) whether the same person can remain throughout a change in the thinking substance, (2) whether the same substance can at different times have different persons annexed to it? Consistency requires that Locke answer both questions in the affirmative, and he proceeds to do so.

The first question has really been already answered. The problem is grounded in our lack of knowledge of thinking substance, and Locke is content to assert that the continuity of personality throughout a change of substance is at least possible, although we can have no knowledge thereof.[18] Locke clearly recognizes the historical and religious significance of the second question. He sees that it involves the further question: whether an immaterial substance may be wholly stripped of all consciousness of its past existence beyond the power of ever recalling it, and have, as it were, a new beginning.[19] This is obviously the assumption underlying the doctrine of transmigration, and although Locke must acknowledge that the idea of such a state of affairs is not self-contradictory, he proceeds to show that it is one to which we can attach no determinate sense. For what, he argues, can it mean to say of a person that he is the same as Socrates, if he has no memory of Socrates' life. Let him suppose that he has the same soul ('for souls being, as far as we know anything of them, in their nature indifferent to any parcel of matter, the supposition has no apparent absurdity in it . . .').[20] But without knowledge of any of Socrates' thoughts or actions, how can he conceive of himself as the same person? The ensuing discussion is highly repetitious. Locke constantly reiterates the same point: viz. the distinction between personal and substantial identity. However, in Section Eighteen he turns to the ethical implications of his position, and it would seem that the previous account is essentially propaedeutic to this discussion. He begins with the statement quoted previously. Personal identity is the ultimate source of all the right and justice of reward and punishment. Moral responsibility is based upon and coextensive with

[18] II, xxvii, 13.   [19] II, xxvii, 14.   [20] Ibid.

personal identity, and this, we have seen, means consciousness or memory. Thus, he argues, if Socrates waking and Socrates sleeping do not partake of the same consciousness (the hypothetical Dr. Jekyll and Mr. Hyde situation), it would be completely unjust to punish the one, Socrates, for the thoughts and deeds of the other.[21]

After making this assertion Locke anticipates possible objections. One might suppose, he reflects, that a person has wholly lost the memory of some part of his life, with no possibility of recall. Yet is he not the same person who performed the forgotten deeds? Locke shows that the answer to this question depends upon the understanding of the concept person, and on his own analysis, where 'person' is defined in terms of consciousness, and distinguished from the idea of man, he would not be the same person, although he would be the same man.[22] Or it might be asked whether or not a somnambulist in his waking and sleeping states, or a man drunk and then sober, are the same 'person', and if not, how can the waking and the sober man be justifiably punished for the actions of the sleepwalker and the drunkard? In reply to this Locke relies on the distinction between human laws, which punish both 'with a justice suitable to their way of knowledge', and divine laws which, based upon perfect knowledge, are absolutely just. Human laws, he reasons, must punish the drunkard because 'they cannot distinguish certainly what is real, what counterfeit; and so the ignorance in drunkenness or sleep is not admitted as a plea'. But, Locke writes:

. . . in the Great Day, wherein the secrets of all hearts shall be laid open, it may be reasonable to think no one shall be made to answer for what he knows nothing of, but shall receive his doom, his conscience accusing or excusing him.[23]

Locke's analysis of the drunkard and the sleepwalker was criticized by Molyneux, who insisted upon distinguishing between the two examples. The sleepwalker, Molyneux argued, is not responsible for his condition, and should not therefore be punished for anything he might do while in it. But since drunkenness is itself a crime, the drunkard is subject to punishment for any further crimes committed while in this condition.[24] To this Locke replied that whatever merit this argument may have, it is irrelevant to his purpose since it has nothing to do with consciousness, and moreover, he adds: '. . . it is an argument against me, for if a man may be punished for any crime which he committed when drunk, whereof he is allowed not to be conscious, it

[21] II, xxvii, 19.
[22] II, xxvii, 20.
[23] II, xxvii, 22.
[24] Letter of Molyneux to Locke, 23 Dec. 1693, *The Works of John Locke* (London, 1794), VIII, 329.

overturns my hypothesis.'[25] However, when Molyneux restated the argument, and contended that drunkenness is a voluntarily induced state, and thus the drunkard is responsible for all of the consequences thereof, while sleepwalking is involuntary, and therefore the somnambulist should not be held accountable for his actions,[26] Locke capitulated. He admits that 'want of consciousness ought not to be presumed in favor of the drunkard'.[27]

In view of this admission one is strongly tempted to ask what has become of Locke's theory. He admitted that, if valid, Molyneux's argument would overturn his hypothesis, but he was finally forced to argue that the drunkard is justifiably punished for his crimes, although he is not conscious of them. Locke never bothered to revise his theory in subsequent editions, so that his final opinion on the subject remains a mystery. Nevertheless, it is quite clear that by admitting the validity of Molyneux's contention, Locke recognized a case where moral responsibility extends beyond consciousness. It is only, however, near the end of the chapter, that Locke discloses the full implications of his position. He has been so careful to separate the notion of person from the notion of soul or immaterial substance that one is in doubt as to the status of that which is signified by the term 'person'. But here he tells us: 'It is a forensic term, appropriating actions and their merit, and so belongs only to intelligent agents, capable of a law, and happiness and misery.'[28]

The recognition of the forensic character of the idea entails a modification of Locke's first definition of 'person' as a thinking, intelligent being, etc. The earlier formulation suggests that 'person' is an idea of reflection, acquired by immediate self-awareness. The above passage, however, would seem to imply that 'person' is an abstract idea. As such, it is not in itself an entity of any sort, standing alongside of the man and the substance, but is simply one aspect of the concrete man, i.e. that aspect in virtue of which he is morally responsible, considered apart for ethical purposes. Moreover, such a conception is perfectly consistent with Locke's doctrine of abstraction, which is in essence: the considering as separate, ideas which are united in their 'real existence'.[29] This separation is the process whereby we abstract, and it is also the process whereby Locke is able to distinguish the idea of person from the idea of man understood as a psychosomatic organism.

Thus considered, the notion of 'person' enables Locke to provide a clear and decisive basis for moral responsibility. However, it also raises the serious question, to be discussed in the third section of this paper, that perhaps this consistency was bought at the price of relevance. By abstracting one aspect

[25] Letter of Locke to Molyneux, 19 Jan. 1694, ibid. 331.
[26] Letter of Molyneux to Locke, 17 Feb. 1694, ibid. 334.
[27] Letter of Locke to Molyneux, 26 May 1694, ibid 336.
[28] II, xxvii, 26.
[29] See for instance II, xii, 1.

from the concrete man, and calling that the 'person', he can account for
personal identity and moral responsibility; but in gaining this too easy victory,
he may have ignored the more serious problem of the identity and responsibility
of the man. Yet, before judging Locke too harshly, it may be well to ponder
his own evaluation of his theory:

I am apt enough to think I have, in treating of this subject, made some suppositions
that will look strange to some readers, and possibly they are so in themselves. But
yet I think they are such as are pardonable in this ignorance we are in of the nature
of that thinking thing that is in us and which we look on as our *selves*. Did we know
what it was or how it was tied to a certain system of fleeting animal spirits, or whether
it could or could not perform its operations of thinking and memory out of a body
organized as ours is, and whether it has pleased God that no one such spirit shall
ever be united to any but one such body, upon the right constitution of whose organs
its memory should depend, we might see the absurdity of some of those suppositions
I have made. But taking, as we ordinarily now do (in the dark concerning these
matters), the soul of a man for an immaterial substance, independent from matter
and indifferent alike to it all, there can from the nature of things be no absurdity at
all to suppose that the same soul may at different times be united to different bodies
and with them make up, for that time, one man. . . .[30]

III

Locke's attempt to ground personal identity in consciousness or memory
was soon attacked from all sides. His treatment of the issue seems to have
convinced his contemporaries of its relevance to the question of the possibility
of a rational demonstration of the immortality of the soul, but his own theory
was generally repudiated precisely because it did not appear to provide an
adequate foundation for that doctrine. Thus it is not surprising to find that
among Locke's most influential critics was the theologian and moralist Bishop
Butler. Butler attempted to demonstrate the circularity of Locke's argument.
His main contention was that the definition of personal identity in terms of the
consciousness of personal identity presupposes the very thing in question.
Thus he writes: '. . . one should really think it Self-evident, that Consciousness
of personal Identity presupposes, and therefore cannot constitute, personal
Identity; any more than Knowledge, in any other Case, can constitute Truth,
which it presupposes.'[31]

A somewhat similar objection was voiced by Thomas Reid:

It may be observed that in this doctrine, not only is consciousness confounded with
memory, but which is still more strange, personal identity is confounded with the
evidence which we have of our personal identity.[32]

---

[30] II, xxvii, 27.

[31] Joseph Butler, Dissertation I: Of Personal Identity, appended to the *Analogy of Religion*,
3rd edition (London, 1740), 441.

[32] Thomas Reid, *Essays on the Intellectual Powers of Man*, in *Works of Thomas Reid*, ed. Sir
William Hamilton, 8th edition (Edinburgh, 1895), II, 351.

And finally, we must mention the famous example of the gallant officer, which is intended to illustrate the absurd implications of Locke's analysis. This objection was first formulated by Berkeley, and later amplified by Reid, who wrote:

Suppose a brave officer to have been flogged when a boy at school, for robbing an orchard, to have taken a standard from the enemy in his first campaign, and to have been made a general in advanced life. Suppose also, which must be admitted to be possible, that when he took the standard he was conscious of his having been flogged at school, and that when made a general he was conscious of his taking the standard, but had absolutely lost the consciousness of his flogging.[33]

The clear implication of this example is that on Lockean grounds, the general and the boy both *cannot* be, but at the same time *must* be, the same person, a consequence which is manifestly absurd.

Each of these criticisms points to a fundamental confusion in Locke's thought, but none of them really takes cognizance of the difficulties which Locke recognized or the spirit in which his solution was offered. Thus, while superficially valid, they nevertheless remain below the insight achieved by Locke. This is true of Reid, who failed to grasp the pragmatic and ethical orientation of Locke's theory, but it is especially evident in Butler, who while criticizing Locke for presupposing that which is to be proven, himself dogmatically assumes the very concept of substance which for Locke had become problematical, and which had driven him to his admittedly untenable position. Thus, we find Butler asserting a few pages after the above quoted criticism:

. . . Person or self, must either be a Substance, or the Property of some Substance. If He, if Person, be a Substance; then Consciousness that He is the same Person, is Consciousness that He is the same Substance. If the Person, or He, be the Property of a Substance; still Consciousness that He is the same Property is as certain a Proof that his Substance remains the same, as Consciousness that he remains the same Substance would be: since the same Property cannot be transferred from one Substance to another.[34]

The English thinker who came closest to grasping the true nature of Locke's problem was David Hume. Like Locke, Hume realized that the question of personal identity arose as a consequence of problems concerning the notion of thinking substance, and that memory must play a central role in any adequate analysis of the problem. Hume differs from Locke in his more radical attitude towards the '*res cogitans*' (rejecting as nonsensical what Locke regarded as problematical) and in his essentially psychological orientation. Locke's analysis grew out of an attempt to determine the

[33] Ibid. 352.
[34] Butler, op. cit., 449

limits of moral responsibility, but Hume's aim is to describe the origin of a belief.[35]

Hume rejects the doctrine of an abiding, substantial self in the light of his fundamental tenet that for every idea there must be a corresponding impression. Reflection upon one's mental life discloses only a succession of fleeting and distinct perceptions. There is no single impression from which the idea of self could be derived, hence there is no such idea. Yet all men believe in an abiding self, and it thus became Hume's task to explain the origin of this persistent belief. This, like all 'natural beliefs', is viewed as a product of the habitual operation of the imagination, acting in accordance with the principles of the association of ideas. There is no real bond among the distinct perceptions which constitute our mental life, and their apparent identity is shown to be 'merely a quality, which we attribute to them, because of the union of their ideas in the imagination, when we reflect upon them'.[36]

The principles of this union are the relations of resemblance and causality, and it is in his analysis of how these relations give rise to the fiction of an abiding self that Hume comes to grips with Locke's account. He begins by describing how the relation of resemblance is produced by the memory, which is defined as the faculty which creates images of past perceptions. Since an image necessarily resembles its object, the production of these memory images, and their frequent placement in the 'chain of thought', inevitably leads the imagination to confound the succession of perceptions with the continuance of an identical self. Thus Hume concludes:

In this particular, then, the memory not only discovers the identity, but also contributes to its production, by producing the relation of resemblance among the perceptions.[37]

However, the agreement with Locke concerning the constitutive role of memory is more apparent than real. For whereas Locke actually equates the identity of a person with the continuity of his memory, Hume regards the memory as the source of a fictitious belief. Their basic disagreement becomes evident when we consider Hume's analysis of the role of the causal relation in the constitution of this belief. Here he suggests that 'the true idea of the human mind, is to consider it as a system of different perceptions or different existences, which are link'd together by the relation of cause and effect'. Hume illustrates this by comparing the soul to a commonwealth, which remains identical throughout a complete change in its laws and members

---

[35] Hume makes this quite clear when he writes: *Treatise of Human Nature*, ed. cit., 253, '. . . we must distinguish between personal identity, as it regards our thoughts or imagination, and as it regards our passions or the concern we take in ourselves. The first is our present subject. . . .'

[36] Ibid. 260.

[37] Ibid. 261.

because the various parts stand in a causal relation to one another. From this standpoint, Hume argues, 'memory does not so much produce as discover personal identity, by shewing us the relation of cause and effect among our different perceptions'.[38] Thus, Locke is right in that without memory we would never become aware of that causal chain which constitutes our person. However, once we acquire an awareness of that relationship, we can extend the same chain of causes, and hence extend the identity of our persons beyond the limits of our memory. Moreover, Hume concludes:

'Twill be incumbent on those, who affirm that memory produces entirely our personal identity, to give a reason why we can thus extend our identity beyond our memory.

Here Hume is at one with the rest of Locke's critics in recognizing that personal identity cannot be arbitrarily confined within the limits of memory. However, since Hume was concerned with delineating the psychological grounds of a belief, rather than with defining the nature of personality and the limits of moral responsibility, he really ignores the main point of Locke's analysis. He could readily point out that the belief of mankind in an identical self cannot be grounded solely in memory, but as he himself admits in the appendix to the *Treatise*, his principles of association likewise fail to explain the nature and unity of the self.[39]

Unquestionably the most important treatment of Locke's theory of personal identity is contained in Leibniz's *New Essays concerning Human Understanding*. Although Leibniz succeeds in pointing out the main weaknesses in Locke's argument, his own analysis betrays the influence of his English contemporary. In fact, Leibniz's very formulation of the problem is modelled after Locke's, and as we shall later see, it was primarily through the mediation of Leibniz that Locke's theory acquired its historical significance. The Lockean stimulus is most evident in Leibniz's distinction between the self, the apparent or phenomenal self, and consciousness (*consciosité*), and the correlative distinction between real and apparent identity. These categories are well grounded in the Leibnizean metaphysics, but since they are not explicitly formulated in any of his earlier writings, it seems fair to assume that they were suggested, or at least provoked, by Locke's distinction between the substance, the man and the person, to which they are intended as a corrective. The result, in any event, is that both Leibniz and Locke analyse the concept of the self at three levels, and both see that the problem of personal identity arises in conjunction with the question of the relation between these levels.

[38] Ibid. 262.

[39] Ibid. 635–6 where he makes the notable confession that he could only conceive of this unity if 'our perceptions either inhere in something simple and individual, or did the mind perceive some real connexion among them . . .', thereby suggesting, with Butler, that the only solution lay in a pre-Lockean, substantial conception of the self, a conception which Hume had clearly repudiated.

Furthermore, although Locke and Leibniz stand at opposite poles of the philosophical spectrum, they nevertheless share a common Cartesian heritage, which they criticize in different directions. Thus, Leibniz begins his critique by agreeing with Locke that the ability to say I, or self-consciousness (*consciosité*), proves a moral or personal identity, and it is upon this basis that he distinguishes between the mere perpetuity (*incessabilité*) of animal souls or monads, and the immortality of rational spirits. Since both are monads, i.e. indestructible, simple substances, they both preserve their real or physical identity. However, a rational soul, which for Leibniz, as for all Cartesians, is one capable of self-awareness, also maintains its moral identity, and it is just this which renders it susceptible of rewards and punishments. Now Locke, Leibniz argues, believes that this apparent or personal identity (disclosed through self-consciousness) could be preserved if there were no real or substantial identity, and while Leibniz admits that this might be possible through a miracle, he contends on the basis of his metaphysical position that:

... according to the order of things, identity apparent to the person himself who perceives the same, supposes real identity to every proximate transition, accompanied by reflection or perception of the ego, a perception intimate and immediate, naturally incapable of deception. If man could be merely a machine and with that have consciousness, it would be necessary to be of your opinion, sir; but I hold that this case is not possible, at least naturally.[40]

At first glance this seems to parallel closely Butler's objection: personal or apparent identity must be grounded in, and presuppose some sort of real or substantial identity. This is demanded by the main principles of the Leibnizean metaphysics. However, Leibniz introduces a whole new dimension into the discussion with his reflection that Locke would be right if man were merely a machine with consciousness added. He does this by relating Locke's thesis to the Cartesian context in which it originated. Leibniz seems to be suggesting here that, while Locke is basically correct in his critique of the Cartesian conception of the soul, his own theory reflects a failure to find an adequate replacement for this conception. Because of this failure, and because he continues to adhere to a Cartesian conception of body as a machine, he is more or less forced to locate the seat of personality in a bare consciousness. The moral which Leibniz wishes to derive from this is, of course, that these Cartesian conceptions must be replaced by his own theory of monads. It is significant too that although Leibniz rejects Locke's equation of 'person' with consciousness or memory, he nevertheless shares his conception of self-consciousness as the defining characteristic of a rational being, and like Locke

[40] Leibniz, *New Essays concerning Human Understanding*, English translation by A. G. Langley, 3rd edition (La Salle, Ill., 1949), 246.

he distinguishes this consciousness and its unity from the unity of the real or substantial self.

Finally, it may, I believe, be argued that Leibniz's admission of the conceivability of apparent (personal) identity without a corresponding real or substantial identity lends support to one of Locke's basic contentions. It is true that Leibniz grants only the barest possibility to such a state of affairs (declaring that it would require a miracle), but Locke never actually claimed that personal identity does in fact exist without substantial identity, but only that, because of the limitations of our understanding, it is necessary to separate the two conceptions. It was no doubt with this in mind that Locke wrote: 'I agree the more probable opinion is that this consciousness is annexed to and the affection of one individual immaterial substance.'[41]

Thus we can see that although Locke and Leibniz start from radically different standpoints (Locke from reflective observation, and Leibniz from a deductive metaphysics wherein the concept of simple, immaterial substance is central), their analyses of the concept of personality suggest a good deal of common ground. This is partly due to Leibniz's characteristic desire to find a measure of truth in the views of his opponent, but the deeper reason lies in their common Cartesian heritage. It is because of this heritage that both thinkers start with the *cogito*, which they distinguish from substance or the 'real self', and it is upon the basis of this distinction that they are led to the recognition that the problem of the nature and identity of the self must be analysed on several levels.

Leibniz's critique of the ethical implications of Locke's theory is more decisive, but far from original. His main contention is the obvious one that the limitation of personal identity to consciousness or memory is too narrow to provide an adequate basis for moral responsibility. This was first expressed by Molyneux, with his insistence upon the distinction between the drunkard and the somnambulist, tacitly admitted by Locke, and later suggested by Berkeley and by Reid with his example of the gallant officer. Leibniz adopts the same line of criticism, but broadens it to include the possibility of amnesia. It is in this connection that he writes:

Neither would I say that personal identity and even the self do not dwell in us and that I am not this ego which has been in the cradle, under pretext that I no more remember anything of all that I then did. It is sufficient in order to find moral identity by itself that there be a *middle bond of consciousness* between a state bordering upon or even a little removed from another, although a leap or forgotten interval might be mingled therein. Thus if a disease had caused an interruption of the continuity of the bond of consciousness so that I did not know how I came into the present state, although I remember things more remote, the testimony of others could fill the void in my memory. I could even be punished upon this testimony, if I had just done

[41] *Essay*, II, xxvii, 25.

something bad of deliberate purpose in an interval that I had forgotten a little after on account of this disease. And if I had just forgotten all past things and would be obliged to let myself be taught anew even to my name and even to reading and writing, I could always learn from others my past life in my previous state, as I have kept my rights without its being necessary for me to share them with two persons, and to make me the heir of myself.[42]

Here we see the discussion carried out on an ethical and legal level, divorced from any metaphysical considerations, and the clear result is that there are important instances where moral responsibility must be extended beyond memory. Not explicit awareness, Leibniz argues, but merely 'a middle bond of consciousness' (*une moyenne liaison de consciosité*) between two distinct states is enough to establish this identity, and hence, the accountability of the person. Even if an individual suffers a temporary loss of memory, so that he cannot recall the immediate past, the testimony of others is sufficient to establish the necessary unifying bond, and the individual should not only regard himself as the author of the deeds attributed to him, but be willing to accept their consequences. Moreover, as Leibniz seems to imply, this principle holds even in the case of total amnesia. Even here the testimony of others suffices to establish identity, and the amnesia victim is not only justifiably held responsible for his past actions, but also fully entitled to the rights which he formerly possessed. This last point, i.e. the maintenance of rights, was not discussed by Locke, who was primarily interested in determining the limits of moral responsibility, but it is certainly an important dimension of the problem, and it is not surprising that it was first recognized by Leibniz, who was deeply interested in the philosophy of law.

If Molyneux, Berkeley, Reid, and Leibniz have succeeded in demonstrating wherein Locke's theory of personal identity is too narrow there is another sense in which it is too wide. This has been pointed out by Professor Flew, who shows that it is a direct consequence of Locke's acceptance of the fallibility of memory. If we take this fallibility seriously, we see that a person can not only forget things he has done but 'remembers' things he has not done. This phenomenon finds its most striking manifestation in the case of paramnesia, and as Flew points out, such honest memory claims, wherein a person actually believes he has done something which he in fact never did, are not empty logical possibilities, but fairly common occurrences. In support of this contention, Flew writes:

... George IV in his declining years 'remembered' his gallant leadership at the battle of Waterloo though only a very Lockean or a very ambitious courtier would pretend that the King assisted at that battle; and today we find that no sooner are the evening papers on the streets than a queue is forming at New Scotland Yard of those who 'remember' committing the latest murder.[43]

---

[42] Leibniz, op. cit., 246.   [43] Flew, op. cit., 57.

Such examples are graphic illustrations of the inadequacy of Locke's theory, but they become even more relevant when viewed in the light of a decisive passage in the chapter on personal identity, which I have not yet discussed. Here Locke writes:

But that which we call the *same consciousness* not being the same individual act, why one intellectual substance may not have represented to it, as done by itself, what it never did, and was perhaps done by some other agent: why, I say, such a representation may not possibly be without reality of matter of fact, as well as several representations in dreams are, which yet whilst dreaming we take for true, will be difficult to conclude from the nature of things.[44]

This passage contains the *reductio ad absurdum* of Locke's theory. After repeatedly distinguishing between the identity of the person and that of the man, he here makes manifest the full implication of this distinction. He is able arbitrarily to locate responsibility in the person, but is forced to admit that this may result in an injustice to the man. However, instead of altering his theory in face of this implied consequence, he merely falls back upon the goodness of God (*à la Descartes*) as a guarantee against its occurrence.

Here Locke's theory fails at its most decisive point, for as Flew suggests, Locke is admitting what is quite fatal to his whole analysis: that it is not self-contradictory to say that someone 'remembers' doing something which he has not done.[45] Such an admission makes manifest nonsense out of Locke's theory, and since it is grounded in his conception of the person as an abstraction from the man it cannot be dismissed as a mere linguistic confusion. According to Cartesian principles (and in this respect Locke is certainly a good Cartesian), if the identity of the person can be conceived apart from the identity of the man, then is it not self-contradictory to assert that the two identities can exist independently of one another:

For there is no doubt that God possesses the power to produce everything that I am capable of perceiving with distinctness, and I have never deemed that anything was impossible for Him, unless I found a contradiction in attempting to conceive it clearly.[46]

IV

We have seen in sufficient detail: that Locke's theory of personal identity involves a *petitio principii*, that it leads to absurd consequences, and that it can be considered as at once too narrow and too wide. In view of this one may quite legitimately ask how such a confused and inadequate account can possibly be of any philosophical significance. Yet to approach the matter in

[44] II, xxvii, 13.
[45] Flew, op. cit., 58.
[46] Descartes, Vth Meditation, op. cit., 185.

this light, which is the light in which it has been regarded by most of Locke's critics, is to miss the point entirely. For the true importance of Locke's theory lies not in what it achieved, but in what it attempted, not in the solution which it provided, but in the further problems which it raised.

Most of the difficulties and absurdities to which Locke's theory falls prey are the direct result of his ambiguous relation to the philosophy of Descartes, a relation which not only characterizes the chapter on personal identity, but the *Essay* as a whole. The ambiguity is clearly manifest in the fact that while he rejects the Cartesian contention that the human mind possesses clear and distinct ideas of the nature of substance, both thinking and extended, Locke nevertheless continually assumes the existence of such substances. A similar confusion may be found in Locke's whole attitude towards scientific know-ledge, i.e. knowledge of the 'real essence' of substances. In his account of perception, and especially of the basic distinction between ideas of primary qualities, which correspond to entities actually existing *in rerum natura*, and ideas of secondary qualities, which are merely the subjective results of the operation of the primary qualities upon the sense organs, Locke certainly presupposes such knowledge. But when we turn to Locke's analysis of the nature and limits of knowledge in Book IV, we find that the very knowledge in terms of which he explains sense perception is beyond the power of the human mind. There Locke's confusion leads to the affirmation of a world of matter in motion, as described by the new physics, the knowledge of which is held to be impossible of attainment. Here it induces him to posit a 'person' who stands in no cognizable relation to the substance to which Locke believes it is 'probably annexed'. Thus, while it is his critique of Descartes which first forced the problem of personal identity upon him, it is the inconsistent manner in which the critique is carried out that leads to the absurd consequences which his theory entails.

However, this ambiguous relation to Descartes is, paradoxically enough, the source of the significance as well as the absurdity of Locke's theory. In the first place it enabled Locke to adopt an ethical and essentially prag-matic approach to the problem. Although the particular results of his analyses are far from happy, his basic orientation nevertheless constitutes a real advance. For from this pragmatic standpoint, which is really a con-sequence of his scepticism in regard to knowledge of substance, Locke is able to show the meaningless of all speculations concerning the pre-existence or transmigration of souls, with its implication that I might be the same person as Socrates, although I can have no possible recollection of that state. It is against just such a conception that Locke quite cogently argues:

For supposing a man punished now for what he had done in another life, whereof he could be made to have no consciousness at all, what difference is there between that punishment and being created miserable?[47]

Locke's implicit pragmatism is not to be ignored, but his main contribution lies in his separation of the concept of the identity or unity of consciousness, which he equated with personal identity, from the metaphysical doctrine of the identity of an immaterial substance, and his consequent recognition of the different levels at which the concept of the self must be analysed. It was this recognition which first constituted personal identity as a distinct philosophical problem, apart from the more general issue of the *principium individuationis*. In this regard it must be noted that Locke's error lies not in the separation of the *cogito* from the 'thinking substance', but in his too facile identification of this separated *cogito* with the person. This is, as we have seen, readily apparent in Leibniz's critique. For although Leibniz rejects Locke's identification of the 'person' with consciousness, he nevertheless shares his conception of the *cogito* as the decisive characteristic of rationality. In Leibniz, the *cogito* (*consciosité*) is distinguished from the person, or phenomenal self, as well as from the real or substantial self, and the result is that it is no longer viewed with Locke, as a quasi-substantial entity, but rather as a purely formal principle, a mere capacity to say 'I'.

Now Kant was a close student of the *New Essays*, and it is in the *Critique of Pure Reason* that Locke's doctrine found (through the mediation of Leibniz) its logical culmination. Kant's basic distinction between the noumenal self, the phenomenal self, and the transcendental unity of apperception closely parallels Leibniz's categories which, as we have seen, were ultimately derived from Locke. However, it is in the concept of the transcendental unity of apperception, the 'I think' which 'must be capable of accompanying all other representations',[48] that we find the full fruition of the Lockean insight. Here the unity of the 'I think' is not only viewed with Leibniz as a purely formal principle, which must be distinguished from the notion of personal or substantial identity, but it is totally divorced from all metaphysical conceptions. This divorce underlies the *Paralogisms of Pure Reason*, where Kant writes:

The identity of the consciousness of myself at different times is therefore only a formal condition of my thoughts and their coherence, and in no way proves the numerical identity of my subject.[49]

This total repudiation of the metaphysics of the substantial self is a direct outgrowth of the Lockean doctrine that the identity of consciousness must

[47] II, xxvii, 26.
[48] Kant, I., *Critique of Pure Reason*, B 132, English translation by Norman Kemp Smith (London, 1958), 153.
[49] Ibid. A 363, 342.

be considered apart from the identity of any substances to which it may be attached. Since Locke was led to this insight by ethical considerations, he erroneously identified this consciousness with the person, an identification which Kant as well as Leibniz repudiated. Yet the underlying thought remains the same, and it is because of this that we can conclude that Locke, Leibniz, and Kant constitute three stages in the modification of the Cartesian conception of consciousness. Moreover, of the three Locke's contribution is the most decisive. He was the first to separate the *cogito* from the concept of a thinking substance, thereby paving the way for the formalistic conception of consciousness suggested by Leibniz's *consciosité*, and explicitly affirmed in Kant's transcendental unity of apperception.

VIII

THE MAIN THESIS OF LOCKE'S
SEMANTIC THEORY

NORMAN KRETZMANN

I N the third book of his *Essay concerning Human Understanding* (first published in 1690) John Locke produced the first modern treatise devoted specifically to philosophy of language.[1] No work had a greater influence over the development of philosophical semantics during the Enlightenment than did this Book Three, entitled 'Of Words'. Naturally it acquired importance simply as a result of being a part of the enormously influential *Essay*, but the source of its special influence lay in the fact that Locke had expressly connected semantic inquiry with theory of knowledge. He had set out to investigate 'our knowledge' and along the way found himself unexpectedly compelled to investigate the 'force and manner of signification' of words (*Essay*, III, ix, 21), having discovered that 'there is so close a connexion between *ideas* and words . . . that it is impossible to speak clearly and distinctly of our knowledge, which all consists in propositions, without considering first the nature, use, and signification of language' (II, xxxiii, 19). Semantic inquiries during the Middle Ages and the Renaissance had been intimately associated with logic and grammar. The new epistemological orientation of semantics, apparent even in the logic books of the Enlightenment, was first explicitly established in Locke's *Essay*.

Nevertheless, the doctrines to be found in Book Three were not novel in principle, nor were they clearly stated or fully developed. Locke never claimed that they were new, and I am not now concerned with showing that they were

From *Philosophical Review*, 77 (1968), pp. 175–96. Reprinted by permission of the author and the editor of the journal.
[1] I am indebted to my colleagues at Cornell and especially to the referee on this paper for having shown me several ways in which to improve it. Some portions of Part I are paraphrases of the section on Locke in my article 'Semantics, History of' in *The Encyclopedia of Philosophy*, ed. by Paul Edwards (New York, 1967).

not. Suffice it to say that many of the most fundamental of them had been anticipated in Kenelm Digby's *Two Treatises* (1664), in Richard Burthogge's *Organum vetus et novum* (1678)[2] and in the works of Thomas Hobbes, and that they were not novel in those earlier appearances either. What I do want to show in this paper is the character of the semantic theory that has been obscured by Locke's own unclear statements and incomplete development of it and by the tradition of misguided criticism to which those characteristically Lockean shortcomings have given rise.

Locke evidently thought of the material of Book Three as serving two purposes in his philosophy. On the one hand he characterized his new 'way of ideas' as nothing more than 'the old way of speaking intelligibly',[3] which he reduced to a few commonsensical maxims for the avoidance of 'jargon', very much in the spirit of Bacon's treatment of the Idols of the Market Place. The semantic theory in Book Three was developed partly in order to serve as a support for these 'remedies of the . . . imperfections and abuses' of words (III, xi), and Locke's preoccupation with that practical aim may help to explain some of the imprecision and inconsistency in his theoretical statements. He did, on the other hand, clearly recognize a more strictly theoretical purpose in the semantic inquiries of his third book, a purpose he set forth at the end of the *Essay* in his description of the third branch of science—'σημειωτική, or *the doctrine of signs*', the consideration of ideas as the signs of things and of words as the signs of ideas (IV, xxi, 4). In this paper I shall have nothing to say about ideas as the signs of things except in so far as that part of Locke's doctrine of signs bears directly on his view of words as the signs of ideas.

II

'The great instruments of knowledge' (IV, xxi, 4), Locke says, are the two sorts of 'signs we chiefly use' (II, xxxii, 19)—words and ideas. His general account of the relation between signs of these two sorts varies in its terminology but may be fairly summarized in the formula 'words signify ideas'. This account is the main thesis of Locke's semantic theory, elaborated in Book Three and frequently applied in Books One, Two, and Four.

Although Locke was by no means the first or the last to say that words signify ideas, it is in his presentation of it that this thesis has become established as one of the classic blunders in semantic theory, alongside such other classics as the view that names have a natural connection with their bearers and the view that the meaning of a name is the name's bearer. No doubt one

---

[2] On these and other relevant predecessors of Locke see John Yolton, *John Locke and the Way of Ideas* (Oxford, 1956).

[3] Third Letter to Stillingfleet; cf. the chapter on words in *The Conduct of the Understanding*, first published in 1706.

reason why the critical tradition has associated the view that words signify ideas with Locke in particular is that the tradition begins with Berkeley. In several early entries in his private 'Philosophical Commentaries' (1707–8) Berkeley presented this much of Locke's semantic theory as an 'axiom' in support of his otherwise anti-Lockean position—for example, '1. All significant words stand for Ideas.'[4] But he attacked it with a series of what he took to be counterinstances[5] when he thought he discerned in it the root of Locke's doctrine of abstract general ideas.[6] Berkeley's second thoughts about the thesis that words signify ideas mark the beginning of a tradition of criticism so uniformly and intensely negative that the thesis seems now to be considered beneath criticism, or at any rate beneath careful criticism.[7] Some of the better-known lines of attack, such as the one taken by Mill ('When I say, "the sun is the cause of day," I do not mean that my idea of the sun causes or excites in me the idea of day'[8]), completely fail to touch Locke's thesis on any fair interpretation of it, however. And those lines of attack that seem most damaging often rest on the accidents of Locke's haphazard terminology rather than on what he is clearly committed to. It is easy, for example, to find passages (where he is applying the thesis rather than arguing for it) in which he speaks as if it were his view that every word is a proper name of some idea in the mind of the user of the word,[9] passages that look as if they could have been what started Wittgenstein thinking about the notion of a private language. Yet for all its shortcomings the main thesis of Locke's semantic theory is not as bad as it looks; and it looks as bad as it does because it looks simpler than it is.

Its apparent simplicity masks not only complexities essential to Locke's own conception of what it means to say that words signify ideas, but also a confusion, far reaching in its effects on Locke and his interpreters, that could easily have been avoided. This confusion has its source in the fact that Locke presents his argument for the thesis in two interdependent parts but treats those parts as if they were two complete and independent arguments for it. He then compounds the confusion by applying and extending the thesis in a misleading terminology that is appropriate at best only to the first part of his two-part argument.

In what follows I am going to present (in Part III) a more detailed statement of the main thesis of Locke's semantic theory, then examine (in Parts

---

[4] Luce and Jessop (eds.), 1.45; cf. 1.33, 39, 43, 53.

[5] Beginning with *Philos. Comm.* 1.62, and going on through the remainder of the *Commentaries* and all the later works.

[6] Beginning with *Philos. Comm.* 1.70, and going on through the remainder of the *Commentaries* and all the later works.

[7] See, e.g., William P. Alston, *Philosophy of Language* (Englewood Cliffs, N.J., 1964), pp. 24–5.

[8] *A System of Logic*, 1.2.1.

[9] e.g. in III, ii, 5 or II, xxxi, 6.

IV and V) each of the two parts of Locke's explicit argument for this thesis that words signify ideas, and finally suggest (in Part VI) that Locke's own 'way of ideas' actually afforded him a simpler basis for a more general and historically more distinctive account of the semantic relation between words and ideas than is supported by the complex, confused argument he does offer. My purpose in this paper is not to defend what has usually been taken to be the main thesis of Locke's semantic theory but to spell out the thesis more carefully than Locke himself or his critics have done. When it is seen for what it is, however, some traditional lines of attack against it will have to be given up.

III

More or less detailed statements of the thesis that words signify ideas can be found in every book of the *Essay* and in every chapter of Book Three. It is even partially argued for in Books Two and Four.[10] But the most careful statements of it and the most fully worked-out argument for it occur, quite naturally, in the first two chapters of Book Three. Locke's wobbly terminology makes it impossible to find any single statement of the thesis in his own words that expresses all and only his evident intentions, but this one from Chapter Two is perhaps the least unsatisfactory: '*words, in their primary or immediate signification, stand for nothing but the* ideas *in the mind of him that uses them*' (III, ii, 2). One obviously crucial ingredient in this statement is the phrase 'stand for'. That it is not a technical term in Locke's use of it may be seen in a comparison of this with various similar statements in the *Essay*—statements in which Locke, without intending to draw any semantic distinctions, can be found saying, for example, that words are signs of, or are marks of, or are names of, or signify, or mark, or correspond to, or are annexed to ideas. The uncovering of a single, explanatory, Lockean sense for Locke's many semantic connectives is, I think, one of the results of the present investigation; but in conducting it I am going to shut out this terminological noise by adopting the neutral verb 'signify' for use in my statements of the thesis and argument under investigation. Thus I propose to take the following close paraphrase as a standard version of the main thesis of Locke's semantic theory. *Words in their primary or immediate signification signify nothing but the ideas in the mind of him that uses them.*

Did Locke intend this as a completely general claim regarding words of every kind? His critics have usually assumed that he did, and he does speak almost everywhere in the *Essay* as if that were his intention. In the short chapter on 'particles', however, he makes explicit exceptions of propositional connectives, the copula, and the word 'not'; and it seems clear that in that

[10] e.g. in II, xxxii, 7–8 and IV, xxi, 4.

chapter he means to be ruling out all words that others called 'syncategore-matic'. These are, he says, *not* 'names of *ideas* in the mind', but are 'made use of to signify the *connexion* that the mind gives to *ideas or propositions, one with another*'. Such words, then, do *not* in their primary or immediate significa-tion signify nothing but the ideas in the mind of him that uses them. Instead they 'show or intimate some particular action' of the mind of him that uses them, some action 'relating to those *ideas*' (III, vii, 1).

Is the main thesis of Locke's semantic theory then intended as a claim regarding all 'categorematic' words—verbs, nouns, and adjectives, especially? Locke does briefly consider the signification of verbs in Book Two and at the beginning of Book Three,[11] but in a way quite detached from the semantic theory developed later in Book Three, where verbs are not discussed as such. While he does not explicitly exclude verbs from the scope of his main thesis, he never explicitly includes them either; and what he has to say about words in Book Three shows that his governing and perhaps exclusive concern was with nouns and adjectives, or 'names'.[12] And even in regard to names alone Locke was led by his rejection of negative ideas to devise a curious variation on the main thesis of his semantic theory in order to accommodate '*negative* names', such as 'insipid', 'silence', 'nothing', which he thinks 'stand not directly for positive *ideas* but . . . denote positive *ideas*, v.g., *taste, sound, being* with a signification of their absence' (II, viii, 5; cf. III, i, 4).

Thus, despite the critical tradition and the many broad passages in the *Essay* on which the tradition is founded, the only kind of word unmistakably referred to by Locke in his thesis that words signify ideas is the 'name'. Much of Book Three is understandable only if this veiled restriction is kept in mind. Locke could, however, have developed his semantic theory regarding words without restricting its scope so severely, as we shall see.

IV

In examining Locke's argument it is only fair and prudent to begin by supposing, as he himself seems to do, that each of its two parts is an in-dependent, complete argument supporting the conclusion that words in their primary or immediate signification signify nothing but the ideas in the mind of him that uses them. What I take to be only the first part of a single argument I shall accordingly designate Locke's argument from the uses of words. In its fullest form it runs as follows.

Men require society, and society requires communication. Communication

---

[11] II, xviii, 2; II, xxi, 72; and III, 1, 5.

[12] Notice that in the opening chapter of Book Three it is 'names' almost as often as 'words' that figure as the projected main topic of the book.

is the disclosure of one's ideas to another. One man cannot disclose his ideas *as such*, or *immediately*, to another man. Consequently,

it was necessary that man should find out some external sensible signs whereby those invisible *ideas*, which his thoughts are made up of, might be made known to others. For this purpose nothing was so fit, either for plenty or quickness, as those articulate sounds which with so much ease and variety he found himself able to make. Thus we may conceive how *words*, which were by nature so well adapted to that purpose, came to be made use of by men as *the signs of* their *ideas* [III, ii, 1].

This is not the end of the argument, but even at this stage of it Locke has already derived a special case of an incomplete version of the thesis—namely, *words used in communication signify ideas in the mind of him that uses them.* On my view of the role actually played by the argument from the uses of words no more than this is required of it. Locke evidently thought, however, that it could be extended to show that words in every use, and not just in communication, signify the user's ideas. His attempt to provide such an extension rounds off his argument from the uses of words, in the following passage.

The use men have of . . . [words] being either to record their own thoughts for the assistance of their own memory or, as it were, to bring out their *ideas* and lay them before the view of others: *words, in their primary or immediate signification, stand for nothing but the* ideas *in the mind of him that uses them* [III, ii, 2].

Although Locke thus presents the complete statement of the thesis as if it were to be concluded from the argument from the uses of words, there is to begin with nothing at all in this argument to support or even to explain the restrictive phrase 'in their primary or immediate signification'. As one would naturally suppose, this phrase does express an essential aspect of Locke's semantic theory, but he provides explicit support for it only in his *second* argument, which he introduces for the first time *following* these passages. (I shall consider the restriction in connection with the second argument in Part V below.) It is likewise natural to suppose that the phrase 'nothing but' occurs in the complete statement of the thesis only because of the restriction to the 'primary or immediate signification' of words. In any case, there is, again, nothing in the argument from the uses of words to support the claim that words signify *nothing but* the user's ideas, not even if the argument as extended should be taken to show that words *always do* signify the user's ideas. The only portion of what I am calling the standard version of the thesis that has a chance of being supported by the argument from the uses of words, then, is this: *Words . . . signify . . . ideas in the mind of him that uses them.*

Locke seems sometimes to have realized this, as in the following shorter version of the same argument, where the stated conclusion is a very close parallel to the weak version of the thesis we have just arrived at.

When a man speaks to another, it is that he may be understood; and the end of speech is that those sounds, as marks, may make known his *ideas* to the hearer. That then which words are the marks of are the *ideas* of the speaker [III, ii, 2].

But even such incomplete, weakened versions of the thesis are not supported by the argument from the uses of words unless either we weaken them still further by inserting the phrase 'in at least some uses of them' or we take the argument to include an exhaustive survey of the uses of words. Locke evidently thinks he has supplied an exhaustive survey in the extended version of the argument, where he cites recording one's own ideas and communicating them to others as '*the* use men have' of words. Neither in these passages nor anywhere else in the *Essay*, however, does he give any reason for supposing that the communicative and recordative uses are the only, or even the only legitimate, uses of words. Moreover, Book Four contains a good deal of discussion of the use of words in thinking. Locke does consider that third, ratiocinative use of words a misuse, however, mainly because he supposes that words used in thinking often *supplant* rather than *signify* ideas. But he certainly views words in this third use also as signifying the user's ideas when they signify anything at all. Locke's own recognition of a third use of words, then, does no serious damage to his argument from what the argument itself suggests are the only two uses of words.

Regardless of how many other uses of words Locke recognizes or fails to recognize, he plainly considers their use in communication *primary*, every other use deriving from the communicative use. In the fullest version of the argument under consideration he shows that he considers the communicative use primary in the sense of earliest; and in the short version of the argument quoted above he describes communication as 'the end of speech' (elsewhere 'the chief end of language'[13]), which makes it primary also in the sense of *raison d'être*. (The primacy of the communicative use of words shows up also in Locke's view of the nature of words, as we shall see in Part VI below.) Thus Locke's argument from the uses of words is essentially an argument from communication, which he takes to be the primary use of words.

Particularly in view of the conclusion Locke seems to think he can draw from this argument, his description of what it is for men to communicate—'to bring out their ideas and lay them before the view of others'—is very likely to suggest that he has failed to consider any more than one special sort of communicative use of words, the sort of use I make of words when I tell someone what I am thinking or how I am feeling or what I am experiencing. If the argument from the uses of words were all he offered in support of the thesis, this incredible oversight might reasonably be attributed to Locke, and

---

[13] III, v, 7; cf. II, xi, 8; II, xviii, 7; II, xxviii, 2; III, v, 11; III, vi, 32; III, ix, 6; III, x, 13; III, xi, 1; III, xi, 5.

he might reasonably be said to claim that the only communicative use of words is to refer to the user's own ideas. We shall see, however, that it is no part of Locke's thesis to deny that in the communicative use of the words 'There's a squirrel in the bird-feeder' one is using words to refer to a squirrel and a bird-feeder rather than to ideas in one's mind. And when the argument from the uses of words is recognized as only one part of the argument for his thesis, and the thesis is interpreted in the way determined by the second part of the argument, it will be clear that everything of theoretical importance in his remarks about communication applies in one and the same way to the communicative use of words in such statements as 'There's a squirrel in the bird-feeder' and in such statements as 'I am perceiving an irregular patch of blue in the upper right quadrant of my visual field'.

Attending for now only to what Locke says and not to what I say he will be shown to mean, we may accept the argument from the uses of words as establishing at most this conclusion, that *words used by a man (1) in communicating his ideas to others, or (2) in recording his ideas to assist his own memory, or (3) in thinking signify his own ideas*. The fact that this conclusion lacks some of the essential ingredients of the thesis this argument is supposed to support is one of two considerations that lead me to recognize it as being only the first part of Locke's argument, the other consideration being the fact that the missing ingredients are supplied in what Locke seems to present as an independent second argument in support of the thesis.

V

What I take to be the second part of the argument for the main thesis of Locke's semantic theory is stronger than the first in most respects, but it is based on theory rather than on commonplace observations and it is more complex formally. Perhaps it was those unattractive aspects of it that led Locke to treat it as if it were a mere gratuitous supplement to the argument from the uses of words. I am going to call it the argument from the doctrine of representative ideas.

There is a passage near the end of the *Essay* containing what may be the most succinct, straightforward statement of the doctrine of representative ideas to be found in the writings of anyone who held the doctrine, and I offer it simply as a reminder of Locke's position:

> ... since the things the mind contemplates are none of them, besides itself, present to the understanding, it is necessary that something else, as a sign or representation of the thing it considers, should be present to it: and these are *ideas* [IV, xxi, 4].

The most detailed and difficult presentation of Locke's argument from the doctrine of representative ideas appears immediately after the short version of the argument from the uses of words considered in Part IV above. It reads as follows:

> ... nor can anyone apply them [words] as marks, immediately, to anything else but the *ideas* that he himself hath, for this would be to make them signs of his own conceptions and yet apply them to other *ideas*, which would be to make them signs and not signs of his *ideas* at the same time, and so in effect to have no signification at all [III, ii, 2].

The clearest thing about this argument is that it is a *reductio ad absurdum* with its indirect conclusion stated at the outset. We may conveniently and fairly paraphrase the indirect conclusion in the following way. *No one can apply words to signify immediately something other than one's own ideas.* Here are the ingredients that were lacking in the conclusion supported by the argument from the uses of words. All there is in the complete standard version of the thesis that is not in this present conclusion is the assertion that one does (and therefore can) apply words to signify one's own ideas, and that much *was* provided by the argument from the uses of words. Thus this argument from the doctrine of representative ideas is evidently meant to support just those aspects of the main thesis of Locke's semantic theory that were left unsupported by the argument from the uses of words. Moreover, it strengthens the standard version of the thesis by introducing a denial of the *possibility* of any other immediate signification for words. Words *do* signify ideas in the mind of him that uses them and *in their primary or immediate signification* they *can* signify *nothing but* the ideas in the mind of him that uses them.

Now, does the argument from the doctrine of representative ideas succeed in supporting all that it appears designed to support? Locke's first explicit premise in this argument reads: 'this would be to make them signs of his own conceptions and yet apply them to other ideas'. If we fill out the place occupied by the pronoun 'this', using Locke's exact words as nearly as possible, we obtain the following as the complete first premiss:

> [for a man to] apply [words] as marks, immediately, to anything else but the *ideas* that he himself hath ... would be to make them signs of his own conceptions and yet apply them to other *ideas* ....

Part of what makes this premiss difficult to grasp at first is Locke's proliferating terminology. The point he is trying to make emerges a little more clearly even when we make the slight adjustments of replacing 'conceptions' with 'ideas' and 'make them signs of' with 'make them signify'. But less obvious and more helpful replacements are available, too. At first glance it might seem reasonable to suppose that applying the word 'gold', for example, as a mark is just the same as using the word 'gold' to refer to something, and hence that Locke is here flagrantly committing what has come to be thought of as his characteristic blunder in semantic theory, claiming that one can use such words as 'gold' only to refer to one's own ideas. The charge is so preposterous that one would disdain to defend Locke against it if it had not been made so often. And the flimsiness of the case against him is pointed up by the fact that there are relatively clear passages in the near vicinity of this argument to show that such an identification is certainly not what Locke intends. What Locke does mean by speaking of one's *applying a word to something* is one's *giving the word a meaning*. (Since he clearly does not imagine that this is always the result of an *action* on my part, it might be more generally correct to say that in Locke's view my application of a word to something is that word's acquiring a meaning for me.) If there is any single locution regularly used by Locke that is parallel to 'using the word "gold" to refer to something' it is the plain English phrase 'calling something "gold"''; and of course I could not call a thing 'gold' if the word had not already acquired a meaning for me. This distinction between applying the word 'gold' to something and calling something 'gold' is brought out in the very next section of the chapter, where Locke says of the world 'gold' that 'each can *apply* it only to his own idea' and describes a child who, 'having taken notice of nothing in the metal he hears *called* "gold" but the bright shining yellow colour . . . *applies* the word "gold" only to his own idea of that colour and nothing else, and therefore *calls* the same colour in a peacock's tail "gold"'.[14] All that it is essential to notice now is that in the premiss under discussion Locke does not use the phrase 'apply words as marks to' in order to introduce a distinction between what a word is used to refer to and what it signifies. It seems, then, that we can fairly and advantageously revert to our neutral semantic connective between words and ideas and replace the phrase 'apply words as marks to' with 'apply words to signify', thereby avoiding the unintended appearance of such a distinction in the premiss.

If we now make use of these replacements in a rewritten version of the first premiss of Locke's argument from the doctrine of representative ideas, we can see that the heart of the *reductio* is contained in the beginning of the premiss: *to apply words to signify immediately something other than one's own ideas would be to make them signify one's own ideas*. That is, my applying (or attempting to apply) a word to signify something other than an idea of mine presupposes that I have an idea of that thing associated with that word. If I had no idea of that thing I could not make it the object of my attention or of any action of mine. Thus, whenever I genuinely use and do not just mouth a word, parrot fashion, that utterance of mine signifies *immediately* some idea of mine, whatever other meaning I may give or think I give to the word.

---

[14] III, ii, 3; emphasis and internal quotation marks added. Cf., however, II, xxxi, 2, where Locke speaks of sugar producing in us 'the *ideas* which we call whiteness and sweetness'.

Therefore, if X is something other than an idea of mine, to suppose that I can apply a word to signify X *immediately* is to suppose that I can apply a word to signify X while I have no idea of X, which is impossible. Consequently the phrase 'to apply words to signify immediately something other than one's own ideas' contains a contradiction in terms, the absurdity to which the denial of the main thesis of Locke's semantic theory is to be reduced. (Part of what is difficult in Locke's own presentation of the argument is that he obscures the absurdity under apparent efforts to reinforce it.)

I have been calling this the argument from the doctrine of representative ideas because it is *representative* ideas, those that Locke thinks have corresponding non-ideas as their originals, that constitute the cases in which Locke's main thesis applies in full detail. Once it becomes clear that it is only *immediately* that words signify *nothing but* the user's ideas, it is clear also that where the ideas immediately signified are *themselves* signs—that is, are representative ideas—their originals may be *mediately* signified by those words. Our ideas of substances are Locke's paradigm cases of representative ideas, and regarding common names of substances he says:

> . . . our names of substances being not put barely for our *ideas*, but being made use of ultimately to represent things, . . . their signification must agree with the truth of things as well as with men's *ideas*. And therefore in substances, we are not always to rest in the ordinary complex *idea* commonly received as the signification of that word [III, xi, 24].

There are, as I have acknowledged, many other passages in the *Essay* that seem to leave Locke open to the charge of taking the untenable position that one cannot use a word except as a proper name for an idea in one's mind; but that is not the position to which his argument commits him, and that cannot be read into the main thesis of his semantic theory as long as the phrase 'primarily or immediately' is properly emphasized and understood,[15] even if many other details implicit in the thesis are ignored.

I think that the thesis and even Locke's own distortions of it can be better appreciated when one recognizes that he *was* concerned to distinguish between a name's signification and what the name was used to refer to, and that this concern was part of what motivated his semantic theory. Suppose I imagine that because the substance in the ring on my finger is correctly *called* 'gold', that substance itself is the *signification* of the name 'gold'. In Locke's view this would be to imagine that the name 'gold' was applied (*per impossibile*) to signify that substance *immediately*. Of such a case Locke says:

---

[15] This phrase or some near equivalent of it occurs in the appropriate context at least twelve times in Book Three: e.g. III, i, 6; III, ii, 1; III, ii, 2 (twice); III, ii, 4; III, ii, 6; III, ii, 7; III, iv, 1; III, iv, 2; III, ix, 13; III, ix, 18; III, x, 3; cf. II, xxxi, 7; II, xxxii, 1; II, xxxii, 26; III, x, 18; IV, vi, 7; IV, vi, 8; IV, xviii, 3; and Locke's marginal heading for III, ii, 2 (see Fraser's edition).

. . . by this tacit reference to the real essence of that species of bodies, the word 'gold' (which, by standing for a more or less perfect collection of simple ideas, serves to design [i.e. to designate] that sort of body well enough in civil discourse) comes to have no signification at all, being put for somewhat whereof we have no idea at all, *and so can signify nothing at all when the body itself is away*.[16]

Near the beginning of this examination of the argument for the main thesis of Locke's semantic theory I said that the thesis might be fairly summarized as 'Words signify ideas'. In the critical tradition that summary formula, or one equally abbreviated and simplified, has often been taken to *be* the thesis. I hope it is clear by now that the formula 'Words signify ideas' summarizes a thesis of more subtlety and insight than is usually discerned in Locke's semantic theory, a thesis never better stated by Locke himself than in this explanatory passage from the third chapter of Book Three:

. . . the signification and use of words depending on that connexion which the mind makes between its *ideas* and the sounds it uses as signs of them, it is necessary, in the application of names to things, that the mind should have distinct *ideas* of the things, and retain also the particular name that belongs to every one, with its peculiar appropriation to that *idea* [III, iii, 2].

VI

So far I have been trying to show that the main thesis of Locke's semantic theory is not as bad as Locke's presentation of it and the critical tradition have made it look. I want to conclude by suggesting that Locke could have given it a presentation that was simpler, stronger, and more obviously unified with his way of ideas if he had appreciated the implications for his semantic theory in his own conception of the nature of a word.

Locke never considers the nature of a word as a topic for discussion in its own right, but he often alludes to it in the *Essay*, and the clearest among his many scattered remarks tend overwhelmingly to suggest that he takes words to be *identical with* articulate sounds. For example, at the very beginning of the Book entitled 'Of Words', where he might be expected to be most conscious of and conscientious about the question of the nature of a word, he speaks of '*articulate sounds*, which we call words'.[17] Such an identification of course obliterates ordinary distinctions between words and nonsense syllables, between utterances and inscriptions, between type and tokens. As we shall see, Locke cannot, even within his own theory, maintain quite so radical a view; and there is evidence enough to show that he did not intend to maintain it in quite so pure a form as that in which he often expresses it. Still, this *is* the form

[16] III, x, 19; emphasis and single quotation marks added.
[17] III, i, 1; see also III, ii, 1, quoted above.

in which he most often expresses it, and it has the advantage of great simplicity; and those seem to be two good reasons for examining it to begin with.

It is unmistakably clear from the discussions in Book Two that Locke holds that *every sound is an idea*, and so every articulate sound is an idea.[18] Locke brings this out explicitly in his discussion of 'simple modes of the simple ideas of sensation':

The like variety have we in sounds. Every articulate word is a different *modification of sound*; by which we see that from the sense of hearing by such modifications the mind may be furnished with distinct *ideas* to almost an infinite number [II, xviii, 3].

Thus if words are articulate sounds (which he suggests here as well as elsewhere), *every word is an idea*.

Now of course Locke does recognize inscriptions as well as utterances, and the use of words in thought without any sound, but since he recognizes words to be *originally* articulate sounds (in their primary, communicative use), he is likely to speak of words even as used in recording thoughts and in thinking as 'articulate sounds'. This is not so surprising when we remember that inscriptions can themselves be considered (according to the way of ideas) as ideas of visual sensation, associated with those ideas of auditory sensation, and that words used in thinking will be ideas of reflection having those ideas of auditory sensation as their originals.[19] And of course Locke does tacitly employ something like a type/token distinction; he often speaks, for example, of several persons using the same word. The type (on this view) will be the abstract idea derived from sufficiently similar particular ideas of auditory sensation, and they, as we have seen, will constitute the primary tokens.

Thus although Locke does not strictly maintain what he sometimes says—namely, that words are identical with articulate sounds—he does hold that words are primarily articulate sounds, and the modifications that must be made in that overly strict form of his view of the nature of words are all completely compatible with the position that every word is an idea.

Locke did not *recognize* this to be his position, however, as is clear from any number of considerations[20]—most obviously from his regular distinction between words and ideas as two sorts of signs. Locke seems to have meant by this distinction that words and representative ideas were two sorts of entities, alike in their signifying. It is my contention that he ought to have recognized that they were entities of a single sort—ideas—but different sorts of signs, in

[18] See esp. II, viii, 8 together with II, viii, 17.

[19] On the use of reflective ideas of sounds in thought see the latter (unquoted) half of II, xviii, 3.

[20] See, e.g., III, ii, 1, quoted above, and IV, xi, 7, where Locke concludes that 'there will be little reason left to doubt that those words I write do really exist without me, when they cause a long series of regular sounds to affect my ears, which could not be the effect of my imagination, nor could my memory retain them in that order'.

that a representative idea cannot be said to signify in the way in which a word can be said to signify, as we shall see. If he had recognized this as his position and drawn on it, the presentation of his theories of knowledge and of meaning would surely have been far more unified. There is, moreover, at least one historically important weakness in the way of ideas that might have been discovered by Locke himself if he had founded his semantic theory on the recognition that within the way of ideas words *are* ideas.

Before saying what that weakness is, I want to examine the effect of Locke's position on the nature of words on his doctrine of the three sorts of perception. It is, I think, the most instructive single illustration of the changes that would result from the recognition that words are ideas. The doctrine of the three sorts of perception is stated in the following passage.

The power of perception is that which we call the *understanding*. Perception, which we make the act of the understanding, is of three sorts: (1) The perception of *ideas* in our minds. (2) The perception of the signification of signs. (3) The perception of the connexion or repugnancy, agreement or disagreement, that there is between any of our *ideas* [II, xxi, 5].

I take it that whatever else may count as a case of Perception 2, a case of my understanding a word used by someone else must count. Suppose, then, that someone drops a lump of metal into my hand and I say 'What is it?' and he says 'Gold' and I know what he means. How is my end of this paradigm case of Perception 2 to be analysed in terms of the three sorts of perception and the realization that the way of ideas implies that every word is an idea? I see and feel the lump of metal: that is, I perceive a particular complex idea of sensation in my mind—an instance of Perception 1. Next, I hear the sound 'gold': that is, I perceive a particular simple idea of sensation in my mind—a second instance of Perception 1. Next, I perceive an abstract complex idea in my mind (yellow-heavy-malleable-fusible-fixed-etc.)—a third instance of Perception 1. Next, I perceive that the sound 'gold' is in my mind associated with, or 'annexed to', that abstract complex idea: that is, I perceive a connection between two of my ideas—an instance of Perception 3. Finally, I perceive a connection between my abstract complex idea of gold and my particular complex idea of the lump of metal—a second instance of Perception 3—or else I fail to perceive such a connection: that is, either I think my interlocutor is right or I am (at best) uncertain about it.

The result is that when Perception 2, the perception of the signification of *signs*, is considered as the perception of the signification of *words*, it is analysable entirely in terms of Perceptions 1 and 3; and the signification of words is shown to be simply a special case of the connection of ideas. Special in what respects? Not in respect of some special status for words among other ideas of auditory sensation. As Locke says toward the end of Book Four,

'Words, by their immediate operation on us, cause no other *ideas* but of their natural sounds' (IV, xviii, 3). (Locke does speak here of words as causing rather than being ideas, but that mode of expression is of no special importance. He frequently, and apologetically, uses expressions that properly apply only to ideas as convenient means of referring to those 'powers' of which the ideas are the perceivable effects.[21] In the case of articulate sounds those powers would, I suppose, consist of the motions of the vocal apparatus and the resultant motions of the air.)

There are, I think, at least and perhaps only four respects in which the signification of words is to be differentiated as a special case of the connection of ideas.

In the first place, if the connection is the sort that can be called 'signification' it must be a *perceived* connection. When I hear and understand the word 'gold' I do not merely, upon perceiving that particular simple idea 'of sensation in my mind, undergo a second Perception 1 and perceive the appropriate abstract complex idea in my mind. I do, of course, perceive that complex idea, but its appearance on this particular occasion in no way surprises me. I am not tempted to say, 'Whatever made that pop into my head?' because I know what made it pop into my head; and if I did not know that, I could not be said to have understood the word 'gold' even though I did hear the sound and immediately perceived the appropriate abstract complex idea. I must perceive the connection between those ideas, at least in the sense that if asked at once why I now perceived that abstract complex idea, I could answer, 'Because of the connection between it and the sound "gold" in my mind.' To perceive the signification of a sign cannot be simply to perceive what it signifies, for one might perceive that without realizing that it was what the sign signified; one might, in fact, perceive that in the absence of the sign. Not every case of a perceived connection between one's ideas is a case of the signification of a word, needless to say; but every case of a connection between one's ideas that can count as a case of the signification of a word is a perceived connection. That is the first respect in which the signification of a word must differ from some other sorts of connections of ideas for Locke.

The second respect is that the idea perceived to be connected with the sound as that which the sound primarily, immediately signifies must be abstract rather than particular. If the idea connected with the sound is particular, the connection may be one of proper-naming rather than of signifying, as if the child in the example quoted on page 132 above had applied the sound 'gold' to signify the particular yellow colour in one particular peacock's tail and hence had equipped himself to call nothing 'gold' but that. Or it may be some more or less idiosyncratic, non-semantic association between the sound and

[21] See esp. II, xxxi, 2.

some experience of the person who hears (whether or not he also produces) the sound. In his chapter on the 'association of ideas' Locke provides a perfect example of the sort of connection of ideas in which just one of the two ideas is a word or articulate sound and in which the connection between that idea and the other is a perceived connection and that must nevertheless be distinguished from the signification-connection in this respect. 'A grown person surfeiting with honey', Locke observes, 'no sooner hears the name of it, but his fancy immediately carries sickness and qualms to his stomach' (II, xxxiii, 7). The particular complex idea constituting the feeling of nausea is not what 'honey' signifies or any part of what it signifies, even for this surfeiting grown person.

In the third place, the signification-connection must admit of arbitrary change. (Locke stresses this condition of the signification of words and sometimes overstresses it,[22] though not, of course, in just this context.) The man who feels nauseated even on hearing the sound 'honey' surely can distinguish between his feeling of nausea and the nominal essence of honey. Moreover, he could continue to draw that distinction even if every other English-speaking person were likewise and invariably subject to that association between the sound 'honey' and the feeling of nausea, as may be illustrated by the case of obscene words. And it seems to me that another important ground of this distinction (besides the one mentioned in the paragraph immediately above) is that he could readily change the *signification* of 'honey' (at least for himself, as in a private code) and could not readily alter this other perceived connection between that sound and the particular complex idea constituting his feeling of nausea, not even—at least not in the short run—by altering the signification of that sound.[23]

The fourth and perhaps the final respect in which applying a word to signify an idea is to be distinguished from other cases of connecting ideas is that, despite the alterability of the connection, the person in whose mind the connecting takes place must be disposed to act in accordance with it. Connecting a word with some abstract idea will count as applying that word to signify that idea only if one intends to go on to call such particulars as match the abstract idea by the name connected with the idea. Locke saw that it was important to guard the signification of words against 'inconstancy', but in

---

[22] See, e.g., III, ii, 8: '[words] *signify* only men's peculiar *ideas*, and that *by a perfect arbitrary imposition*'.

[23] Cf. the discussion of an interesting parallel example in Paul Ziff, *Semantic Analysis* (Ithaca, N.Y., 1960), pp. 54 ff. 'Roughly speaking, if one finds out with respect to the woman in question that if she hears the word "date" uttered then generally she experiences abdominal discomforts one has found out nothing whatever about her language or dialect or idiolect . . . a necessary but not a sufficient condition of a regularity being semantically relevant in the analysis of a corpus is that the speakers of the language associated with the corpus can deviate from the regularity at will.' (pp. 56 f.)

keeping with his practical concerns he concentrated on inveighing against such kinds and degrees of inconstancy as are merely symptomatic of 'great folly or greater dishonesty' in the user of the word rather than destructive of the character of the signification-connection itself:

Words being intended for signs of my *ideas* to make them known to others, not by any natural signification but by a voluntary imposition, it is plain cheat and abuse when I make them stand sometimes for one thing and sometimes for another [III, x, 5].

Occasionally, however, he seems also to have understood that constancy is an *essential* aspect of the signification-connection:

But so far as words are of use and signification, so far is there a constant connexion between the sound and the *idea* [III, ii, 7].

On page 126 above I presented a standard version of the main thesis of Locke's semantic theory: *Words in their primary or immediate signification signify nothing but the ideas in the mind of him that uses them.* What this thesis might have been if Locke had recognized all the implications in his way of ideas for his semantic theory may be suggested by glossing the thesis in the light of this discussion. *Words* (that is, such concrete particular [simple or complex] ideas of auditory sensation as are ordinarily described as articulate sounds, together with their related abstract ideas of sensation and ideas of reflection) *in their primary or immediate signification* (that is, in the connection with something other than themselves that is essential to their being used to refer to anything at all) *signify* (that is, are in a perceived, arbitrarily alterable, action-governing connection with) *nothing but the ideas* (that is, nothing but certain abstract [simple or complex] ideas) *in the mind of him that uses them* (that is, in the mind of the person who produces those articulate sounds as devices by means of which to refer to something).

While Locke himself never maintained this thesis in all these details, it came to be maintained in some of the most noteworthy though not all of its details by men who considered themselves Locke's philosophical heirs—David Hartley (especially in Chapter III, Section I, 'Words, and the Ideas associated with them', of his *Observations on Man*, first published in 1749) and James Mill (especially in Chapters IV and XIV of his *Analysis of the Phenomena of the Human Mind*, first published in 1829).

I have said something about the advantages I think there would have been for Locke's semantic theory if he had recognized that his own way of ideas implied that words are themselves ideas and that the signification of words is a special case of the connection of ideas. This move, however, provides no account of the signification of non-ideas by representative ideas; and, since the only account of signification provided by this move is in terms of the connection of ideas with one another, it suggests no particular way in which an account of the signification of representative ideas might be devised.

The difficulties over *that* sort of signification, which have often been thought of as constituting the most formidable obstacle on the way of ideas, are the familiar difficulties with Locke's perception theory. In this paper my concern has been to examine and refurbish only Locke's semantic theory.

IX

SOME REMARKS ON LOCKE'S ACCOUNT OF KNOWLEDGE

A. D. WOOZLEY

LOCKE's account of knowledge in *Essay* Book IV has led commentators either to reach for their hatchets or to shake their heads in sorrowful despair; the former eagerly point out, the latter sadly admit, the collapse of the theory of ideas of Book II when subjected to the pressure of supporting the relation of knowledge as the bridge between our ideas and the reality which they are about. *Prima facie* Locke is fair and embarrassingly easy game for his critics. If 'our knowledge is only conversant about' our ideas (IV, i, 1), how could anything be known, whether *a priori* or empirically, about the world outside ideas? and how could any existential proposition be known to be true—or be known to be false? Alternatively, if empirical knowledge is to be possible, such as, for example, that this is a table in front of me, or that tables have level tops, that cows ruminate, that aluminium is rustless, etc., how can knowledge be so narrowly characterized as the perception of 'the agreement or disagreement of two *ideas*' (IV, ii, 1)? What sort of agreement is coexistence? and how is real existence agreement of any sort?

And yet, if these objections are so obvious, why were they not obvious to Locke? The *Essay*, after all, was not the explosion of an excited young man's genius, as Berkeley's *Principles* and Hume's *Treatise* arguably were. It was the fruit of long, patient and cautious nurture, and was almost twenty years agrowing; surely even an under-labourer should in that time have spotted weeds that rank and obvious?

Locke is usually taken to define knowledge as the perception of the agreement (or disagreement) *between* ideas. (For brevity I shall, from now on, omit references to disagreement.) But is it possible that that view is wrong? Certainly he does not in the *Essay* explicitly so *define* knowledge. The explicit definition (IV, i, 2) is of knowledge as the perception of the agreement *of*

From the *Locke Newsletter*, 3 (1972), pp. 7–17. Reprinted by permission of the author and the editor, Roland Hall.

'any of our ideas'. Of our ideas with what? He never actually *says* that the perceived agreement must be between ideas and ideas, so maybe he meant that sometimes it could be between ideas and things other than ideas, e.g. physical objects. This would account for his listing coexistence and existence together with identity (or diversity) and relation (IV, i, 3). It would not necessarily acquit him of the charge of inconsistency in his theory of knowledge, but it would explain his thinking that there was none. That this is the correct reading of Locke, that he did suppose that the second term of the perceived relation might be something other than an idea, has recently been maintained by J. W. Yolton:

the knowledge relation . . . does not always require two ideas, is not always *between* ideas but is in some cases a feature *of* ideas. The perception of any kind of relation between or of ideas can produce knowledge. The term 'agreement' signals an intimation of something beyond the idea itself. Sometimes the intimation is of other ideas contingently coexisting with the idea, other times it is of other ideas necessarily connected with the idea, still other times the agreement intimates some physical cause producing the idea. [J. W. Yolton, *Locke and the Compass of Human Understanding*, p. 110; Cambridge: Cambridge University Press, 1970.]

But it is not as easy as that. There is a distinction which Locke carefully preserves, but which Yolton in that passage does not, the blurring being perhaps foreshadowed by the ambiguous expression 'knowledge relation' which he uses, when he says that according to Locke it is not always between ideas. If taken as the relation of knowing, the knowledge relation is not between ideas, it is the relation of perceiving between the mind as the first term and as the second term the relational complex consisting of the agreement between an idea as the first term of that complex and whatever else is allowable as the second term of that complex. If taken as the relation known, the knowledge relation is the relation of agreement composing that complex. Now, there is no doubt (1) that Locke believed that the second term of an agreement relation was sometimes something other than an idea. Evidence from the text of the *Essay* will be produced for that. But it does not follow (2) that he believed that the agreement could be perceived in the case where the second term was not an idea. We cannot conclude from

(1) not all *agreements* are between ideas

that (2) not all *perceived* agreements are between ideas.

Yolton has Locke sliding from (1) to (2) in a way which would not be defensible, and in a way in which I think he did not. I am convinced that Locke did not believe (2); I am unaware of any textual evidence that he believed it, let alone that he believed it because he believed (1).

Evidence that he believed (1) is plentiful. In Book II, chapters xxx–xxxii, devoted respectively to questions of the reality, adequacy and truth of ideas, are full of references to agreement between ideas on the one hand and that of which they are ideas on the other. 'By *real ideas*, I mean such as have a foundation in nature, such as have a conformity with the real being and existence of things, or with their archetypes' (II, xxx, 1). All simple ideas are real, 'all agree to the reality of things' (II, xxx, 2), while complex ideas of substances are real only to the extent that 'they are such combinations of simple *ideas* as are really united and co-exist in things without us' (II, xxx, 5). Similarly, all simple ideas are adequate: 'being nothing but the effects of certain powers in things, fitted and ordained by God to produce such sensations in us, they cannot but be correspondent and adequate to those powers; and we are sure they agree to the reality of things' (II, xxxi, 2). (Note that there he says not only that simple ideas agree to the reality of things, but that we are *sure* that they do. He is clearly there maintaining proposition (1), and might be taken also to be maintaining proposition (2). But he is not: he does not say that we *know* that simple ideas agree to the reality of things, but that we are *sure* that they do. There may be a difference, in Locke's scheme, between knowing and being sure; at least we cannot assume that there is not.) While simple ideas are '*copies*, but yet certainly *adequate*' (II, xxxi, 12), complex ideas of substances are '*copies* too, but not . . . *adequate*', for the mind cannot be sure of such a complex 'idea, or collection of simple ideas, that it 'exactly answers all that are in that substance' (II, xxxi, 13).

Having argued that correspondingly all simple ideas are true, while complex ideas of substance may not be, Locke summarizes the whole discussion of those three chapters in a final paragraph:

Upon the whole matter, I think that our *ideas*, as they are considered by the mind either in reference to the proper signification of their names or in reference to the reality of things, *may* very fitly *be called right or wrong* ideas, according as they agree or disagree to those patterns to which they are referred [II, xxxii, 26].

When Locke turns in Book IV from discussing ideas and their relations to things other than ideas to discussing knowledge, he shows himself well aware that in the case of existential knowledge it is required, if such knowledge is to be possible, that there be the relation of correspondence or agreement between an idea and 'the existence of anything without us which corresponds to that *idea*' (IV, ii, 14). The presence of this relation is a necessary condition of such knowledge, but it is not yet sufficient; we need also to be able to 'certainly infer' its presence. (Note here that he says, not that we have to be able to *know* or *perceive* this relation of agreement between idea and object, but that we have to be able certainly to *infer* it. And whatever inferring is for Locke, it does not seem to be a way of perceiving. The word 'infer', which might have been thought appropriate to an analysis of demonstrative knowledge and of its distinction from intuitive knowledge, nowhere occurs in Locke's account of demonstration; there he followed familiar Cartesian lines, demonstration consisting in a sequence of linked intuitions, perceptions or seeings following the chain of proof from premisses to conclusion; but nothing is said about inferring conclusion from premisses. Inferring appears to be something which is not perceiving.)

The point that knowledge of existence requires there to be a relation of agreement between an idea and what is not an idea is elaborated in IV, xi where, having in the preceding two chapters dealt with the question of his knowledge of his own existence, and of the existence of God, he turns to the problem of knowledge of the existence of other things, the problem being as before that on the one hand such knowledge requires the presence of a relation of agreement between ideas and reality, while on the other hand 'the having the *idea* of anything in our mind no more proves the existence of that thing, than the picture of a man evidences his being in the world, or the visions of a dream make thereby a true history' (IV, xi, 1).

Locke then certainly believed proposition (1), that ideas can be related by agreement to things other than ideas. But did he believe proposition (2), that such an agreement (i.e. where the second term is not an idea) is perceivable? If he did believe it, why did he never in so many words say so? Why did he make such heavy weather of empirical knowledge in general, and of what he called sensitive knowledge in particular? Why, when talking of 'the notice we have by our senses of the existing of things without us', did he persistently talk, not of 'knowledge', but of 'assurance' (IV, xi, 3)? And why did he say (in that same paragraph) that assurance 'deserves the name of knowledge', if he could have said more simply that assurance *is* knowledge? On the other hand, if he did not believe proposition (2), i.e. if he did believe that all knowledge was perception of agreement *between* ideas, how does he escape the familiar charge that, closed within the circle of ideas, he failed to realize both that the claim to existential knowledge must be vacuous, and that it is inconsistent with his definition of knowledge?

I think that all these questions can be answered by paying faithful enough attention to his own words.

First, I think the conclusion is unavoidable that Locke did not believe proposition (2). If he did, it is beyond comprehension why he never said so, especially when he had so many opportunities in Book IV for doing so. I have cited two passages where, if he had believed that we could perceive agreement between ideas and objects that are not ideas, the terminology of knowing would have been appropriate, but instead he used the terminology of assurance and of being sure. There is one more very important paragraph,

IV, iv, 18 (which I inexcusably omitted from my abridged edition, but which is to be added in the next impression). It runs:

Wherever we perceive the agreement or disagreement of any of our *ideas*, there is certain knowledge; and wherever we are sure those *ideas* agree with the reality of things, there is certain real knowledge. Of which agreement of our *ideas* with the reality of things having here given the marks, I think I have shown wherein it is that *certainty, real certainty*, consists.

Here we have it all in summary form: (a) where we have agreement between ideas and other ideas, and when we *perceive* that agreement, we have certain knowledge; (b) where we have agreement between ideas and the reality of things, and where we are *sure* of that agreement, we have certain real knowledge. (Locke is not always consistent in his use of 'real knowledge'. Here, it is knowledge of what is real, so that knowledge within pure, as opposed to applied, mathematics would be certain but not real; whereas my knowledge that I now have a sheet of white paper before me is both certain and real. On the other hand, he elsewhere uses 'real knowledge' to mean what really is knowledge, so that within pure mathematics real knowledge is possible; cf. IV, iv, 6 and *Conduct of the Understanding*, §15.)

However, the clearest evidence that Locke did not believe proposition (2) is his denial of it. Passages in the *Essay* are not totally without ambiguity, although IV, ii, 15 ('our knowledge consisting in the perception of the agreement or disagreement of any two *ideas*') and IV, iii, 1 might be thought fairly definite. In any case, the posthumously published *Conduct of the Understanding* is absolute conclusive. 'Knowledge consists in nothing but the perceived agreement or disagreement of those ideas' (§9), where the context makes clear that he means the perceived agreement or disagreement of those ideas (of obligation and of justice) with each other. 'It is in the perception of the habitudes and respects our ideas have one to another, that real knowledge consists' (§15). Finally and clinchingly, 'knowledge consists only in perceiving the habitudes and relations of ideas one to another' (§31). If knowledge consists *only* in that, it cannot consist *also* in something else, i.e. it cannot ever consist in perceiving the relations of ideas to non-ideas.

In that case how is knowledge of existential matters of fact, and specifically sensible knowledge, possible at all? And why does Locke ever use the word 'knowledge' in this area, when the relation of agreement (between ideas and the reality of things), which is necessary to the possibility of such knowledge, is itself such that, on Locke's own view of knowledge, it cannot be perceived? In the case of purported sensitive knowledge is there any agreement which is perceived? Objections along these lines were raised by Stillingfleet, and prompted the following response from Locke.

In the last place, your lordship argues, that because I say, that the idea in the mind
proves not the existence of that thing whereof it is an idea, therefore we cannot know
the actual existence of any thing by our senses: because we know nothing, but by the
perceived agreement of ideas. . . . Now the two ideas, that in this case are perceived
to agree, and do thereby produce knowledge, are the idea of actual sensation (which
is an action whereof I have a clear and distinct idea) and the idea of actual existence
of something without me that causes that sensation. And what other certainty your
lordship has by your senses of the existing of any thing without you, but the perceived
connexion of those two ideas, I would gladly know. [*Second Reply*, Works IV, 360.]

Yolton (p. 112) criticizes Locke's response as 'misleading, even on his own
account of thinking, perceiving, etc. . . . it is not the *idea* of actual sensation
which carries the agreement with physical causes but the receiving of sensory
ideas. To translate the real-existence relation as holding between the idea of
actual sensation and the idea of actual existence without me leaves the nature
of the agreement in this case unclear'. But here it is not Locke who is misleading, it is Yolton who is confused. Locke, of course, agrees that it is not
the idea of actual sensation, but the receiving of sensory ideas, which carries
the agreement with physical causes. But Locke did *not* translate the real existence relation (between idea of actual sensation and actual existence without
me) into a relation between the idea of actual sensation and the idea of actual
existence. Locke keeps the two relations perfectly distinct. Only the relation
between idea of sensation and idea of existence is perceived; and this perception amounts to knowledge only when it is *both* the case that the other relation,
between the idea of actual sensation and actual existence without me, is there,
and the case that I am *sure* (or have assurance) that it is. To requote *Essay*
IV, iv, 18. 'Wherever we perceive the agreement or disagreement of any of
our *ideas*, there is certain knowledge; and wherever we are sure those *ideas*
agree with the reality of things, there is certain real knowledge.' Knowledge
of existence, like the other three categories of knowledge, is still perception of
the agreement or disagreement of ideas, with in its case the qualification added
that we have to be sure that there is the further agreement or disagreement
between ideas and actual existence without us.

   This presents Locke's account as coherent, and makes sense of his hesitation
whether or not to admit as knowledge supposed 'sensitive knowledge of
particular existence' a perception which 'passes under the name of knowledge'
(IV, ii, 14). The hesitation is there because we do *not* perceive the relation
of agreement between ideas and the reality of things. 'How shall the mind,
when it perceives nothing but its own *ideas*, know that they agree with things
themselves?' (IV, iv, 3). The hesitation is removed when Locke is satisfied
that in a limited set of cases, notably in the case of present sensation, although
we do not *know* that this agreement is there (given his definition of knowledge,
it is in principle impossible to know that the agreement is there), we are *assured*

that it is. In such a case we do have sensitive knowledge of particular existence, for what we know (the agreement perceived between ideas of sensation and of existence) is backed by assurance of the further agreement between ideas and things themselves; while the definition of knowledge precludes that assurance from *being* knowledge, it is reasonable to say that 'it is an assurance that *deserves the name of knowledge*'.

But coherence is not enough; justification is another thing. Did Locke have any good reason for characterizing sensitive knowledge, even in part, as a perception of a relation *between ideas*? And how, on such a view, as Stillingfleet persistently asked, could scepticism be avoided; how could the assurance, on which Locke's whole scheme depended, be possible?

On the primitive dualism of ideas and things which has long persisted as the accepted interpretation of Locke's epistemology, he is not to be taken seriously at all. But that interpretation is itself hardly to be taken seriously at all, as Yolton argues (pp. 133–4), and as I have argued elsewhere (*Essay*, abridged ed., Fontana Library, 1964, pp. 24–35). When Locke spoke, in his reply to Stillingfleet, of perceiving an agreement between an idea of actual sensation and an idea of actual existence of something without, he was not talking about a couple of mental images, or about any pair of items from his private mental inventory. The view which he was presenting was much less silly than that. Suppose that in fact there is a table in front of me: I believe there is one because I believe I am seeing one. In what I take to be a veridical case (whether or not it actually is one), I perceive a match (agreement) between what it is that I think is there and what it is that I think I see. In what I take to be a non-veridical case (whether or not it actually is one), I perceive a mismatch (disagreement) between what it is that I think is there and what it is that I think I see. Sometimes I believe my eyes, sometimes I don't; and neither the belief nor the disbelief is self-certifying. It looks as though what I see is a stage magician sawing his assistant in half; I may believe that he is, I may disbelieve that he is; and in either case I may be right, or I may be wrong. There is, in principle, no problem about verifying my perceptual and my existential claims, but the verification is subject always to the limitation that it is done (using sight as the example) by what I think I see. The 'I think' there is not the 'I think' of hesitation, of feeling doubt or uncertainty, or of playing safe by not being totally committal. It is the 'I think' which marks the subjectivity of awareness, that seeing is seeing as, that the only way in which I can see anything is as I see it. Consequently, if awareness has to be what it is, how can I ever get from knowing that what I see I see as a rose to knowing that what I see is in fact a rose?

To bridge this gap Locke relies on principles like Reid's explicit and Moore's less explicit principles of common sense: that, in the ordinary course of events, we have no problem in discriminating between sensings on the one hand and imaginings or rememberings on the other; that sensings have to be caused by external objects; and that perceptual claims are safe as long as they are confined to claims about objects causing present sensings (IV, ii, 14; IV, xi, *passim*). 'Of the *existence* of anything else [than of oneself and of God], we have no other but a sensitive knowledge, which extends not beyond the objects present to our senses' (IV, iii, 21). Locke took one step beyond the red-here-now school, but only one, just as far as the a-rose-here-now position.

If Locke has an Achilles' heel, it will be in the acceptance of the principles which give the assurance which makes knowledge possible. And if he has that Achilles' heel, who hasn't?

X

THE NATURE AND SOURCES OF LOCKE'S VIEWS ON HYPOTHESES

LAURENS LAUDAN

I

IT has often been assumed that John Locke was primarily an epistemologist with only a casual and superficial interest in the physical sciences. Despite the fact that he studied medicine and spoke glowingly of figures like Newton and Boyle,[1] Locke's *Essay* seems—at least on the surface—to be concerned with the epistemology of common sense rather than with the logic and methods of theoretical science. Philosophers, by reading history backwards, have written as if Locke accepted the view of Berkeley and Hume that the empiricist philosophy should not be based on a 'scientific' metaphysics. Furthermore, in so far as the *Essay* does deal with scientific matters, it usually seems to treat them with derision and condescension. Consequently, some commentators have inferred that Locke was an opponent of the corpuscular philosophy which dominated the physics of his day and have viewed his *Essay* as an attempt to develop a theory of knowledge with no corpuscularian, or other quasi-scientific, bias. They suggest that Locke was opposed not only to the atomic hypothesis, but to the use of virtually all hypotheses in science. Those commentators who do not explicitly attribute an anti-hypothetical view to Locke generally leave unmentioned his remarks about scientific method, as if meta-science was foreign to the spirit of the *Essay*,[2] Recently, however, Maurice Mandelbaum has pointed out not only that Locke was sympathetic to the corpuscular programme, but that an atomic view of nature is essential to

From *Journal of the History of Ideas*, 28 (1967), pp. 211–23. The paper has been amended and a postscript added. It is reprinted by permission of the author and the editor of the journal.

[1] In a classic piece of understatement, Locke speaks of himself as an 'under-labourer' to the scientists Boyle, Sydenham, Huygens, and 'the incomparable Mr. *Newton*' (*Essay*, 'Epistle to the Reader').

[2] Among those who have taken the above interpretation of Locke, the most prominent are probably R. I. Aaron, *John Locke* (Oxford, 1955), J. Gibson, *Locke's Theory of Knowledge* (Cambridge, 1960), and J. W. Yolton, *John Locke and the Way of Ideas* (Oxford, 1956).

Locke's epistemology and metaphysics.[3] Rather than read Locke in the light of Berkeley's criticisms, Mandelbaum urges us to approach the *Essay* with the atomic theories of Boyle and Newton in mind. It is surely as important to understand Locke in terms of his contemporaries and predecessors as it is to view him as a forerunner of Berkeley.

In this paper, I want to build upon Mandelbaum's analysis by looking carefully at the theory of scientific method implicit in the *Essay*. For if Mandelbaum is right that Locke was vitally concerned with corpuscular physics, then we have every reason to expect that the *Essay* will provide guidelines for the way in which Locke—a lifelong scientist himself—wanted to see science develop. Although it is hoped that this paper will substantiate Mandelbaum's reading of Locke as a corpuscularian, from a slightly different point of view, its primary aim is to ascertain Locke's attitude on the role of hypotheses in science. The bearing of this latter problem on Mandelbaum's thesis should be clear; if Locke was as anti-hypothetical as most writers have made him out to be, then he could not conceivably have embraced so hypothetical a theory as the atomic one. Conversely, if Locke was sympathetic to the use of hypotheses in physics, then it would not be surprising if he adopted the corpuscular philosophy as enthusiastically as Mandelbaum maintains he did.

Perhaps the best place to begin is in response to one of the most detailed studies of Locke's methodology; namely, that of R. M. Yost.[4] In his lengthy analysis of the methodology of the *Essay*, Yost comes to the conclusion that Locke was not only sceptical about the scientific value of the atomic philosophy, but that he objected—on epistemic and methodological grounds—to all scientific theories which employed hypotheses about unobservable events or objects. More specifically, Yost claims that 'unlike many scientists and philosophers of the seventeenth century, Locke did not believe that the employment of hypotheses about sub-microscopic events would accelerate the acquisition of empirical knowledge'.[5] Yost insists that while Locke allowed, albeit grudgingly, the use of hypotheses about observable events, he was categorically opposed to all hypotheses dealing with the behaviour and properties of unobservable forces and atoms. He contrasts Locke's views on this subject with those of such seventeenth-century atomists as Boyle and Descartes, who endorsed the use of hypotheses about unobservable events. Yost suggests that Locke's opposition to hypothetical reasoning was a radical

---

[3] Mandelbaum, *Philosophy, Science and Sense Perception* (Baltimore, 1964), 1–60. I can do no better than cite Mandelbaum's own summary of his thesis: 'The conclusion which I wish to draw . . . is that Locke, throughout his career, was an atomist, and that he accepted both the truth and the scientific usefulness (or, at least, the scientific promise) of the corpuscular, or new experimental, philosophy' (ibid. 14).

[4] R. M. Yost, Jr., 'Locke's Rejection of Hypotheses about Sub-Microscopic Events', *Jrnl. of the History of Ideas*, XII (1951), 111–30.

[5] Ibid. 111.

departure from the hypothetical methodology which accompanied the atomism of his contemporaries. Unfortunately Yost's analysis seems to overlook many of Locke's crucial pronouncements on methodology while it obscures the meaning of others. For not only did Locke look favourably on many uses of the hypothetical method, but in doing so he was squarely within, rather than aligned against, the corpuscularian tradition. To develop this argument, I shall work in two directions. To begin with, I want to determine precisely what Locke's attitude towards sub-microscopic hypotheses was. I shall then turn to consider his debt to the corpuscular philosophers who preceded and influenced him.

II

The casual reader of Locke's *Essay* invariably comes away from that volume with the firm suspicion that Locke was uniformly pessimistic about the natural sciences. Apart from the general scepticism which forms the dominant motif of the fourth book of the *Essay*, there are numerous specific passages which reinforce this impression. Thus, Locke asserts:

As to a perfect *science* of natural bodies ... we are, I think, so far from being capable of any such thing that I conclude it lost labour to seek after it.[6]

If it is ill-conceived even to attempt to develop a science of mechanics, how hopeless must the situation be for other branches of scientific inquiry? Elsewhere, he writes that 'scientifical' knowledge of nature is for ever out of our reach.[7] Or again, he sadly proclaims that mechanics must not 'pretend to certainty and demonstration', and that there can never be a 'science of bodies' (ibid.). Locke's pessimism seems especially pronounced whenever he discusses the corpuscularian programme for explaining the observable world in terms of the motion and concretions of unobservable atoms. Thus,

Because the active and passive powers of bodies and their ways of operating consisting in a texture and motion of parts which we cannot by any means come to discover. ...[8]

Or,

I doubt not but, if we could discover the figure, size, texture, and motion of the minute constituent parts of any two bodies, we should know *without trial* several of their operations upon one another. ... But whilst we are destitute of senses acute enough [to perceive such corpuscles] ... we must be content to be ignorant of their properties and ways of operation.[9]

---

[6] *Essay*, IV, iii, 29.
[7] Ibid. IV, iii, 26. Cf. also IV, xii, 10.
[8] Ibid. IV, iii, 16.
[9] Ibid. VI, iii, 25. Italics added. Elsewhere, he writes: 'Thus having no *ideas* of the particular mechanical affections of the minute parts of the bodies that are within our view and reach, we are ignorant of their constitutions, powers, and operations. ...' Ibid. IV, iii, 26.

Passages like these have disposed many historians to interpret Locke as a critic of hypothetical science in general, and of corpuscularian theories in particular. But in fact Locke was neither of these. To see the flaws in caricaturing Locke as an anti-hypotheticalist, we need only recall that he devoted an entire section of the fourth book of the *Essay* (IV, xii, 13) to the 'true use of hypotheses' and that he frequently spoke as if the phenomena of the visible world ultimately derived from interactions on the corpuscular level.[10] But if such remarks indicate Locke's acceptance of the hypothetical method, we are confronted, when we compare them with *obiter dicta* like those cited above, with an apparent tension between Locke's simultaneous denunciation and acceptance of hypotheses.

To resolve this seeming contradiction, we need only invoke Locke's pivotal distinction between knowledge and judgement. Knowledge, for him, is based on a true and infallible intuition of the relation of ideas. To know that a statement *x* is true is to perceive that we could not conceive things to be other than the state of affairs which *x* specifies. In this way, we 'know' the truth of mathematics. But we do not 'know' anything about the physical world.[11] Many statements the scientist makes may be highly probable, but they are not indubitably true and, because of this deficiency, are not in the domain of knowledge. When Locke says that we cannot 'know' anything about the 'minute parts of bodies', he is using 'knowledge' in this technical sense. Since science is the name given to the body of our knowledge, natural philosophy can never be 'scientifical'.[12] But Locke was not so rash as to restrict our discourse rigidly to strictly 'scientific' statements.[13] He recognized clearly that one can say some informative and highly probable things about the

---

[10] As one of the numerous passages where Locke overtly takes a corpuscular view, consider his remark that heat and cold are 'nothing but the increase or diminution of the motion of the minute parts of our bodies, caused by the *corpuscles* of any other body'. Ibid. II, viii, 21 (italics added). Cf. also his *Elements of Natural Philosophy*: 'By the figure, bulk texture, and motion of these small and insensible corpuscles, all the phenomena of bodies may be explained.'

[11] Yolton (in his *Locke and the Compass of Human Understanding*, Cambridge, 1970, p. 117) rightly observes that I have badly oversimplified Locke's views on the nature of certainty.

[12] 'Therefore I am apt to doubt that, how far soever human industry may advance useful and *experimental* philosophy *in physical things, scientifical* [knowledge] will still be out of our reach....' Ibid. IV, iii, 26.

[13] Locke expresses himself thus: 'The understanding faculties being given to man, not barely for speculation, but also for the conduct of his life, man would be at a great loss if he had nothing to direct him but what has the certainty of true *knowledge*. For that being very short and scanty, as we have seen, he would be often utterly in the dark, and in most of the actions of his life perfectly at a stand, had he nothing to guide him in the absence of clear and certain knowledge. He that will not eat till he has demonstration that it will nourish him, he that will not stir till he infallibly knows the business he goes about will succeed, will have little else to do but sit still and perish' (ibid. IV, xiv, 1). Again, he remarks: 'How *vain*, I say, it is *to expect demonstration* and certainty *in things not capable of it*, and refuse assent to very rational propositions . . . because they cannot be made out so evident as to surmount every the least . . . pretence of doubting' (ibid. IV, xi, 10).

physical world. Such statements belong, however, not to knowledge, but to *judgement*:

The faculty which God has given man to supply the want of clear and certain knowledge, in cases where that cannot be bad, is *judgment*: whereby the mind takes . . . any proposition to be true or false, without perceiving a demonstrative evidence in the proofs.[14]

The natural philosopher, Locke tells us, may be able to make many very likely statements but 'the highest probability amounts not to certainty, without which there can be no true knowledge' (ibid., IV, iii, 14). Knowledge, then, consists in those statements which are already clearly and distinctly perceived to be true; judgement consists of all those statements which are merely probable or conjectural. 'Judgement is the presuming things to be so, without perceiving it.'[15]

Having decreed that judgement deals with probable statements, Locke proceeds to argue that there are two sorts of such statements: (1) those dealing with strictly observable phenomena, or 'matters of fact', and (2) speculations dealing with unobservable phenomena.[16] Locke then turns his attention to the second sort of probable statement, viz., speculations about unobservables. Wielding again the logician's axe to split hairs, he argues that there are two types of such speculations: (1) conjectures about purely spiritual beings (e.g. angels, demons, etc.) and (2) hypotheses about the unobservable causes of such natural phenomena as generation, magnetism, and heat.[17] Locke's remarks on this second class are particularly of interest to our argument.

Suppose, Locke reasons, that we want to understand the ultimate nature of heat. Because we do not clearly perceive, or even dimly observe, the causes of heat, we cannot claim to 'know' anything about it.[18] All we can hope to pronounce are *probable* statements about its nature and causes. Since Locke believes that any tentative explanation of heat will be couched in terms of the behaviour of unobservable corpuscles, he insists that observation can tell us nothing *directly* about the behaviour of the heat-producing atoms. How then can we formulate any useful hypotheses at all? Locke's answer is straightforward: by conceiving submicroscopic corpuscles on the *analogy* of bodies which we do perceive, viz., we must picture the smallest particles as miniature instantiations of the gross objects of perception. Indeed, 'in things which

---

[14] Ibid. IV, xiv, 3.

[15] Ibid. IV, xiv, 4.

[16] '. . . the propositions we receive upon inducements of *probability* are *of two sorts*: either concerning some particular existence or, as it is usually termed, matter of fact which, falling under observation, is capable of human testimony; or else concerning things which, being beyond the discovery of our senses, are not capable of any such testimony' (ibid. IV, xvi, 5).

[17] Cf. *Essay*, IV, xvi, 12.

[18] '. . . effects we see and know; but the causes that operate, and the manner they are produced in, we can only guess and probably conjecture.' Ibid. IV, xvi, 12.

sense cannot discover, analogy is the great rule of probability' (ibid.). In the case of heat, the analogy we should make is obvious:

Thus, observing that the bare rubbing of two bodies violently one upon another produces heat, and very often fire itself, we have reason to think that what we call heat and fire consists in a violent agitation of the imperceptible minute parts of the burning matter [ibid.].

We must resort to analogies and models in conceiving the nature of submicroscopic events because, since our conjectures about them cannot be directly verified, the only reason we have for believing them to be even probable is that 'they more or less agree to truths that are established in our minds' and because such conjectures are at least compatible with 'other parts of our knowledge and observation' (ibid.). 'Analogy', he notes, 'in these matters [viz. relating to unobservable events] is the only help we have, and it is from that alone we draw all grounds of probability' (ibid.).

It was a basic tenet of Lockean epistemology that all our ideas of external objects derive from sensation. Thus, it was perfectly natural for him to insist that our ideas about unobservable corpuscles must be based on, and derived from, ideas which visible bodies impress on our senses.

These remarks about analogy-based hypotheses dealing with submicroscopic events are not merely a grudging concession Locke makes to his scientific colleagues. On the contrary, he insists that the enunciation of analogical hypotheses is the most productive and theoretically fertile method which the sciences possess:

This sort of probability, which is the best conduct of rational experiments, and the rise of hypothesis has also its use and influence; and a wary reasoning from analogy leads us often into the discovery of truths and useful productions, which would otherwise lie concealed.[19]

Having said as much, we can see how misleading Yost's remark is that Locke's method employed hypotheses, but they were hypotheses about correlations of observable qualities and did not refer to sub-microscopic mechanisms'.[20] Equally untenable is Yost's view that Locke 'thought that one could infer *something* about submicroscopic mechanisms, but not enough

[19] Ibid. Elsewhere he writes that an accomplished experimenter can often make valuable hypotheses: 'I deny not but [that] a man, accustomed to rational and regular experiments, shall be able to see further into the nature of bodies and guess righter at their yet unknown properties than one that is a stranger to them; but yet, as I have said, this is but judgment and opinion, not knowledge and certainty . . . [hence] natural philosophy is not capable of being made a science' (ibid. IV, xii, 10). Again, he notes: 'Possibly, inquisitive and observing men may by strength of *judgment* penetrate further and, on probabilities taken from wary observation and hints well laid together, often guess right at what experience has not yet discovered to them. But this is but guessing still: it amounts only to opinion and has not that *certainty* which is requisite to knowledge' (ibid. IV, vi, 13).

[20] Yost, op. cit., 127.

to help us in making discoveries'.[21] In the passage cited above, Locke explicitly states that the use of corpuscular hypotheses could lead us 'into the discovery of truths and useful productions'. Elsewhere, he writes that '*hypotheses*, if they are well made, are at least great helps to the memory and often direct us to new discoveries'.[22] Yet another misleading claim in Yost's paper is his assertion that Locke never mentioned the hypothetical method 'whenever he spoke of the methods of increasing empirical knowledge'.[23] The same passage cited above stands as an obvious counter-example to this statement.

In enunciating his hypothetical account of scientific explanation, Locke likened nature to a clock whose external appearances (e.g. hands moving, wheels grinding, etc.) are visible but whose internal mechanisms are for ever excluded from view. The scientist's conception of nature is even 'more remote from the true internal constitution' of the physical world than a 'countryman's *idea* is from the inward contrivance of that famous clock at *Strasbourg*, whereof he only sees the outward figure and motions'.[24] If we knew the 'mechanical affections of the particles' of bodies, 'as a watchmaker does those of a watch',[25] then we would not need to make hypotheses, but could have infallible, first-hand knowledge of nature's mechanisms. But because we can never get inside of nature's clock, we must be content to hypothesize about the possible arrangements of its parts on the basis of its external configuration.

Though Locke believed that scientific explanations should be based on hypotheses about corpuscular events, he insisted that the scientist should be very circumspect in his use of such hypotheses. Hypotheses must never be called 'principles', because such an honorific title makes them sound more trustworthy than they are.[26] Furthermore, we should never accept an hypothesis unless we have carefully examined the phenomena which it is designed to explain, and even then, only if the hypothesis saves all the phenomena efficaciously. Locke is quite sensitive to the dangers of an unbridled hypothetical method and he often warns us against its excesses. Thus, one of the major sources of error which he cites is the clinging tenaciously to preconceived hypotheses and prejudging the facts on the basis of those hypotheses.[27]

---

[21] Ibid. 125. Further on, Yost puts it this way: 'Speaking generally, Locke said that the observable clues are so scanty that there is no hope of making good guesses about any kind of specific submicroscopic mechanisms' (ibid. 126).

[22] *Essay*, IV, xii, 13. He prefaces the quoted passage by an endorsement of hypotheses which is quite unequivocal: 'Not that we may not, to explain any *phenomena* of nature, make use of any probable *hypothesis* whatsoever' (ibid.).

[23] Yost, op. cit., 127.   [24] *Essay*, III, vi, 9. Cf. also III, vi, 39.   [25] Ibid. IV, iii, 25.

[26] 'And at least that we take care that the name of *principles* deceive us not, nor impose on us, by making us receive that for an unquestionable truth which is really at best but a very doubtful conjecture, such as are most (I had almost said all) of the *hypotheses* in natural philosophy' (ibid. IV, xii, 13).

[27] Cf. ibid. IV, xx, 11.

But it is a mistake to say that Locke's critique of the extravagant exaggerations of the hypothetical method indicates his aversion to all forms of that method. At one point, Locke explicitly acknowledged that his animadversions upon hypotheses were not designed to preclude the scientist from hypothesizing, but only to make him wary about it:

> But my meaning is that we should *not take up any one* [hypothesis] *too hastily* (which the mind, that would always penetrate into the causes of things and have principles to rest on, is very apt to do) till we have very well examined particulars and made several experiments in that thing which we would explain by our hypothesis and see whether it will agree to them all, whether our principles will carry us quite through and not be as inconsistent with one *phenomenon* of nature, as they seem to accommodate and explain another.[28]

To sum up: the traditional account of Lockean epistemology is certainly correct in its insistence that Locke believed we could not have *knowledge* about unobservable events; it is equally true that Locke was exceedingly scornful of those who believed one could make indubitable statements about the properties of unobservable corpuscles. But he was not opposed to the use of atomic hypotheses—or other hypotheses which invoked unobservable entities—so long as they made sense of the phenomena and were treated as merely probable judgements.

III

We may conclude from the foregoing discussion that Locke was neither opposed to hypotheses (if properly conceived) nor an adversary of the corpuscularians who used hypotheses about submicroscopic events. Indeed, so far as one can judge from the texts, Locke enthusiastically accepted the view that changes in the observable world are caused by, and explicable in terms of, changes on the atomic level.[29] I now want to suggest that the major features of Locke's hypothetical method, as well as many of the epistemological arguments whereby he justifies his hypotheticalism, are derived from, or at best are variations on, the methodological ideas of his corpuscularian predecessors. In particular, I want to claim that Locke probably derived the following methodological ideas from the corpuscularians: (1) the insistence upon the provisional and tentative character of all scientific theories, (2) the view of nature as a clock whose internal mechanisms are not susceptible of direct analysis or observations, (3) the doctrine that hypotheses must be

---

[28] Ibid. IV, xii, 13.

[29] For some of the relevant passages in which Locke takes a corpuscular position, cf. *Essay*, II, viii, 13–21 and II, xxi, 73; III, vi, 6; IV, iii, 16 and 25; IV, x, 10; IV, xvi, 12; IV, vi, 10 and 14. As Locke's nineteenth-century editor, Fraser, notes: 'It is to the "corpuscularian hypothesis" that he [Locke] appeals in the many passages in the *Essay* which deal with . . . the *ultimate physical cause* of the secondary qualities . . .' *Essay* (ed. Fraser), Vol. II, 205 n.

constructed on analogy with the behaviour of observable bodies, and (4) the insistence, related to (3), that the hypotheses about submicroscopic events must be compatible with laws of nature and phenomena other than those which they were devised to explain.

(1) Locke's insistence that there was a legitimate mode of inquiry and belief which did not exhibit the certainty usually associated with *'scientia'* comes directly out of the corpuscularian tradition.[30] It was the corpuscular philosophers who first realized that many of our beliefs about natural processes were necessarily conjectural and who made it a *sine qua non* of natural philosophy that its fine-grained assumptions can only be probable and hypothetical. Robert Boyle, for example, wrote that scientific theories should be 'looked upon only as temporary ones; which are not entirely to be acquiesced in, as absolutely perfect, or incapable of improving alterations'.[31] In a similar vein, Hooke warns against treating any scientific theories as if they were indubitable:

If therefore the reader expects from me any infallible deductions, or certainty of *axioms*, I am to say for myself that those stronger works of wit and imagination are above my weak abilities. . . . Wherever he finds that I have ventur'd at any small conjectures, at the causes of the things I have observed, I beseech him to look upon them as *doubtful problems*, and uncertain ghesses [*sic*], and not as unquestionable conclusions, or matters of unconfutable science. . . .[32]

Another mid-century corpuscularian, Joseph Glanvill, puts the point similarly in his *Scepsis Scientifica* (1661). True philosophers, he says, 'seek truth in the great book of nature, and in that search . . . proceed with wariness and circumspection without too much forwardness in establishing maxims and positive doctrines. . . . [They] propose their opinions as hypotheses, that may probably be true accounts, without peremptorily affirming that they are'.[33] Like Locke after him. Glanvill insists that all scientific principles are conjectural; there is nothing we can say with certainty about the physical world:

For the best principles, excepting divine and mathematical [precisely Locke's exceptions], are but hypotheses; within which, we may conclude many things with security from error. But yet the greatest certainty, advanced from supposal, is still hypothetical. So that we may affirm that things are thus and thus, according to the principles we have espoused: But we strangely forget ourselves, when we plead a necessity of their being so in nature, and an impossibility of their being otherwise.[34]

[30] Alongside the stress of the corpuscularians that science was 'merely probable', there was a different tradition—the sceptical one—which stressed the utter impossibility of reliable knowledge of nature. For reasons indicated below, I classify Locke with the optimistic, fallibilistic corpuscularians rather than with the pessimistic sceptics.

[31] Robert Boyle, *Works*, ed. Birch (London, 1772), I, 303.

[32] R. Hooke, *Micrographia* (London, 1667), preface, n.p.

[33] *Scepsis Scientifica* (London, 1665), 44.

[34] Ibid. 170–1.

All three writers—Boyle, Hooke, and Glanvill—were widely read in the 1660s and 1670s, when the ideas for the *Essay* were taking shape. It is highly likely that Locke knew the works of Hooke and Glanvill and it is certain that he knew Boyle's works, as the two were close friends for more than thirty years and, as Leyden has noted, Locke 'followed with interest each new publication of his friend Robert Boyle'.[35] Furthermore, Locke met frequently with Boyle's scientific circle at Oxford (of which Hooke was also a member) in the 1660s, and one presumes that among the topics for conversation was the nature of scientific knowledge and the tentative character of its hypotheses. It is not unreasonable to suggest that Locke's ideas on this topic stemmed, in part, from the discussions with, and readings of, the Oxford corpuscularians who, like him, were alarmed that hypothetical systems were being passed off as infallibly true theories.

(2) We have seen that, in explaining why the corpuscular philosophy can never be more than an hypothesis, Locke metaphorically likened nature to a clock whose internal mechanisms could never be observed. Just as we can only conjecture about the possible internal mechanisms of an unfamiliar clock, the scientist can only hypothesize about nature's hidden mechanisms. We know no more about the real natural processes than a seventeenth-century country bumpkin knew about the 'famous clock at Strasbourg', which was accompanied by ingenious automata of every description. This clock-analogy[36] was widely exploited among Locke's predecessors—Descartes, Boyle, Glanvill, and Power—in justification of their insistence on the necessarily hypothetical character of scientific principles.[37] Given the

[35] J. Locke, *Essays on the Laws of Nature* (ed. Leyden, Oxford, 1954), 20. Maurice Cranston, Locke's biographer, records that 'Locke, as Boyle's pupil, absorbed much of the Boylian conception of nature before he read Descartes and became interested in pure philosophy'. *John Locke* (London, 1957), 75–6.

[36] Locke uses the analogy on at least two occasions: *Essay*, III, vi, 9; IV, iii, 25.

[37] The relevant tests are the following:

(1) Descartes: 'It may be retorted to this, that, although I may have imagined causes capable of producing effects similar to those we see, we should not conclude for that reason that those we see are produced by these causes; for just as an industrious clockmaker may make two watches which keep time equally well and without any difference in their external appearance, yet without any similarity in the composition of their wheels, so it is certain that God works in an infinity of diverse ways, each of which enables Him to make everything appear in the world as it does, without making it possible for the human mind to know which of all these ways He has decided to use. And I believe I shall have done enough if the causes that I have listed are such that the effects they may produce are similar to those we see in the world, without being informed whether there are other ways in which they are produced.' *Principles*, Part iv, §204.

(2) Boyle: '. . . many atomists and other naturalists, presume to know the true causes of the things they attempt to explicate, yet very often the utmost they can attain to in their explications, is, that the explicated phenomena may be produced after such a manner as they deliver, but not that they really are so. For as an Artificer can set all the wheels of a clock a going, as well with springs as with weights . . . so the same effects may be produced by diverse causes different from one another; and it will often be difficult if not impossible for our dim reasons to discern surely which of those several ways, whereby it is possible to produce the same phenomena, she has actually

fact that this analogy occurred prominently in the works of several of the most important of Locke's predecessors, it is implausible that he did not borrow it, either consciously or unconsciously, from one of them.

(3) Locke was adamant in his insistence that hypotheses about submicroscopic events must construe atoms and their properties as natural extensions of the properties of macroscopic bodies. Locke believes there was a continuity in nature such that the laws governing macroscopic phenomena must be similar to, if not identical with, the laws governing submicroscopic phenomena. One finds almost identical formulations of this argument in Descartes, Boyle, and Hooke.

It is well known that Descartes's scientific treatises are packed with analogies: the mind as a piece of wax, light transmission as a revolving stick, light corpuscles as grapes in a vat. It is not so well known that analogy plays an important role in Descartes's philosophy of science as well. In the *Regulae*, for example, Descartes argued that since light is a force whose nature we cannot perceive directly, we should imagine light on the analogy of other natural forces which we do understand.[38] Again, in the *Dioptrique*, Descartes talks of the importance of analogies in understanding light.[39] But his most explicit discussion of analogies occurs in the *Principles*, which Locke undoubtedly read. There he writes:

---

made use of to exhibit them.' *Works*, II, 45. It should also be mentioned that Boyle likens nature not merely to any clock, but specifically to the 'clock of Strasbourg' (ibid.). Was this perhaps the source for Locke's allusion to 'that famous clock at Strasbourg'?

(3) Glanvill: 'For nature is set a going by the most subtil and hidden instruments; which it may have nothing obvious which resembles them. Hence judging by visible appearances, we are discouraged by supposed impossibilities which to nature are none, but within her sphear of actions. And therefore what shews only the outside, and sensible structure of nature, is not likely to help us in finding out the *Magnalia* [i.e. inner mechanisms]. 'Twere next to impossible for one, who never saw the inward wheels and motions, to make a watch upon the bare view of the circle of hours, and index: And 'tis as difficult to trace natural operations to any practical advantage, by the sight of the cortex of sensible appearances.' *Scepsis Scientifica*, 155.

(4) Power: 'For the old dogmatists and notional speculators, that onely gazed at the visible effects and last resultances of things, understood no more of nature than a rude countrey fellow does of the internal fabrick of a watch, that only sees the index and horary circle, and perchance hears the clock and alarum strike in it.' Henry Power, *Experimental Philosophy* (London, 1664), 193. Locke's formulation of the analogy is particularly close to Power's when he talks of a 'countryman's idea' of the clock at Strasbourg 'whereof he only sees the outward figure and motions'. *Essay*, III, vi, 9.

For a detailed discussion of this metaphor within an epistemological context, see my 'The Clock Metaphor and Probabalism', *Annals of Science*, 22 (1966), pp. 73–104.

[38] 'If he [the scientist] finds himself ... unable to perceive the nature of light, he will, in accordance with Rule 7, enumerate all the natural forces in order that he may understand what light is, learning its nature, if not otherwise, at least by *analogy* ... from his knowledge of one of the other forces.' *OEuvres* (ed. Adam & Tannery), X, 395. Italics added.

[39] He says that he intends to offer 'two or three comparisons, which will help us to understand it [viz. light] in the most convenient manner, in order to explain all those of its properties that experience allows us to know, and to deduce thereafter all the others which may not be so easily noticed. ...' Ibid. VI, 83.

Nor do I doubt that anyone who uses his reason will deny that we do much better to judge of what takes place in small bodies which their minuteness alone prevents us from perceiving, by what we see occurring in those that we do perceive than, in order to explain certain given things, to invent all sorts of novelties that have no relation to those that we do perceive.[40]

The sentiments of this passage are Locke's as well as Descartes's.

Boyle was the next to take up this theme. He argues that it is absurd to assume anything but that submicroscopic corpuscles obey the same laws as macroscopic bodies do. To say, for example, that the principles of mechanics apply to visible masses but not to invisible ones would be 'as if a man should allow, that the laws of mechanism may take place in a town clock, but cannot in a pocket-watch'.[41] For corpuscular hypotheses to be even intelligible, they must attribute the same type of behaviour to atoms as we observe taking place in perceptible bodies.

In his *General Scheme* (c. 1667), Hooke too argues for the importance of models and analogies in the construction of hypotheses: 'A most general help of discovery in all types of philosophical [i.e., scientific] inquiry is, *to attempt to compare the working of nature in that particular that is under examination, to as many various, mechanical and intelligible ways of operating as the mind is furnisht with.*'[42] What matters here is not whether Locke borrowed his beliefs about analogies from Descartes, Hooke, or Boyle, but rather that the use of hypotheticals, based on analogies with observed phenomena was a basic and explicit tenet of the corpuscularism which Locke so warmly embraced.

(4) Finally, I want to consider the likely sources of Locke's belief that corpuscular hypotheses must be compatible with 'truths that are established in our minds' and with 'other parts of our knowledge and observation'.[43] The writer who comes most quickly to mind in this connection is Robert Boyle, who frequently emphasized that the two requirements of any sound hypothesis are that it accord both with other known laws and with observations. Boyle goes so far as to say that the function of an hypothesis is 'to render an intelligible account of the causes of the effects, or phenomena proposed, without crossing the laws of nature, or other phenomena'.[44] Elsewhere, he insists that a good hypothesis must 'not be inconsistent with any other truth or phenomenon of nature'.[45] Varying the wording yet again, he says that an hypothesis is acceptable if we can show 'its fitness to solve the phenomena for which (it was) devised, without crossing any known observation or law of

[40] *Principles*, Part iv, §201.
[41] *Works*, IV, 72.
[42] Hooke, *Posthumous Works*, ed. Waller (London, 1705), 61. Italics in original.
[43] *Essay*, IV, xvi, 12.   [44] *Works*, IV, 234.   [45] Ibid. I, 241.

nature'.[46] Locke's remarks in the *Essay* at IV, xvi, 12 seem to be little more than stylistic variations on this Boyleian theme.

The object of this historical exercise has not been to belittle Locke's originality nor, even more trivially, to decide 'who said what before whom'. It is no criticism of Locke to point out that he adhered to certain conventions of the philosophical and scientific *milieu* in which he matured. There was a cluster of beliefs—methodological as well as scientific—which many adherents of the 'new philosophy' accepted; among them was the conviction that scientific knowledge was conjectural. In sharing this conviction, Locke was in distinguished company.

POSTSCRIPT: 1976

Yost's reading of Locke, which served as the springboard for the analysis in this paper, has received a spirited defence from John Yolton (especially in his *Locke and the Compass of Human Understanding*). Unfortunately, the interpretative and exegetical divide which separates the Yost–Yolton reading of Locke from the Mandelbaum–Laudan one probably cannot be settled by further citations of 'definitive' texts from the *Essay*; taken in isolation, that work provides evidence for both interpretations. What may help settle the issue is to ask a larger question about where Locke fits into the major intellectual traditions of the seventeenth century.

In brief, Yolton—like Yost—is inclined to see Locke in the natural history tradition of Bacon, Sydenham and some members of the Royal Society. Viewed against that background, Locke emerges as the apostle of, and apologist for, an inductive–descriptive science of purely observable entities and events. On this analysis, resort to unobservable objects in order to explain or to discover the properties or causes of observable ones is otiose and (literally) 'unscientific'.

For my part, I am more impressed by the filiations between Locke, Boyle and Descartes and am inclined to see Locke's problems as emerging from a tradition which placed a higher priority on the mechanical philosophy of unobservables than on a descriptive science of observable properties.

In all of this (so it seems to me), Robert Boyle is the key to the puzzle. We know how closely Locke worked with Boyle, how highly he regarded him, and, in some cases (e.g. *vis-à-vis* primary and secondary qualities), how much the argument of the *Essay* derived from Boylean concerns. This is acknowledged by Yolton as well as by Mandelbaum and myself. It seems likely that if we can get clearer about what Boyle was up to, we shall have moved a long way toward deciding how to explicate the problematic (and often contrary) texts in Locke about scientific methodology.

[46] Ibid. IV, 77.

Yolton's Boyle was a true Baconian, sceptical about hypotheses postulating unobservable entities, optimistic about the emergence of infallible knowledge from data compilations and natural histories. I have shown elsewhere[1] that this reading of Boyle is almost certainly ill-founded. Boyle saw clearly that the establishment of the mechanical philosophy—a programme to which he was fully committed—could *never* be achieved by the method of natural history, and that a conjectural method was the only path to a knowledge of the 'hidden well-springs of nature'.

Locke's groping efforts to find a place for the methods of hypothesis and analogy are serious attempts to provide a cognitive rationale for the speculative natural philosophy of his countrymen such as Boyle, Hooke, Willis, Wren and Charleton. To deny this claim, as Yolton and Yost do, requires us to imagine that Locke—despite his acknowledged scientific interests and concerns—was hopelessly out of touch with the leading intellectual currents of his time; for, by the appearance of the *Essay*, Baconianism of the type Yolton and Yost attribute to Locke had been convincingly discredited by the likes of Boyle, Hooke, Hobbes, Glanvill, Barrow and Newton.

Of course, these considerations in themselves *prove* nothing about Locke's beliefs; it remains conceivable that he was a Neanderthalian figure, fully oblivious to the most progressive scientific movements of his epoch. But they do add a modicum of historical plausibility to an interpretation of the Lockean corpus which is already compatible with (though by no means uniquely supported by) the available *obiter dicta* from Locke.

[1] Op. cit., note 37 above.

NOTES ON THE CONTRIBUTORS

GRENVILLE WALL is a senior lecturer in philosophy at the Middlesex Polytechnic. He has published a number of papers in the journals, mainly on questions of political and moral philosophy.

JOHN HARRIS taught philosophy at Manchester University from 1971 until 1975, when he became a social worker. He is co-editor of and contributor to *Animals, Men and Morals* (1971).

DOUGLAS GREENLEE is a member of the Department of Philosophy at Temple University, Philadelphia. His publications include *Peirce's Concept of Sign* (1973), and he has edited *The Semiotical Writings of C. S. Peirce* (forthcoming).

GUNNAR ASPELIN is Professor Emeritus at the University of Lund.

H. E. MATTHEWS is a senior lecturer in the Department of Logic at the University of Aberdeen. He has published a number of papers in the journals and is about to publish a volume of translations of the selected works of Max Weber.

PETER ALEXANDER is Professor of Philosophy at the University of Bristol. His publications include *Sensationalism and Scientific Explanation* (1963), *A Preface to the Logic of Science* (1963), and *An Introduction to Logic* (1969).

M. R. AYERS is a Fellow of Wadham College, Oxford. His book *The Refutation of Determinism* appeared in 1968, and he has edited the new Everyman's University Library edition of *George Berkeley: Philosophical Works* (1975).

HENRY E. ALLISON is a member of the Department of Philosophy at the University of California, San Diego. His publications include *Lessing and the Enlightenment* (1966), *The Kant–Eberhard Controversy* (1970), and *Benedict de Spinoza* (1975).

NORMAN KRETZMANN is in the School of Philosophy at Cornell University. He has published widely in the journals and produced editions of works by William of Sherwood and William of Ockham. His *Elements of Formal Logic* appeared in 1965

A. D. WOOZLEY was Professor of Philosophy at St. Andrews until 1967 when he moved to the University of Virginia. His publications include *The Theory of Knowledge* (1949), an abridged version of Locke's *Essay* (1964), and (with R. C. Cross) *Plato's Republic: a Philosophical Commentary* (1964).

LAURENS LAUDAN is a professor at the University of Pittsburgh. He has published widely on the history and philosophy of science, and he is co-editor of the ten-volume *Collected Works of William Whewell* (1968–   ).

BIBLIOGRAPHY

This bibliography suggests some further reading for topics covered in this collection. The emphasis is on recently published material. For a full bibliography see (a) H. O. Christophersen, *A Bibliographical Introduction to the Study of John Locke* (Oslo, 1930), (b) Hall and Woolhouse, 'Forty Years of Work on John Locke (1929–1969)', *Philosophical Quarterly*, 20 (1970), and (c) the *Locke Newsletter* (1970–   ).

General
The best general survey of Locke's philosophy is R. I. Aaron's *John Locke*, first published in 1937 and now in its third edition (Oxford, 1971). D. J. O'Connor's *John Locke*, first published in 1952, is now available from Dover Books (New York, 1967). More recent books include:

John L. Kraus, *John Locke: Empiricist, Atomist, Conceptualist and Agnostic* (New York, 1968).
John W. Yolton, *Locke and the Compass of Human Understanding* (Cambridge, 1970).
R. S. Woolhouse, *Locke's Philosophy of Science and Knowledge* (Oxford, 1971).
François Duchesneau, *L'Empirisme de Locke* (The Hague, 1973).
J. D. Mabbott, *John Locke* (London, 1973).

C. B. Martin and D. M. Armstrong (eds.), *Locke and Berkeley* (London, 1968) contains reprinted papers on Locke; and Yolton (ed.), *John Locke: Problems and Perspectives* (Cambridge, 1969) contains original articles.

J. L. Mackie's *Problems From Locke* (Oxford, 1976) appeared while this collection was in the press.

Though not devoted entirely to Locke, the following books have been influential:
Maurice Mandelbaum, *Philosophy, Science, and Sense Perception* (Baltimore, 1964).
Gerd Buchdahl, *Metaphysics and the Philosophy of Science* (Oxford, 1969).
Jonathan Bennett, *Locke, Berkeley, Hume: Central Themes* (Oxford, 1971).

For papers on the general character of Locke's *Essay* see for example: Douglas Odegard, 'Locke as an Empiricist', *Philosophy*, 40 (1965); Yolton's 'Locke's Concept of Experience' in Martin/Armstrong; P. A. Schouls, 'The Cartesian Method of Locke's *Essay Concerning Human Understanding*' (with comments by Duchesneau and Yolton), *Canadian Journal of Philosophy*, 4 (1975); and Neal Wood, 'The

Baconian Character of Locke's "Essay"', *Studies in History and Philosophy of Science*, 6 (1975).

Innate knowledge
Recent papers include: H. M. Bracken, 'Innate Ideas—Then and Now', *Dialogue*, 6 (1967); Jonathan Barnes, 'Mr. Locke's Darling Notion', *Philosophical Quarterly*, 22 (1972); and Douglas Greenlee, 'Locke and the Controversy over Innate Ideas', *Journal of the History of Ideas*, 33 (1972). Useful material will also be found in Aaron's book; in Yolton's *John Locke and the Way of Ideas* (Oxford, 1956); and in Stephen P. Stich (ed.), *Innate Ideas* (Berkeley, 1975). For Chomsky's 'vindication' of the rationalist view see for example his *Aspects of the Theory of Syntax* (Cambridge, Mass., 1965); his *Cartesian Linguistics* (New York, 1966); and his *Language and Mind* (Enlarged Edition: New York, 1972). Chomsky's claims have been very widely discussed and the reader can be referred for example to material in Stich's collection and in Gilbert Harman (ed.), *On Noam Chomsky: Critical Essays* (New York, 1974). See too: David E. Cooper, 'Innateness: Old and New', *Philosophical Review*, 81 (1972); and Chomsky and J. Katz, 'On Innateness: a Reply to Cooper', *Philosophical Review*, 84 (1975).

Ideas, perception, representative realism
On the various uses to which Locke puts the word 'idea' see for example O'Connor's book, pp. 33–9; Woolhouse's book, Ch. 2; and Stephen L. Nathanson, 'Locke's Theory of Ideas', *Journal of the History of Philosophy*, 11 (1973). There is a long discussion of Locke's views on the mechanics of sense-perception in P. J. White's 'Materialism and the Concept of Motion in Locke's Theory of Sense–Idea Causation', *Studies in History and Philosophy of Science*, 2 (1971). For contributions on Locke's (alleged) representationalism see Reginald Jackson, 'Locke's Version of the Doctrine of Representative Perception', originally published in 1930 and reprinted in Martin/Armstrong; Aaron's book, pp. 101–5; Woozley's introduction to his abridged edition of the *Essay* (London, 1964); Yolton's book, Ch. 5; and Douglas Lewis, 'The Existence of Substances and Locke's Way of Ideas', *Theoria*, 35 (1969). Further useful material will be found in Ch. 4 of Buchdahl's book and in Bennett's book. Yolton has more to say on Locke's idea of 'idea' in 'On Being Present to the Mind: a Sketch for the History of an Idea', *Canadian Journal of Philosophy*, 4 (1975).

Primary and secondary qualities
Very useful material on this topic will be found in the books by Mandelbaum (Ch. 1), Buchdahl (Ch. 4), Yolton (*passim*), and Bennett (Ch. 4). The paper by Reginald Jackson entitled 'Locke's Distinction between Primary and Secondary Qualities' has been much discussed. This originally appeared in 1929 and it is reprinted in Martin/Armstrong together with a reply from W. H. F. Barnes which originally appeared in 1940. Recent papers on the topic include: D. M. Armstrong, 'The Secondary Qualities', *Australasian Journal of Philosophy*, 46 (1968); E. M. Curley, 'Locke, Boyle and the Distinction between Primary and Secondary Qualities', *Philosophical Review*, 81 (1972); Alexander's 'Curley on Locke and Boyle', *Philosophical Review*, 83 (1974); David Palmer, 'Locke and the "Ancient Hypothesis"' (with a comment by E. M. Curley), *Canadian Journal of Philosophy*, Supp. Vol. 1 (1975); and Robert Cummins, 'Two Troublesome Claims about Qualities in Locke's Essay', *Philosophical Review*, 84 (1975).

Substance

The reader will find a convenient list of references in Ayers's n. 2 in the paper reprinted in this collection. The following papers are also relevant: Douglas Odegard, 'Locke and Substance', *Dialogue*, 8 (1969); R. S. Woolhouse, 'Substance and Substances in Locke's *Essay*', *Theoria*, 35 (1969), and 'Things', *Philosophy and Phenomenological Research*, 33 (1972); and R. J. Butler, 'Substance Un-Locked'. *Proceedings of the Aristotelian Society*, 74 (1973–4). See too Bennett's 'Substance, Reality, and Primary Qualities' which is reprinted in Martin Armstrong; and Ayers's examination of this paper in his 'Substance, Reality, and the Great, Dead Philosophers', *American Philosophical Quarterly*, 7 (1970). In his paper reprinted in this collection Ayers refers to his forthcoming 'Substance, Substrate, Essence and Accident: Some Antecedents to Locke's *Essay*'.

The person and personal identity

Recent papers have included: Douglas Odegard, 'Locke and Mind–Body Dualism', *Philosophy*, 45 (1970); Baruch Brody, 'Locke on the Identity of Persons', *American Philosophical Quarterly*, 9 (1972); and M. W. Hughes, 'Personal Identity: a Defence of Locke', *Philosophy*, 50 (1975). I have had sight of H. E. Matthews's 'Locke's Account of the Person' which was read to the Locke Conference in Alberta in 1975 and which should be published shortly. Antony Flew's paper 'Locke and the Problem of Personal Identity', originally published in 1951, is reprinted in Martin/Armstrong. There is currently a revival of interest in personal identity and a number of important books and papers have been published in which Locke may play a peripheral role but in which questions that concerned him are to the fore. These include: Sydney Shoemaker, *Self-Knowledge and Self-Identity* (Ithaca, N.Y., 1963), and 'Persons and their Pasts', *American Philosophical Quarterly*, 7 (1970); David Wiggins, *Identity and Spatio-Temporal Continuity* (Oxford, 1967); and Derek Parfit, 'Personal Identity', *Philosophical Review*, 80 (1971). Also relevant are a number of the papers by Bernard Williams which are reprinted in his *Problems of the Self* (Cambridge, 1973).

Language

The paper by Kretzmann reprinted in this collection is discussed by Douglas Odegard in 'Locke and the Signification of Words', *Locke Newsletter*, 1 (1970); and by Yolton in his book, pp. 208–14. See too Charles Landesman, 'Locke's Theory of Meaning', *Journal of the History of Philosophy*, 14 (1976). Bennett's discussion of Locke on language in Ch. 1 of his book ('Ideas and Meanings: Locke') and its development in Ch. 2 is recommended; as is a very relevant chapter—'Nobody's Theory of Meaning' —in Ian Hacking's *Why Does Language Matter to Philosophy?* (Cambridge, 1975). There are useful chapters on Locke on language in the books by Aaron and O'Connor. Two recent papers on Locke on real and nominal essences and the common names of substances are J. L. Mackie, 'Locke's Anticipation of Kripke', *Analysis*, 34 (1974), and John Troyer, 'Locke on the Names of Substances', *Locke Newsletter*, 6 (1975). In his 'Meaning and Communication', *Philosophical Review*, 80 (1971), D. M. Armstrong develops what he takes to be the Lockean insight that the communicative function of words gives '*the* clue to an analysis of the notion of linguistic meaning'. On Berkeley's famous attack on Locke or abstraction, E. J. Craig's 'Berkeley's Attack on Abstract Ideas', *Philosophical Review*, 77 (1968), is recommended.

Knowledge

Useful material on Locke's account of knowledge will be found in the books by Aaron,

Buchdahl, Woolhouse, and Yolton, for example. See too David L. Perry, 'Locke on Mixed Modes, Relations, and Knowledge', *Journal of the History of Philosophy*, 5 (1967); and R. E. A. Shanab, 'Locke on Knowledge and Perception', *Journal of Critical Analysis*, 2 (1971). For reading on Locke's attitude to hypotheses, see my introduction, p. 9 (above). There is a paper on 'Boyle, Locke, and Reason' by G. A. J. Rogers in *Journal of the History of Ideas*, 27 (1966); and in the same area there is Margaret J. Osler's 'John Locke and the Changing Ideal of Scientific Knowledge', *Journal of the History of Ideas*, 31 (1970). Only lack of space prevented my seeking to include Margaret D. Wilson's 'Leibniz and Locke on "First Truths"', *Journal of the History of Ideas*, 28 (1967). I would also have liked to include something on Locke on *faith*. On this topic see Richard Ashcraft, 'Faith and Knowledge in Locke's Philosophy', in Yolton (ed.), John Locke: *Problems and Perspectives*; and Paul Helm, 'Locke on Faith and Knowledge', *Philosophical Quarterly*, 23 (1973).

INDEX OF NAMES

(not including authors mentioned only in the Bibliography)

◊ Animals have only
a disunified consciousness
correlated w/ neurological
event-flow. Correlation
upheld by God.

Diff betw us and
animals is not that
we have ideas and they
don't but that our
consciousness is unified
because ~~one~~ we
perceive our ideas
in a way that
animals can't.
They simply ~~are~~ a
contingently combined set
of mental ~~states~~
particulars and physical
particulars such that
the ~~the~~ mental particulars
may be conscious which are
(units of)
directed upon physical
states of affairs but
these units of consciousness
cannot be directed upon
themselves as can the
intentional states of spirits